The Constance Spry Encyclopedia of Flower Arranging

Constance Spry began working with flowers in the late 1920s, when she opened a small shop behind Victoria Station in London. By the start of World War II the present shop in South Audley Street was established. She started a floristry school and in 1945, together with Rosemary Hume, she founded the Cordon Bleu Cookery School. Later, the residential school, Winkfield Place, near Windsor, was opened. Her flower decorations became renowned throughout the world and she was responsible for the floral arrangements at a great many social and royal occasions, including the Queen's wedding and coronation. Constance Spry wrote twelve books on flower decoration and cooking, including her biggest bestseller, *The Constance Spry Cookery Book*, which is also available in Pan Books. She died in 1960.

Members of Constance Spry Limited who contributed to this book are Anthony Marr, Constance Spry's son; Harold Piercy, NDH, who wrote a large number of the general articles on practical aspects of flower arranging; Barbara Pearce, who did the flower arrangements photographed at the School; and George Foss who wrote the article on the history of flower arranging.

Other expert contributors to this book include Roy Genders, who provided a number of articles on subjects closely related to horti-culture, such as ferns and bottle gardens, and Ann Bonar, BSc (Hort) who wrote the large section on house plants. The article on shows was written by Grace L. Young, founder chairman of Bearsden Flower Club and past chairman of the Scottish Association of Flower Arrangement Societies, whose experience of show administration at various levels has been gained through her work for these societies and through her association with the National Association of Flower Arrangement Societies of Great Britain (NAFAS).

The Constance Spry

Compiled by the Constance Spry School, London

with contributions from

Anthony Marr · Harold Piercy

Barbara Pearce · George Foss

Roy Genders · Ann Bonar

Lorna F. Bowden · Grace L. Young

Roger Grounds

PAN BOOKS LTD · LONDON AND SYDNEY

Encyclopedia of Flower Arranging

and Indoor Plant Decoration

First published in Great Britain 1972 by Ward Lock Ltd
This edition published 1975 by Pan Books Ltd,
Cavaye Place, London SW10 9PG

ISBN 0 330 24091 9

© Constance Spry Ltd and Cordon Bleu Group Ltd
and Ward Lock Ltd 1972

Printed in Great Britain by
Fletcher & Son Ltd, Norwich

Preface

The Constance Spry Encyclopedia of Flower Arranging provides those interested in using flowers and plants decoratively with a complete guide. It is based on the work of the late Constance Spry, to whose inspiration the English traditional style of flower arranging owes so much, and it has been prepared with the help of the Constance Spry Flower School. A number of experts, well-known in their fields, have contributed articles on specialised subjects. The book covers not only the hundreds of flowers and plants used by flower arrangers but it includes sections on buying flowers, composition, colour, preservation, dried arrangements, history and styles, Japanese flower work and bonsai, house and table decoration, garden cultivation, bottle gardens and fern cultivation. The section on house plants includes every type of plant from bulbs to climbers and trailers, cacti and other succulents, their cultivation and conditions for survival.

It has been designed for reference or for browsing through, and looking something up may often lead your eye to something else of interest. As a help to the reader common names have been clearly linked to their botanical names in every title. The book is profusely illustrated, with many pictures taken at the Constance Spry School.

(Chairman, Constance Spry Limited, London)
ANTHONY MARR

Note the reader will notice that after the latin and/or common name of each plant there is a further line of words and symbols. These are provided for quick reference, so that the reader can see at a glance whether a particular plant is useful for its flowers, leaves or seeds, and at what season it is most beautiful

Acacia/mimosa

Flower

The yellow blossoms of *A. dealbata* are excellent for spring arrangements. Store in a plastic bag to keep the blossoms from going dark. Before arranging, dip the flowerheads, first in cold then in hot water for a few moments to preserve the colour. The florists, as well as selling the flowers already wrapped in plastic bags, also supply a special powder which, when mixed with water in the container, will help to preserve the blossoms. The acacia is hardy only in areas free from frosts. See also Mimosa.

Acanthus/bear's breeches

Leaf/Flower

Hardy perennials. These plants (especially *A. mollis*) were an inspiration to the Ancient Greeks, the columns of their temples being sculptured with acanthus leaf designs. Unfortunately, the leaves do not last very long when picked, though they are fine foliage for flower arrangements. It is possible to make them last longer by dipping them in starch or spraying with plastic solution, and they will give you an excellent foil for flowers. The species favoured by the Ancient Greeks is best.

The unusual-shaped flower spikes of the acanthus may be dried by hanging upside down in a warm room. Pick them when they are fully developed. They are also excellent for cut flowers in July and August. You can grow acanthus in any sunny part of the garden. *A. spinosus* has darker, smaller leaves than *A. mollis*. The flowers of the latter are white, pink, or purplish-white in long spikes.

Achillea/yarrow

Flower/Sp/Su

A hardy perennial also commonly known as milfoil. The flowers are usually large, yellow, and appear as plate-like heads, but sometimes form in loose clusters. The foliage is fern-like and also attractive. The flowers, which may be dried in powdered alum for winter arrangements, bloom from spring onwards. The flowerheads can also be dried upright in a dry atmosphere and for this should be picked in full bloom.

Agapanthus see House Plants

Alchemilla

Flower/Leaf

The light lime green flowerheads of *A. mollis*, and interesting leaves of similar colour make this rather low-growing perennial an attractive plant for flower arrangers. The flowers appear from June and both they and the leaves set off other brighter flower blooms.

Allium

Flower/Seed

These are hardy bulbous plants, and the species *A. moly* produces yellow flowers which may be dried by borax treatment. The buds appear from spring to summer and should be picked when almost flowering. The flowers of this and other species may also be dried upside down. They are members of the onion family, so beware of the smell. Some of the other species have blue or rosy-coloured flowers, and *A. schoenoprasum* is the well-known flavouring chives, which provide interesting flowers if cook will let the stalks grow that long.

Aloe see House Plants (Cacti and Succulents)

Alstroemeria/Peruvian lily, herb lily

Flower/Su

These flowers are natives of South America, and are worthy of interest for their large beautifully veined and patterned lily-like flowers which make a distinctive contribution to any flower arrangement. The cut flowers last well and are most suitable for large flower arrangements. The seedheads may be hung upside down in a shed to dry for dried flower arrangements. Astroemerias may also be used for pot plants. If you are thinking of trying to grow them in the garden, choose a sunny, sheltered spot, as few species are fully hardy. Hybrids of *A. ligtu* provide the widest range of colours from pink, rose and red to orange and yellow. The petals have veins of red or brown or purple.

Althaea/hollyhock

Flower/Seed/Su

The tall spikes of hollyhocks have always been popular for mass arrangements, as old paintings

This prize-winning show arrangement called 'Gala Night' makes use of non-floral props such as birds' wings and dancing sandals to highlight its theme.

Fruits can be as colourful as flowers and, if used with care, can add new interest to an arrangement. Here oranges pick up the colour of the alstroemeria, while the pineapple affords a contrast in a different key.

Amaranthus, always popular with flower arrangers, is not the easiest of flowers to arrange owing to its pendulous habit which, contrast wise, is also its main attraction.

show. After cutting, dip the ends of the stalks in boiling water for several minutes and then in deep water in a dark place for about two days. Ripe seedheads are dried by hanging upside down.

Amaranthus/love lies bleeding

Flower/Su/Au

The very beautiful *A. caudatus* is famous for its trailing red tassels of flowers. The favourite with many flower arrangers is *A. caudatus* 'Viridis', which has attractive green tassels adding a note of coolness that contrasts well with the rich colours of other flowers.

The plant can be brought into the house as a pot plant. It needs plenty of room, sunlight and water. In the garden the plants should be planted out in June. Remove the leaves both for cut flowers and before drying the flowers. The rules for drying are to hang the flowers upside down in a warm room with plenty of air circulating round. The best time for drying is towards the end of the flowering season. Some of the colour may fade, but the form of the drooping tassels remains attractive.

Anemone/windflower

Flower

These are generally available at florists for use as cut flowers all the year round, but the lovely red, blue, violet and yellow flowers of the tuberous *A.*

9

coronaria are the cheapest buy in the shops from January onwards and give colour when it is most wanted. *A. blanda*, which has blue and white flowers, opens in early spring and makes a useful pot plant for the house. Then in summer and autumn come the white, pink, red, mauve or purple blooms of *A. hupehensis*, the Japanese anemone. Some of the varieties of *Pulsatilla* (pasque flower) are like anemones. The natural flowering period for *A. coronaria* is in spring and it is quite easy to grow it in good soil in the garden because like most species of anemone it is quite hardy. Most famous varieties of *A. coronaria* are 'St. Brigid' (double flowers) and 'de Caen' (single). The blooms of anemones can be dried by borax treatment. Symbolically the anemone is supposed to indicate love.

Anthemis/chamomile

Flower/Leaf

Notable for aromatic, delicate foliage and daisy-like flowers, these are hardy perennial or biennial plants easily grown in rock garden or border. The fern-like leaves and yellow daisy-like flowers of *Cladanthus arabicus* should not be confused with Anthemis. See also CLADANTHUS. The flowers of Anthemis are good subjects for cut flower arrangements.

Anthurium/palette plant, flamingo flower

Flower/Leaf

A remarkably dramatic-looking plant. Some species have beautifully marbled and decorative leaves with striking heart-shaped flowers with long spadices or tongues. The colours can be really exotic including brilliant scarlet and orange, but the flowers must be carefully arranged to avoid clashing with other plants. They last well in water. Unfortunately for some flower arrangers, they must be grown in tropical conditions in a temperature of between 60°–70°F (16°–21°C). However, in a warm room they can be grown in pots or even in water containing liquid plant food.

Antirrhinum/snapdragon

Flower/Su/Au

These are excellent for summer cut flowers. If you are thinking of growing them for this purpose

select the newer double varieties. They make a fine background in massed summer arrangements or are good on their own in variety. When picking from the garden, place the flowers in deep water. If you buy forced flowers from the shops dip the ends in boiling water before arranging them.

Aphelandra see House Plants

Aporocactus see House Plants (Cacti and Succulents)

Aquilegia/columbine

Flower/Leaf/Seed/Su/Au

These hardy perennials produce delicate flowers and there are fine modern hybrids which give bright-coloured blooms with long spurs on tallish stems. The columbine is associated with the dove and traditionally symbolises the Holy Ghost. Put the stems of cut flowers in boiling water for a few seconds. The seedheads can be dried upside down. The leaves can be pressed to preserve them.

Arctotis

Flower/Su

Attractive cool-looking, daisy-like flowers from South Africa, which in the pure form of *A. grandis* are white with a tinge of pale blue. Hybrids may be cream, yellow, primrose, buff orange, red, crimson or purple. When cutting dip the ends of the stems in boiling water for a few seconds.

Artemesia/wormwood, old man

Leaf/Seed/Flower/Su/Au

Chiefly of interest for the feathery or downy grey or silvery-white foliage, which is often strongly scented. The flowers are generally small and are insignificant. *A. lactiflora*, however, has tall, creamy-white plume-like flowers, which would grace any large group. To preserve the cut flowers hammer the stems, and the seedheads can be dried by hanging upside down. Hardy perennial or annual shrubs or sub-shrubs, the plants will grow in almost any garden soil in sun or partial shade. *A. ludoviciana* provides interesting dried foliage processed by hanging upside down and removing alternate leaves.

Artificial flowers

Artificial flowers are certainly not a new idea,

and today, with the advent of modern materials, they can be made to look very like the real thing. Years ago, especially in Victorian times, they were made from metal, or stiff brown paper covered in oils, and some were fashioned from wax and plaster of paris. The majority of artificial flowers and foliages on sale today are made from plastic. They are stamped out and unfortunately all take on an identical look, a far cry from the infinite variety of nature. The higher-priced flowers are generally better in quality of bloom and are more natural in colour and therefore more life-like. But they still have a stiff rigid look which immediately labels them 'artificial'. A lot can be done to improve them by adjusting the foliage and putting a few small curves into the stem. Good arranging helps to make them look better, and grouping the colours and shapes and using the correct type of container is also useful. Another important point is to keep them seasonal and not to leave them on display from year to year. Of all the artificial flowers on sale at present, plastic flowers are the easiest to use and keep clean. They can be washed at regular intervals, which will help to give them a brighter look.

Silk flowers are to be seen occasionally on sale. They are very expensive, but beautifully made and far more natural in appearance. Paper flowers can be of two kinds: the lovely ones such as those made by Constance Spry herself many years ago, which are exact in every detail and hand-painted, making them very natural-looking; or the simple ones cut out of coloured paper to give just a colourful effect. These are used in big display work and should really be called 'fantasy flowers'. They in no way take the place of real flowers.

The day of wooden flowers, hawked around the towns by the gypsy communities, seems to have gone. These flowers were made by peeling back bark which, when cut in a certain way, resembled a daisy-type flower; they were dyed bright and gaudy colours and often fitted on to stems of wild privet to give them foliage.

Novelty flowers can be made up from skeleton-ised leaves, bound on to cones for a centre and many people will make up this type of thing in the winter months and as Christmas novelties. They are then painted and often give an amusing display.

The modern decorative papers give the clever paper artist much scope. Certain foreign papers in metallic finishes are very easy to mould in one

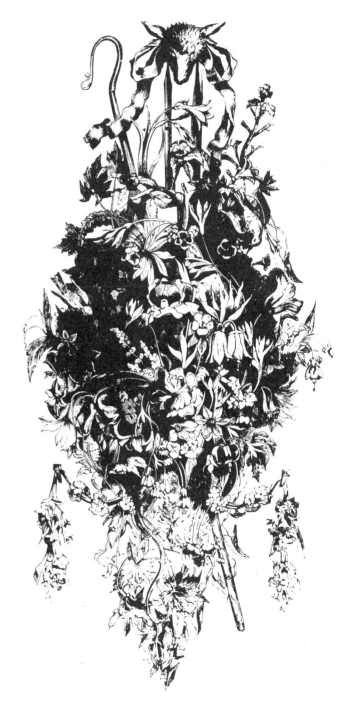

Victorian wood carving representing spring, one of a series of four done for the Great Exhibition 1851. The carving is 5½ ft high, 3 ft wide and contains 47 varieties of plants. (From a contemporary engraving.)

11

Artificial flowers made by a jeweller in silver work in a silver vase. Such pieces are still considered beautiful. (From a contemporary engraving.)

hand, and these can give very realistic finishes to some flowers. Roses, poppies and poinsettias are all easy to make, but each petal should first be made from a template taken from the living plant if anything like the real flower is to be obtained.

There are different ways of looking at artificial flowers. The true grower and plant lover will not tolerate them at any price. The artistic person, who cannot always have fresh materials, may well have in the house some artificial flowers which are well arranged, carefully tended and kept seasonal. Then, of course, there is the small minority who have no aptitude for arranging flowers, but just stick a few stems in a vase to add colour to the room without needing any attention.

The artificial flower, whatever it is made of, will never take the place of the living one, and generally speaking it is a great pity to mix fresh flowers with artificial flowers. There is a place for artificial flowers when real ones are not practical and this is where they should be used. Seen from a distance they can, if they are really good, be most effective and serve a useful purpose. A good example can be seen at the Commonwealth Institute, in London, where flowers from all over the world are on display to illustrate the countries concerned.

At Christmas, one can use plastic flowers and foliages in the home in a big way, and these can be most attractive. The addition of glitter, aerosol sprays and all the modern aids gives one scope to make displays which are striking and pleasing for a short while, but one soon tires of such things. The latest artificial flowers and foliage are made of glass, and this makes a pleasant change.

Perhaps the most pleasing flower arrangements, other than real, are the jade flowers and leaves seen so beautifully arranged in the Far East; exquisite work in perfect materials, which make a very beautiful decoration. The Japanese, incidentally, are extremely expert at making artificial flowers, and Japanese master flower arrangers use them.

Arum see Zantedeschia

Asparagus see House Plants

Aspidistra see House Plants (Pot Plants)

Artificial flowers in a vase. The whole piece is carved from one piece of wood. The circle of flowers on the base represents countries of the British Commonwealth. (From a contemporary engraving.)

Aster/Michaelmas daisy

Flower/Su/Au

A wide selection of flowers with pink, red, blue, mauve or purple petals are found in the aster family including both dwarf and tall varieties, all of which grow well in sunny spots in most gardens. Michaelmas daisies are just one type which make a fine mass of cut flowers. Hammer the stems and dip them in boiling water for a few seconds followed by a good soaking in cold water. A little sugar added to the water is considered helpful. See also Callistephus.

Astilbe/goat's beard

Flower/Seed/Leaf/Sp/Su

Astilbes include many attractive modern hybrids, with interesting divided leaves and plume-like masses of flowers, white and in colours ranging from pink to deepest red. The seedheads should be cut when fully ripe and hung upside down to dry.

Astrantia/masterwort

Flower/Leaf/Au

The star-like flowers are not very exciting, but their papery look is unusual and they blend well in mixed arrangements. They range from red to pink and white, and *A. carniolica* is particularly useful for both foliage and flowers of red, bluish-pink or white. They grow in the shade in ordinary soil.

Auricula/auriculas

Flower/Seed/Su

These gay looking flowers are close relatives of the garden hybrid primulas, but differ from them in their smooth leaves, often covered with a powdery indumentum (fluff) and in the way in which their flowers are curiously edged, the petal tips being a different colour from centre of the flower. There are two types of auricula, those known as the 'florists' auriculas', and the garden auriculas. The florists' auriculas are the finest of all, embracing a remarkable range of colour combinations, including flowers edged with green. The leaves of the florists' auriculas are very mealy and, since this meal is easily damaged by rain, the florists auriculas are usually grown under glass. The garden auriculas, which have less mealy leaves, have flowers just as exciting but in a slightly narrower range of colours. The garden varieties need to be grown in a well-drained soil: every two or three years they should be lifted and the 'carrots'—the roots—divided and replanted. The seedheads provide useful material for dried arrangements, but should be allowed to ripen thoroughly before drying.

Azalea see House Plants (Pot Plants)

Bamboos

The evergreen bamboos are among the most handsome plants of the garden, and the Japanese have long been skilful in arranging their foliage. They are members of the grass family and are suitable for water-side planting, though they do not like to have their roots in perpetually wet land. Many species may be grown in this country but although hardier than generally believed, they are not suitable for a windswept garden. Plant them where they may be protected from prevailing winds, and in the warmer parts of the garden.

As with most evergreens, spring planting is recommended, early April being the best time. They like a deep loamy soil into which peat, leaf-mould or other humus-forming materials have been incorporated. During dry weather give copious waterings and syringe the foliage. Propagate by division of the roots at this time. They will often die after flowering, though this may not take place for many years, and it is advisable to lift and divide every four years so that there will be continuity of stock plants. At the same time, frequent division will ensure healthy plants, free of dead wood at the centre. Bamboos like a yearly mulch of decayed manure or of other humus materials.

The stems of several species, particularly *Arundinaria variegata* 'Fortunei', which has narrow leaves of brilliant green striped with silver, and *A. viridistriata* 'Auricom', the leaves being striped with gold, may be cut during late summer and autumn and used for floral decorations indoors. *Phyllostachys nigra*, is a striking plant with its stems changing to shining purple-black in their second year. It is not advisable to cut the stems until well into summer and during autumn for they are often damaged by the cold winds of spring and take until July to reach their best. It helps to preserve the leaves if you dip the stem ends in boiling vinegar for a couple of minutes.

Basic flower arranging

Flower arranging is a creative art which brings delight and pleasure to the eye and to the heart. If visual art is the communication of feelings and not of abstract ideas or quantitive information, then flower arranging may be said to unite the most natural art with the gentlest feelings. Its strength lies in its spontaneity and freshness— you may spend hours readjusting flowers in a vase only to realise that the first vision of your subject and its chance-taken form were the best. This is because, though practice leads to greater skill, you have missed the sensitive moment when the eye is most alert and the medium itself most responsive to your eye and touch.

So much for the act of creation. There are, however, basic rules and methods which enable you to create within your chosen medium. Other parts of this book will tell you how to gather and care for flowers and the other plant materials. It must be assumed here that you have the subjects for arrangement and need to know the basic requirements for arranging them.

EQUIPMENT The most essential things for modern flower arranging are containers (see the article on containers), scissors and secateurs, pinholders, plasticine, wire netting, flower arranger's putty, clear tape and perhaps a few large elastic bands or thin string. None of these will cost you much, and most will be a good deal less.

The best type of scissors are the stubby-bladed florists' scissors, which may have coloured plastic handles. Secateurs are useful for cutting tree or shrub branches.

Florists' scissors may also be used to cut the thin wire netting which is used to fill pots and other containers so that stems may be poked in the meshes of the wire and held in place. Plastic-covered wire is best for containers which might be spoiled by being scratched. The mesh may be one or two inches wide (two inches is better) and is usually crumpled to fit the shape of the container. The thin wire required can be bought at florists' shops by the yard and cut up as needed.

'Scotch' tape or 'Sellotape' is handy for making an almost invisible criss-cross grid on the top of the glass types of containers to hold stems in position in the style of wire holders. Wire netting may also be adapted for this purpose by placing a double layer of netting over the top of the glass, bending the little ends of wire over the rim to hold it in position. Thin sticks, split and locked, or crossed and lashed together will hold stems in place. They can be secured to the container with string or wire, or wedged into a vase. This method is based on Japanese practice and not used in Constance Spry flower schools. Foliage or moss can be used to hide the 'mechanics'. Wedges and twigs used in Japanese-style arranging will also provide you with natural means of support.

Pinholders consist of upright 'pins' set in a heavy base. It is possible to make a pinholder by melting lead into a mould of clay and setting brass nails in the lead. Alternatively roll a ball of plasticine and press it flat, stick it to the bottom of the container (before filling with water), and fix the pinholder to the plasticine. Plasticine has a fairly tacky quality which makes it quite satisfactory for this purpose. Plasticine is also useful for dried arrangements. Roll it in the hand to make it soft and it will easily support the stiff stems of grasses, etc. when they are pressed into it. It tends to discolour copper and silver. Plasticine will also support candle-cups (see Containers), and can be used to stick a small container to a statuette. It can be used as a base for pieces of driftwood.

Pinholders are often used together with wire netting. The pinholders support the upright flowers or stems which are stuck onto the pins and the wire netting holds the laterally placed flowers at the sides or front. To insert thin delicate stems on a pinholder you can wrap the stem ends with thin paper in a roll and gently tie it with fine copper wire so that the roll of paper will hold the stem to the pin. Cut straws will serve the same purpose. Some pinholders are made complete with cups which render them handy containers.

Modern flower arrangers' putties are sophisticated plastic materials which have revolutionised flower arranging. They even enable you to use containers which are leaky, as when properly soaked they retain the water and may be contained in plastic bags. Be careful the bags do not leak, however, as the water will easily mark polished surfaces. They are especially useful for people who do not have much time to spare, for it is easy to build up arrangements in them and they save the trouble of continual watering if used in quantity. Flower arranger's putty can be cut to fit any container and can be used for several arrangements—if it becomes crumbly, bind it with silver or copper wire. It should be soaked in water for at least an hour before use.

CAGES AND WIRE HOLDERS These are purpose-made holders which fit into matching containers. Some have suction discs which fix on to the bottom of the container, others may be used in conjunction with pinholders.

FUSE WIRE This is handy for securing cups or small water holders inside containers, and for holding wire netting firmly to the container.

FLORISTS' WIRE This is covered with green paper and may be used for wiring broken stems on to firm ones, and for buttonholes, wreaths, etc. It is not used in Constance Spry flower arrangements, and really only applies to floristry.

DIVIDED CUP HOLDERS These are used in Japanese flower arrangements. The divisions in the cups make it easy to insert twigs and wedges in order to fix branches.

SPRAYERS Atomising sprayers are useful for keeping foliage and flowers fresh after arranging, and preventing too much loss of water by transpiration.

GLASS HOLDERS These are often found in old-fashioned rose bowls and florists' containers. They tend to limit the style of arrangement because most of the stems are held upright.

COMPOSITION AND COLOUR (see also Colour) Firstly, you must watch your arrangement and container. Obviously a huge bowl is unsuitable for a small amount of flowers and foliage. Fancy baskets and miniature kettles made of copper may easily be swamped, but a simple bowl on a heavy though small pedestal may offset dramatic and large groups. By using florists' putties you can often use small containers for quite big effects. Big, traditional containers are best for large flowers on long stems like chrysanthemums and peonies. A fluted glass stem vase or porcelain mantelpiece vase will suit delicate flowers such as a few pansies or hellebores. Curiously-shaped containers will enhance curving or cascading effects.

The subject matter of the arrangement will influence the choice of container: modern roses, surely the most adaptable and sophisticated of flowers, will go into almost any container. The colour of the container must blend with, or set off, the flowers and foliage. From the point of view of both colour and composition you must bear in mind where you are going to place the arrangement. A large spreading arrangement will not go in a cramped position, and a tiny spray of flowers would be lost on a large dining table.

Generally speaking, it is best to consider foliage separately from flowers. You will find it much easier if you do not rely on the leaves of the flower stems (most of which often have to be stripped), but on leaves of the same plants on separate stems, or even contrasting foliage. However, plants grown specifically for their foliage effects, such as shrubs and trees, provide the most exciting foliage.

GENERAL A flower arrangement may be compared to a picture. The eye takes it in one glance, but by skilful arrangement the parts can be united to one another and provide interest as the eye gathers detail. Remember that space is important and crowding may reduce everything to to amorphous mess. The flowers should appear in drifts rather than haphazardly, with prominent flowers and interesting foliage used to provide the lines of the arrangement. Where several different type of flowers are used it is best to adopt the principle of using some to give the outline of the arrangement and others to provide the essential balance or weight.

Pointed leaves may be lost at the centre in the bottom of an arrangement, but keep large rounded leaves near the bottom. Startling flowers with unusual shapes, very bright or contrasting colours should not be allowed to take too much attention in a balanced arrangement. On the other hand, an arrangement may be built around one or two very prominent flowers. Placing flowers in groups tends to lessen their individual effect. The arrangement may be considered to have a focal point, or series of focal points. This is a point where a line followed by the eye terminates, or where such a line crosses another line. A striking arrangement may be built around such a point or series of points, but remember the eye does not like to linger too long so that highlighting a single flower requires a good subject and great skill.

Generally it is wise to bear in mind how the plant material appears in nature. This is not a hard and fast rule. For instance, a large flower which appears high up on its plant in nature may shine at the base of a flower arrangement very effectively. If you should strain people's view of the way things appear you should at least justify this by building the whole arrangement in an artificial way. They then may be 'surprised by joy' rather than puzzled by a curious conflict of art and nature.

In general try to achieve good flow, avoid crossed stems, balance the sizes and shapes of your material. The Japanese rule that the arrangement

Five stages in the making of a simple flower
arrangement.

should be as much as or more than $1\frac{1}{2}$ times as high as the container is not absolute, but it is a good rule of thumb. Light feathery arrangements may be taller and wider than heavy solid-centred ones.

All sorts of themes are possible, from seasonal arrangements, which fit in well with the material available, to lines of poetry, books, music and paintings. A visit to a local show in which there is a competition in floral art will give you hundreds of ideas (see SHOWS). Arrangements may be simple or dramatic, quiet or creating an atmosphere of gaiety and wild profusion. The essential quality is good taste, something indefinable, based not upon fixed rules or mere enthusiasm, but an ability to distinguish the visual qualities of your materials and exhibit them in the best possible way.

Begonia see House Plants (Pot Plants)

Beloperone see House Plants (Pot Plants)

Berberis/barbery

Leaf/Berry/Flower/Sp

This is a large genus of evergreen and deciduous flowering shrubs, the deciduous kinds providing beautiful autumn foliage. The red, purple or blue-black berries last into the winter. Berberis will provide you with plant material of one kind or another all the year round. *B. aquifolium* flowers in late winter. *B. darwinii* and *B. stenophylla* are evergreens with orange-yellow flowers in spring. The deciduous *B. thunbergii* is noted for its beautiful spring and unsurpassed autumnal foliage. *B. t. atropurpurea*, as its name implies, provides purple foliage. Hammer the stem ends when preparing arrangements.

Bergenia

Leaf/Flower/Sp

These herbaceous plants come from India, but are hardy in temperate climates. Invaluable, large heart-shaped leaves are provided all the year round by *B. cordifolia* and other species. Plants grown in the garden can be induced to provide leaves that redden in the winter if grown in full sun and exposed to frost. The flowers appear in spring but are less interesting. The leaves should be well soaked, allowed to dry and then arranged.

Billbergia see House Plants (Pot Plants)

Bonsai

Bonsai is the name given by the Japanese to deliberately dwarfed shallowly potted trees. The Japanese have been cultivating these trees for hundreds of years, though bonsai came originally to Japan from China. The idea may have been suggested by finding dwarf trees growing in mountainous country, where the inhospitable environment often resulted in gnarled and interestingly-shaped trunks and stunted, miniature trees. Finding such a tree could be the start of an interesting bonsai collection.

Although many types of tree can be adapted for bonsai, slow-growing evergreens, such as junipers, pines and spruces, are particularly suitable, and deciduous trees of compact growing habit can be made to look interesting without leaves in winter by training them to form a fine tracery of branches.

The big bold *Begonia rex* and bergenia leaves used here act as a foil to the airy tracery of sorrel, rue, larkspur and seed-heads and the dominant rose.

17

Good bonsai subjects may be found growing wild, or may be raised from seeds, seedlings or rooted cuttings (all obtainable from specialist nurserymen). It is possible to obtain them by grafting, but probably the fastest way to produce a bonsai is by air-layering a suitable branch of a mature tree.

Once obtained, the bonsai should be planted in a simple, shallow container, specially designed in shape and colour to display the tree to best advantage. These pots can be obtained from a garden supplier specialising in bonsai, who can also advise on suitable shapes. Bonsai trees are hardy and should be kept out of doors with only a little protection from extremes of climate. They should not be brought indoors for more than a few days at a time, since the warmer atmosphere tends to induce undesirable spurts of growth.

Styles of bonsai include a single straight, slanting, or bent trunk, or a number of trees grown either for group effect or for their roots which form interesting shapes above the surface

Bonsai is the ancient Japanese art of growing little trees in little containers. There are Bonsai societies in both the U.S.A. and Great Britain. (Courtesy of Kenji Nurata and Japan Publications Inc.)

of the soil. Trees or trailing plants may also be grown in the form of a cascade or semi-cascade. Double, treble, even four or five trunks may be cultivated in a single tree, and interesting effects are achieved with trees growing out of stones.

The characteristic appearance of a good bonsai is achieved by a combination of several techniques: root and branch pruning, nipping the buds or leaf cutting, and wiring. Root pruning is carried out when the plant has become pot-bound and needs repotting if it is not to die of starvation, and aims at reducing the root system rather than enlarging the pot. Branch pruning is done to maintain the balance between the small root system and the top growth, and is also an excellent way of creating the overall shape of the tree. Nipping the buds, and leaf cutting for certain deciduous trees, will encourage compact and bushy leaf growth. Gentle wiring with fine copper wire induces the tree to follow its true line of growth.

Bonsai is not a difficult art providing you have patience, and care for your plants in the way that they might be expected to survive in a slightly improved form of their natural environment. However, in order to be sure of success, it is essential to understand both the principles and the techniques of raising, training and general care of your plants. For this reason no detailed instructions are given here, and for more information the reader is referred to one of the several excellent specialist publications on the subject and also to the Bonsai Kai of the Japan Society in London and Washington.

Bottle gardens

Bottles, ten-gallon carboys and old brandy glasses may be converted into semi-permanent 'gardens' of every size and shape. Even television tubes may be made into attractive 'bottle' gardens by the use of those plants of low, trailing habit. The warmth and humid conditions provided by the containers are ideal for growing many of the foliage plants which prove difficult under ordinary room conditions and which with artistic arrangement may be made to look more attractive than by growing in pots. The plants remain clean, which gives them a freshness that pot plants do not have, and the leaf markings take on a new beauty. Once planted, they require very little attention.

The most interesting 'gardens' can be made in

carboys which can be purchased for a very reasonable sum in five and ten-gallon sizes. They should be washed quite clean with warm water before using. To this add a small amount of liquid soap and then wash out with clean cold water. Then prepare a suitable compost.

Using a paper chute placed in the neck of the bottle or jar, first drop in some crushed charcoal. The pieces should be about pea size and there must be sufficient to cover the bottom to a depth of about 1 inch. Over the charcoal, pour in some washed shingle (or use a mixture of sand and peat) to a depth of 2 inches, then top up with 4 inches of compost. This should be made up of 2 parts John Innes Potting Compost and 1 part each of peat and sand. It should be comfortably moist but sufficiently friable to pour easily. The whole will sink down to a depth of about 6 inches. For a bottle placed on its side, pour in a mixture of charcoal, shingle and compost to give a depth of about 2 inches evenly distributed. The charcoal is necessary to assist drainage and to absorb undesirable gases. It will also keep algae away from the surface of the compost. Allow the compost several days to settle before planting.

For the garden choose slow-growing plants of neat, compact habit with small leaves, otherwise the bottles will soon become a tangled mass of plant growth. Get plants as small as possible: they will be easier to manipulate and to get through the neck of the bottle if they are quite small, and only the minimum of soil should be left on the roots.

Before purchasing the plants, make sure that they will be suitable for bottle culture, and if possible make a small drawing of the position each will occupy in the bottle so that once inserted there need be as little manipulation as possible. There should be a happy balance of greens, bronze and silvery leaves and plants of more dwarf habit should be arranged around those at the centre which grow taller while club mosses may be planted in the spaces in between. Six to eight plants and a few club mosses are suitable for carboy. Do not use flowering plants or those with thick hairy leaves.

Planting calls for a degree of skill. Holes should first be made in the compost with a pice of stick or cane. Before inserting the plants, tie up their roots with moss which will hold in place a limited amount of soil, and will enable the plant to be pressed home without damage to the roots. This is done with a cotton reel securely fixed to the end

of a cane. The plants are lowered into the holes made in the compost either by means of black cotton lightly tied to a main stem or by means of strong wire hooked around the main stem immediately beneath a leaf. The thread or wire is then used to hold the plant in position while the roots are made firm with a cotton reel securely fixed to the end of a cane. The wire is then removed or the cotton cut (the piece remaining will not be visible and will soon rot away).

After planting admit air for several hours and lightly spray the plants if necessary before resealing. The 'gardens' should require no further attention for at least three years. The plants require light but are best kept away from direct sunlight. Ordinary living-room temperatures are suitable.

Suitable plants

Aglaonema commutatum, Anthurium, Aphelandra, Begonia, Billbergia, Calathea insignis, Codiaeum pictum (croton), *Cryptanthus bivittatus, Dracaena sanderiana, Euonymous, Fatshedera, Ficus, Fittonia verschaffeltii, Maranta leuconeura* 'Massangeana', *Mesembryanthemum, Pellionia pulchra, Peperomia (P. magnoliaefolia, P. glabella, P. sandersii, P. hederifolia* and *P. caperata), Pilea cadierii, Saintpaulia, Sansevieria, Sarraceanea, Selaginella, Spathiphyllum, Tradescantia, Vriesia splendes.* Avoid large-growing or too rampant varieties. See also Ferns.

Bouquets

A bouquet is simply a bunch of flowers, and it is the way in which it is presented that gives it a special quality. Really a bouquet can be of two kinds: an informal one where the flowers are just tied together to make a very pretty bunch or, if made of short-stemmed flowers, it could really be called a posy. In this latter instance the flowers are in no way wired so it is made up of just natural-stemmed materials. If given as a presentation bouquet, it can easily be untied and placed in water. Some people receiving such a gift would, in fact, leave it just as it is and place it upright in a vase of water when it would last a few days. However, often the tying of the stems tightly to form the controlled pattern of the bunch will restrict the water intake up the stems.

The formal bouquet can be of many shapes and sizes. Some can consist of both natural-stemmed flowers and others of flowers on false stems made from covered wires or, in the case of the very formal bouquets, all flowers mounted on false stems. There is a lot to be said for both types of bouquets. The first group are useful for presentation at theatre and on special occasions when the recipient can make use of the flowers afterwards. The latter type (generally for bridal decoration) is of no use really after the ceremony and will very soon be dead, the lasting quality of the bouquet depending entirely on the flowers in it. One often gets asked how a bridal bouquet can be preserved and really this is a difficult problem; if in good order, straight after the ceremony, it should be lightly dusted all over with silica gel and laid in a box, resting the bouquet on more silica gel. Then seal the whole thing up in an airtight bag for a few days. You will find this will help preserve the flowers.

The basic shapes for wedding bouquets are really the straight and curved hand shower, the crescent, posy, loose posy and Victoria posy. The majority of flowers in these will be on false stems, although where possible a few natural stems should be kept to make the bouquet look more pleasing. The secret of a good bouquet lies in the choice of flower and foliage for use against the dress material, as well as its lightness to carry and the way it balances in the hand, and also its movement. Many bouquets made of perfect plant materials are so stiff and heavy that, when they are carried, they stand out like a ramrod and the beauty of the bouquet is quite lost. A shower bouquet should have movement in the tail and should look as light as a feather. The wires in a bouquet are just there to hold the flowers in place and not to act as a stake does to a plant. The lightest wire which will do the job satisfactorily should be chosen and, when natural stems are used, the wiring of these should be done internally, as far as possible, so that it will not show. Choice of materials in the bouquet is important and one does not want them too mixed, but a range of small, through medium, to large flowers is important in mixed bouquets so that a visual balance can be obtained. Some bouquets call for no foliage, others can be made of all mixed foliages, and these can be quite charming. As a rule, if you can use the foliage belonging to the flower you have in the bouquet, it will be helpful in making it look more natural. The day of the bouquet of just long trails of asparagus fern studded with roses or carnations has gone (unless some person introduces it again), and today

detailed attention is given to shape, so the fussy foliages like fern are no longer used. One of the most beautiful bouquets I have ever seen was made entirely from white azalea flowers, the wired stems covered with gold gauze ribbon to pick up the gold thread in the dress. No foliage was used in this bouquet.

Many wedding bouquets are white and often contain a lily of some type. They can be made of all one type flower, such as lillies-of-the-valley, roses, or can be mixed when they have four or five types of flower and different foliages. Any flower which will stand wiring, and last for at least twenty-four hours after it has been wired without deteriorating, can be used, but it is much easier for the florists (and the florist is the correct person to be asked to make a bouquet) to keep to the more conventional flowers. How many people have been disappointed because, on the special day, the unusual flower discussed a few weeks ago has since died or is not available. When arranging for bouquets to be made, always suggest alternatives so that you are not disappointed with the bouquet on the day. The flowers chosen should be in keeping with the bride's dress material and in the case of coloured bouquets, may also tie up with the colouring of the dresses worn by the rest of the bridal party.

Presentation bouquets give the recipient great joy, especially if given to someone not in the habit of receiving bouquets, and it is very nice if you can find out beforehand the flowers which give the most pleasure. If for a theatre or lady's evening presentation, try to find out the colour of the dress that the lady will be wearing because this also helps to make the picture. Often the best choice is a small bouquet, containing really choice materials and easy to carry. How worrying it is to see the recipient of a bouquet overwhelmed by an enormous bunch of flowers, the poor thing not really knowing how to carry it or what to do with it. That beautiful small bouquet would have been so much more welcome!

Many everyday presentation bunches or bouquets look wrong because they are made of rather stiff flowers instead of the seemingly casual small mixtures. What could be prettier in early spring than a small mixed bunch of Christmas roses, pink hyacinths, white freesias, eucalyptus foliage, violets, and cyclamen flowers and foliage? These should be on their natural stems and after use as a bouquet could be made into a very pretty table centre—so much nicer than the usual bunch of irises, chrysanthemums, tulips, pittosporum and stem or two of lilac.

Brachycome/Swan River daisy

Flower/Su

A delightfully free-blooming daisy-like Australian plant in various colours, including blue, rose and even purple and white. It can be grown in cool temperate gardens as a half-hardy annual making a cheerful addition to summer flower arrangements; or as a pot plant on a sunny window sill in a warm room for early spring.

Buddleia/butterfly bush

Flower/Leaf/Sp/Su/Au

Deciduous shrubs from the Orient, adding to the wealth of summer colour with flowers of white, rose-pink, purple, mauve or orange. The leaves of some varieties have a silvery colour. *B. davidii* in many unusual varieties is the most popular having tall spikes of lavender-blue flowers. Dry the ripe flowers in an upright position.

Bulbs see House Plants (Bulbs)

Buying flowers

Firstly, visit a good flower shop, where flowers are handled with care; this is so important if they are to last well. It is always safer to buy where the flowers are kept standing in deep water rather than from a stall where the flowers may well have had a few days drying out in the open air. The quicker one can get a flower or any plant material into water, once cut, the better chance it will have of lasting well. Mimosa is an excellent example of this and should always be kept sealed up in a polythene bag until wanted for use; it is certainly a case of the flower being fully developed before it is really attractive. The fluffy nature of the flower does not appear until it is covered with pollen, and this does not occur until the flower is nearly over.

Look carefully at flowers. There should not be a lot of pollen showing when they are young and fresh. Any daisy-type flower with a yellow-covered centre disc is better left alone. Flowers when purchased should have plenty of buds unless an immediate display is required, when they should be fully developed. There has recently been a lot of publicity given to bulb flowers from abroad discussing whether they are cut at the correct stage. Certainly in some cases, it seems that narcissi do not develop to their correct size when cut too early. Carnations should be firm and well rounded in shape, with no sign of the white stigma and style showing in the centre. Incidentally, carnations from some countries abroad are cut and packed in a very dry state and they need two or three days to develop up to selling conditions. So if they appear small and rather dry-looking ask what is the country of origin. Carnations do not last long in thundery weather. Roses, poppies and anemones should be tight in the bud. Always be careful of roses sold by street-sellers. The outer petals of the roses may have been peeled off to stop them appearing blown and the stems then packed tightly with all the flowers together to stop them opening! Gladioli, delphiniums and lupins should have just a few of the basal flowers showing colour; tulips should just be showing colour. Freesias are another flower that will last well if purchased when only the first flowers are open on each stem. Chrysanthemums should have good foliage well down the stem. If single blooms, they should be a good shape, with plenty of centre still to open. Large incurved blooms should be flat and not too deep—once they are fully developed, they appear nearly as round as a tennis ball.

Pots of narcissi bulbs should just be showing the buds between the young leaves. Cyclamen are better when they have short compact foliage, and the plant should be carrying a number of buds. Again, plants should be fresh from the nursery and have travelled under protected conditions and not, as one sees from time to time, on top of an open lorry!

As a general guide, it is better to pay a little more for good flowers which have been grown well and looked after carefully.

Cacti and Succulents see House Plants (Cacti and Succulents)

Calceolaria see House Plants (Pot Plants)

Calendula/common, or pot marigold

Flower/Su/Au

These orange or yellow flowers are familiar in gardens, but it is often forgotten that they will grow in bowls in the house, which makes them a godsend to people on low budgets. The cut flowers last well given plenty of water, and if you are tired of the orange variety there are also yellow ones. See also Tagetes.

Callistephus/China aster

Flower/Su/Au

These flowers bloom in a wide range of colours including pink, red, yellow, mauve and white. Some varieties resemble chrysanthemums, others peonies and others the ordinary asters, or Michaelmas daisies. Several varieties are easily grown in pots and all can be grown in good garden soil. For cut flower arrangements, hammer the stem ends.

Calluna/ling

Flower/Su/Au

This is the heather with purple flowers found on moorlands in Scotland. There are many cultivated varieties with white, pink or carmine flowers, one or two with attractive bright green or golden foliage and some, such as 'H. E. Beale', are quite tall and make very useful long-lasting cut flowers. Dry upright in a little water. See also Erica.

Camellia/tea plant

Flower/Leaf/Su/Au

Camellias are evergreen shrubs producing, mainly in spring, single, semi-double or double flowers in shades of white, pink and red, often fimbricated and frequently striped, splashed or edged with another colour or shade. The species most commonly grown is *C. japonica*, of which there are more than 1,000 named cultivars: the foliage of this species is glossy and is useful as a foil in arrangements. *C. reticulata*, is, since *C. japonica* is called the 'king of garden shrubs', the undisputed emperor of garden flowers. The flowers are immense, and of the most beautiful shades of pink, with gracefully curled petals: the foliage is matt. *C. saluenensis* is like a smaller version of *C. reticulata*, both in leaf and in flower, and crosses between this and *C. japonica* are known as *C.* x *williamsii*: this group contains some of the loveliest camellias raised in modern times. *C. sasanqua*, though less spectacular than the other species, is especially useful for flower arranging because it produces its red, white or pink flowers during mild spells throughout the winter months.

Camellias will not tolerate lime in the soil. The end of the stems should be crushed before arranging.

Campanula/bellflower, Canterbury bell

Flower/Su/Au

These are popular flowers which can be hardy garden varieties, slender and delicate trailers or tall, upright pot plants. The blooms appear mostly in varying shades of blue or mauve. For arrangements steep the flowers in water and remove faded blooms. Place the woody stems of Canterbury bells in boiling water for about a minute.

Capsicum/sweet pepper

Berry

Sometimes known as chillies (these are the smaller-fruited varieties), or red or yellow peppers, the red and green glossy-skinned fruits may be used in conjunction with foliage, flowers or other fruits. Some varieties make good pot plants. They are not hardy in cool temperate regions, and ripen their fruits in late summer.

Carnations

Flower/Leaf

There are two main kinds of carnations: the border carnations, which are hardy in cool temperate gardens, and the perpetual-flowering type which needs a minimum winter temperature of 50°F (10°C) and is generally grown in a greenhouse in regions subject to frost. The border varieties include single-coloured flowers (Selfs), striped flowers (Flakes), flowers marked with two or three tints (Bizarres), flowers with distinctively coloured edges (Picotees) and unclassified varieties (Fancies). In the Middle Ages the carnation (pink or gilly flower) was regarded as a symbol of the Virgin Mary.

The wide range of colours includes crimson, scarlet, white, heliotrope and grey, yellow and red, orange and heliotrope, mauve-pink, etc. The tall stems and delicate foliage of carnations may stand alone and last well in a cut-glass vase. You can mix them with other flowers and foliage, say with the fine tracery of nigella (love-in-a-mist), or any silvery or pale foliage, but great care should be taken with stronger colours.

Border carnations are always popular with flower arrangers. Here are some of the many different shapes and forms in which they can be obtained. Carnations can be bought from florists' shops at all times of the year.

Carthamus/distaff flower, safflower, saffron flower

Flower/Su

A hardy annual producing orange flowerheads which should be dried in an upright position for winter arranging.

Ceanothus/Californian lilac

Flower/Seed/Su/Au

The Californian lilacs, natives of North America, are prized for their beautiful blue flowers which, sadly, are not long-lasting when picked. There are two groups, the deciduous ones, which generally flower in the fall and are frost-hardy in all but the coldest places, and the evergreen kinds which have flowers of the most intense blue and which are usually spring flowering. These are not so hardy as the deciduous kinds and are generally grown against a wall in cold climates. Crush the stems before arranging. The seedheads are attractive and easily dried.

Celastrus

Berry

These deciduous climbing Chinese plants provide long-lasting brilliant gold and scarlet fruits in winter; they are therefore very useful at this time of the year. They grow in most garden soils, but the flowers are not exciting.

Celosia/Prince of Wales' feather, cockscomb

Flower/Su

Striking yellow, scarlet, deep red, orange, salmon, gold or cream grass-like plumes appear from August to October on celosias. They can be grown from seed in the greenhouse and planted outside in June. *C. cristata* (cockscomb) is the most popular. *C. plumosa*'s plumes may reach 18 inches high. Dry at the bud stage by hanging upside down.

Centaurea/cornflower, knapweed, sweet sultan

Flower/Leaf/Su

The vivid blue of cornflowers is to be treasured, but there are also shades of pink, rose, yellow and white in this genus. The delicate and some-times silvery tracery of foliage is attractive. The flowers tend to fade rather quickly in cut arrange-ments, but crush the stem ends before putting them in water.

Chamaerops see House Plants (Palms)

Chaenomeles/quince, japonica

Flower/Leaf/Berry/Sp

A group of deciduous flowering shrubs with bright wax-like flowers in varying shades of red, pink or salmon, which are matched by glossy leaves. The fruits are used for making jelly but also look unusual in displays of other fruit or flowers. *C. lagenaria*, the Japanese quince, may flower from January to June. Hammer the stem ends before placing in water.

Cheiranthus/wallflower

Flower/Sp

These delightful flowers follow the spring bulbs, and are attractive both for their scent and colour after the drabness of winter. Though the flowers do not last long in water, especially if cut on long stems, they mingle well with other flowers such as freesias and spring anemones. The dwarf varie-ties are easier to grow and their short stems sur-vive better. Incidentally, *C. kewensis* is winter-flowering.

The modern garden wallflowers are usually treated as bienniels, and will often seed themselves.

Chimonanthus/winter sweet

Flower/Wi

The fragrant greenish or golden-yellow flowers with brownish-red centres of this hardy deci-duous wall shrub are valuable for displays in winter. The flowers are usually seen around December. *C. praecox* is the species generally found in gardens.

Chlorophytum see House Plants (Pot Plants)

Chrysanthemum

Flower

The proud heads of chrysanthemums are justly famed and doubly valuable because the outdoor ones arrive in high season after the rich choice of summer is over.

The blooms vary in form tremendously from tightly packed incurved florets which are almost globe-shaped, to loosely arranged decorative florets. Quill-like florets are increasingly popular with flower arrangers. There are also pom-pom flowers, and small-flowered cascading types suit-able for hanging baskets.

The Korean varieties, obtained by crossing *C. koreanum* with early outdoor florists' varieties, are popular with flower arrangers. There are a large number of these varieties with double and semi-double flowers in a wide range of colours and with tall or bushy stems.

Chrysanthemums are also divided into types according to their period of flowering. The early-flowering types (July to October) are generally garden grown, the later-flowering ones are brought into the greenhouse about September. The bushy types of chrysanthemums are becom-ing more popular as pot plants for the house; see HOUSE PLANTS (Pot Plants). Greenhouse grown flowers or flowers from mild climates are available all the year round.

C. frutescens, the popular border flower mar-guerite, or Paris daisy, and *C. maximum*, the Shasta daisy, both daisy-like flowers, do well in massed summer arrangements. See also Pyre-thrum, for *C. coccineum*. In preparing chrysan-themums for displays hammer the stem ends, or split them, and give them plenty of water. Strip off all dead leaves as the flowers last longer than the leaves. The flowers do well on their own or with other flowers in large and perhaps rather sombre arrangements.

Church decoration and festivals

Churches have always attracted flower arrangers. One can see in very early paintings examples of flower decoration in churches and there are written records of the use of flowers at the main church festivals. Flower decorations can do much for a church and will add to its beauty if well done. Simplicity is the keynote of successful church decoration, and it is better to rely on good colour sense rather than gimmicks. Modern churches in new architectural styles tend to be more difficult to arrange in than the old stone churches which, with their elegant windows, arches and interesting stonework, set off the flowers to perfection.

A few large arrangements will turn out to be better than many little groups, and flowers on plinths or raised in some way will look better than those standing in containers on the floor. Place the arrangements at strategic points so that they show to good advantage. See Pedestal Arrangements.

Always obtain permission before attempting any decoration. Some clergymen have strong views about the position of flowers in church, and although they are almost invariably helpful, it is important to follow their wishes.

Be careful not to damage the woodwork or fabric of the church by affixing vases or containers, and see that any groups that are liable to be top heavy are placed in containers previously well weighted at the bases. Strong colours are helpful in brightening up dark backgrounds. Some colours are lost to the eye at a distance; blue is particularly bad and seems to be completely absorbed against a background of stonework. When working on an arrangement to go in front of stained glass, try to get colours which blend with it. Vases used in churches are often difficult to arrange, because many of them were designed before the modern era of flower arrangement and do not lend themselves to large displays. They must often be used, however, because they may be memorials to deceased members of the congregation. Sometimes one can fit special bowls in the tops of vases to get a larger display. It is always easier to work with one's own containers, if this is possible.

The majority of spare vases in churches turn out to be jam jars, which in the correct positions may be useful, but they are never suitable for wide-spreading displays. One of the most useful types of containers for window sills, and for the fronts of choir stalls, are baking tins. Check that such containers do not leak, then paint them a neutral colour; fill the base with strips of lead or gravel, and they will then be worth their weight in gold.

It is important to choose the correct containers for the church, and any pedestals should fit into the picture well. Stone ones will look good against stonework, but are heavy to move around. In some churches, brass or even silver pedestals are available and these are excellent. Fibreglass has recently come into use for pedestals, and can be painted to suit the background of the church. The one disadvantage of this material is that it is so light, and must be weighted at the base. This can be done by pouring stones or cement into a hole drilled into the side of the pedestal. Wrought-iron stands are popular these days but are often badly designed. The container is often not made large enough at the top to hold the flowers—a point to remember when buying.

Wooden containers are good and can be simple in design with weighted bases. Try to find ones that are similar in colour to the woodwork of the church. A very large bowl from an old-fashioned washstand, or a large mixing bowl, holds a considerable amount of water and has a wide area in which to work. They can be painted in neutral colours, and when well arranged, should be completely hidden by the flowers and foliage.

Church decoration for weddings

The flowers for a wedding are extremely important and really make the setting for the ceremony. They suggest a note of welcome to the guests before the arrival of the bride and it is at this time that particular notice is taken of them. Many people arriving early just sit and wait, and at the same time study the flowers. The flowers should pick up the colourings of the bridal party and the whole thing should be most carefully planned.

It is nice, if possible, to have flowers in the entrance to the church, either a group on a pedestal or perhaps a hanging basket in the porch roof. A group at the back of the church is the last thing one sees on leaving the church, and helps to hide the conglomeration of oddments which often accumulate at the back of the church because there is nowhere else to put them.

The number of vases of flowers used at a wedding varies considerably, but one should reckon on two groups at the altar, either at the back of the holy table or on either side. These flowers should be simple and there is nothing better than some form of large white lily; just a few stems in each vase, well arranged with clean cut foliages. Lots of different types of flowers do not show up well from a distance. Two large groups always show to good advantage on either side of the chancel rail, where the main part of the service takes place. These can take up the colourings of the bridal party. Another pair of vases at the beginning of the nave looks attractive, and the flowers should be similar in colouring to the large groups. These last arrangements may be on a smaller scale. If doing a pair of vases, always divide the materials equally before starting. If one has to flow one way, then the opposite should be done to the other vase.

Often this will be sufficient. For a large wedding it is very necessary to use the whole of the church area, and then the use of window sills is effective, as well as some pedestals placed at strategic points in various parts of the church. For extra decoration, some people like the pew ends fitted with flowers at intervals down the aisle. Very elegant decorations may be done in lantern vases fixed to the main pillars in the nave, but garlands of flowers and foliages attached to the stonework tend to look gaudy. It is important to know when to stop. Remember, simplicity is the key to success. A few large groups showing up well give the best results. Remember, also, that much of the service is taken standing up, so small flowers low down will not be seen.

Flowers for weddings and festivals are usually done the day before, so make arrangements to look at them early on the day, being prepared to fill up gaps, and always have the odd flower as a replacement. When you have them, they are not often needed, but you can be certain to want one or two when they are not available.

Christmas decorations

Christmas is a very important festival in the church year. Many churches today have a Nativity scene with the crib and stable set up, and it is here that the Christmas tree can also be used. Over the last few years, the Constance Spry Organisation has had the privilege of doing the Nativity scene for Westminster Abbey, in London, where many Christmas trees, together with bay and other evergreens can be used. There is nothing more attractive than a decorated Christmas tree, but it must be well done. It is often necessary to thin the branches slightly, then decorate it in a special colour scheme. Lights, if required, are so much prettier when they are wired up with white or green flex. The little lights are the best ones to use. Keep to red and silver, or green and gold colours and be bold with the decoration to the tree at the base. So often the base does not get finished, and the whole effect is spoilt. Just large bows and bells with streamers can look really good, having first made a good top for the tree.

The artificial materials available today for decorating are superfluous for decorating churches. Christmas calls for holly (green and variegated) with real berries, ivy, evergreen conifers and mistletoe, and really these are the best materials for church decoration. Somehow plastic Christmas flowers do not seem correct. See that the altar is neatly and boldly decorated, and if lilies are too expensive, use white blooms with variegated holly as a background foliage.

The entrance porch will look excellent if decorated and perhaps lit with a carol singers' lantern. The window sills can carry large mantel-pads of evergreens, and at this time a large plaque of evergreen may be hung from the pulpit and the base may be garlanded. Evergreens are longer lasting, so garlanding can be done without the problem of everything dying off quickly. The pieces should be wired and then bound on to strong string. Another quite attractive decoration can be made on a broomstick set in a large flower pot, the broomstick being bound in red ribbon and having a few streamers attached; fix a large ball of moss or polystyrene on to the top of the stick and poke pieces of holly, ivy and evergreen into it. Have them all the same length to get a nice round effect. Remove the leaves from some of the holly to get the berries to show up well. These could stand on either side of the aisle or each side of the chancel rail. A few big red bows of ribbon will give the extra colour and finish off your mixed evergreen groups.

A watch-night service in candlelight is a beautiful sight, and tall candles may well be fitted to the window decorations, care being taken to see that the foliage is kept well away from the naked lights. Evergreen foliage can go up like dry tinder.

Amusing use has been made of the font in this decoration which is in fact for a wedding not a christening. The arrangement shown on page 28 can be seen in the background to the right.

Churches are not always the easiest places in which
to arrange flowers. Wedding arrangements like the
one shown here need to be bold and colourful.

Easter decorations

It is at Easter that one usually finds a wealth of materials to decorate the church, unless it falls too early after a hard winter. The spring flowers, trees and shrubs are in full bloom and the many bulb flowers provide a wide range of colours. White and gold are the colours often used at Easter, and Madonna lilies are associated with this season. Pussy willow (see Trees—Salix) makes a substitute for palms, which are appropriate at Easter as well as on Palm Sunday.

Decorations for Christenings, etc.

Flowers should never be arranged in the font, but at the base or on the top, where they can be easily moved should it be required. For special services, a font edge top, made to fit round the font can be very pretty. This is made on a moss-covered ring-shaped wire frame. The ring can be made like a large wreath (the diameter of the font), covered in bun moss. Small flowers are then wired and stuck into it. Remember to leave a space for the minister to carry out his duties.

Sometimes, the flowers are done in three or five groups rather than all round. Then it is best to have one principal group which is larger and should flow well over the edge of the font. The colour pattern of the flowers is usually blue and white or pink and white, for boy and girl respectively. If there are to be a few christenings, then just have pastel shades, but simple flowers are called for rather than anything exotic.

Often flowers are asked for at funerals and at memorial services. In this case, one or two large groups are all that is necessary and these should be rather sombre in colouring. Whites, greys and greens are good. Large groups in red and purple colouring also look good. Where the service is for a keen gardener, it is nice to use something simple in the way of garden flowers.

Flower festivals

Flower festivals have now become a fund-raising activity which many churches have adopted. They are often combined with a music festival or some special patronal festival, but the flower side is generally the most important part. Some wonderful work has been done at these festivals and great sums of money have been raised. Often, however, the little village churches are the most striking because they are not overdone, whereas the big cathedrals sometimes seem to contain too many collections of flowers, and these take away from the beauty of the building rather than add to it. The ordinary simple, but beautiful decorations seem preferable to the over-elaborate creations and interpretive work which some people do.

Church flowers and foliage

It is difficult to make a list of flowers and foliages that one can use for special occasions, because anything that will stand cut in water for 48 hours is suitable, if the correct shape and colour. Foliages first can be chosen from these: eucalyptus, camellia, lichen branches, guelder rose, laurel, beech, whitebeam (especially *Sorbus aria* 'lutescens'), stripped lime, wych elm and holly. All these are used as large branches. Reeds, *Phormium tenax*, bergenia, cardoon and hosta provide useful foliage; the individual leaves are excellent. Smaller pieces of privet, *Senecio greyii*, snowberry, aucuba and ivy can always be used.

For large groups, the bigger blooms are probably best, and there is a wealth to choose from most of the year. Lilies are always wanted and are always available in some form. Among the most suitable are arum lilies, *L. longiflora*, *L. speciosum* 'Alba' and *L. auratum*. Crinums, carnations, roses, narcissi, chrysanthemums, irises, scabious, *Chrysanthemum maximum* 'Ester Reeds', gladioli, hydrangeas, are but a few of the more common flowers which are suitable for large groups.

Flowering shrubs, such as lilac, cherry, philadelphus, forsythia, guelder rose and rhododendron, can all be forced for early spring work, following on through spring and early summer. If the stems carry a lot of foliage, this must be stripped off to make more of an impact with the flowers. Pampas grass and bullrushes, large seedheads of angelica, cardoon and many sprays of berries seem to fit into autumn and winter decorations.

Cissus see House Plants (Trailing Plants)
Citrus see House Plants (Pot Plants)

Cladanthus arabicus

Flower/Su

Cheerful daisy-like yellow flowers appear in a delicate tracery of fern-like foliage. A sunny spot with sufficient moisture will give you plentiful supplies of the flowers from the garden. They may reach three feet but are usually much shorter.

Clarkia

Flower/Su

A Californian annual that produces elegant flowers of purple, rose, salmon, pink or white. There are several varieties, some reaching two feet. They need a sunny spot in the garden or should be grown in a cool greenhouse in regions subject to frost. This is a good flower for arrangers as it lasts in water and dries easily for winter arrangements. Dip the stems of cut flowers in boiling water.

Clematis

Flower/Sp/Su/Au

These delightful climbing shrubs (mostly deciduous) will give you a wide range of colours mostly in a minor key: dark mauves, purples and pinks, often striped. Some varieties come into flower in spring, others later. They should be used with other stronger-stemmed material for support and the stem ends dipped in boiling water or steeped in medical alcohol. Hang the flowers upside down to dry: many species also have attractive fluffy seedheads which can be dried in the same way.

Clivia see House Plants (Pot Plants)

Cobea see House Plants (Trailing Plants)

Colchicum/autumn crocus, meadow saffron

Colchicums produce flowers very similar to those of the crocuses but are not in fact members of the crocus family. The species and hybrids usually grown produce their flowers in autumn: the leaves, which are massive and strap-shaped, are not produced until spring, when the flowers are over. The flowers may be picked and used in indoor arrangements just like crocus flowers, but there is another decorative indoor use for colchicums: these bulbs possess the remarkable power of being able to produce their flowers without any earth or water. Just place the dry bulbs on a window sill or on a saucer of decorative pebbles close to a window and the bulb will produce its gorgeous flowers. After flowering the bulbs should be planted in the garden to make leaf. They should not be lifted again until the leaves have died down when they should be carefully lifted, washed clean of earth and brought indoors again to perform their miracle once more.

Coleus see House Plants (Pot Plants)

Colour in flower decoration

What is good and what is bad in the use of colour cannot be answered by quick reference to any universally accepted standard or rule. Colour makes up the dominant element in flower decoration; they please or do not please according to the onlooker's sensitivity, but tastes develop and change, so flower arranging is as variable and controversial a pastime as you like to make it. Choice of colours for a group is to some extent governed by the setting. Ideas must take into consideration the background, lighting (artificial or otherwise) and the size of room so there is a measure of discipline when finding the right flowers to fit.

Ideas, the best of them at any rate, have been developed by people with a sure eye for colour and fundamentally good taste and fortunately these people have shown us enough to sharpen our perception by writing about and illustrating much of the work they have carried out in practice. Colours in flowers, however, are almost impossible to record accurately on paper. The texture of petals or leaves, the shape of a stem or the stage of development of any of them will affect the way they reflect light. Because flowers are naturally in the process of change, particularly when cut for arrangement in vases, precise descriptions tend to miss the point and definitions or rules to become questionable. One cannot say why the reddest of red geraniums against the orange yellow of, for example, marigolds, which is recognisable to say the least as a combination lacking in subtlety, happens to be a strikingly unhappy one to some eyes but obviously not so to others—for those flowers are often seen growing together, sometimes with the addition of the bluest lobelia, in gardens and window boxes. The flowers themselves are pleasing, so are the colours, but the juxtaposition of them is a commonplace one rather than a harmonious one, and a subtle eye is unlikely to pick it out, for choice, as desirable for an arrangement.

It is not simply that such primary and intermediate colours cannot be used together but that the texture, shapes and formation of those materials in those colours will form an uncomfortable group. On the other hand, an entirely different impression is made with red, yellow and blue put together, perhaps in a handful of poppies and cornflowers and daisies; such a simple, gay and delicate mixture has an immediate appeal probably for most of us. 'Mixture' incidentally may not be the correct expression, the colours in this context, of course, not being mixed, in the sense that paint can be, but it will serve.

Rules, so many of which are heavily contrived by theorists, may thankfully be laid aside. 'Theorists argue,' wrote Constance Spry, 'that certain combinations of colours are preferable to others. This is no doubt true for many purposes but, in flower arrangement, I have always found it advisable to discard any such preconceived theories. . . . Colour is an intensely personal affair which it would be foolish to be dogmatic about.'

Backgrounds and containers

Whether chosen to suit flowers or the flowers to suit them, these set the scene; they enliven it in more senses than one. Pale walls, plain not patterned ones, matt surfaces in, say, dark green, not dark blue and in light rather than dark yellow make manageable backgrounds. Again, not only their colours but sizes, shapes and textures play a part in the scene. Suitable containers for general purposes should be simple vases, clean in outline, wide open at the brim and well balanced on their bases. Light colours or white (which are reasonably easy to get) and preferably not with glazes that glare. Deeply coloured containers—orange, blue, red or black ones—are by no means impossible to use but the choice of flowers to match them is limited. Few settings are unsuitable for flowers and their infinitely variable colours.

RED seems to come at you with a bang and to glow cheerfully in any setting. The sparkle of scarlet berries in a hedge is evidence enough of what red can do to a background of greens, browns and rusty hues. Reds on their own, boldly put together in every shade from gentle rose to flashing crimson and even orange, almost stir the air; this use of them, often called crashing reds, well describes the rousing effect it can have on the senses.

GREEN calms things down a bit. When stems are stripped of leaves the colours of blooms are the stronger for being deprived of the green that normally tempers their brilliance. Varied greens, arranged to play up the contrasting shapes foliages have (spiky, rounded and angular), will soothe the senses, where reds so conspicuously can disturb them.

YELLOW, which of course lightens the imagination with thoughts of spring, quickly lights up a mixed flower arrangement; it appears in itself to be sensitive and to vary in intensity, noticeably so against greys in particular.

BLUE (heavenly of course) is not entirely an amenable colour when you get the flowers indoors. It seems to need very clear light to respond to, and somehow does not always firmly make its mark among other colours in arrangements. But when allowed to be strongly predominant (a bowl of gentians for example) it seems hardly the cool, receding colour that one usually takes it to be.

WHITE is encouraging to use; when colours have to be grouped which may otherwise seem difficult to put together, the introduction of a little white makes a convenient intervention between one shade and another. Alternatively it can become a highlight among colours, in other words a foil. Flowers in fact are seldom pure white. Arrangements (in a variety of so-called white flowers) give an impression of colour; well lit by artificial light, they solve the problems posed by dark and possibly angular backgrounds.

Fashion in flower arrangement changes, thanks more to an imaginative use of colour than to the influence of directives based on theory.

Columnea see House Plants (Trailing Plants)

Composition

The two main considerations when using flowers as decorative material are: 1, to arrange them in vases and other containers so that they are presented in the most satisfying and effective way, and 2, to place them against an appropriate background. Flowers not well arranged will spoil the beauty of a room, and the most carefully arranged group will only give the greatest pleasure when in the correct setting.

Proportion between flowers and vase is of the utmost importance and it is not a subject about which one can lay down a law. The container may be considered in two ways, firstly merely as a

Amusing china containers such as the one above add extra interest to an arrangement, but can be awkward to use. The visual centre of gravity is the boy's chin.

receptacle for water, and today with the employment of modern water-retaining flower arranger's putty it can be just a dish or tray, not playing any real part in the finished arrangement. Secondly, the container can become an integral part of the whole arrangement. The first way of using a container might be for a large group of fruit and flowers on a chimneypiece for a party. However, a large group on a pedestal would look quite incorrect if part of the vase was not showing, and in this instance the container must be considered an important part of the total composition.

The whole problem is to get the correct proportion and only the discerning eye will guide you in this important factor. Top-heavy effects, squat or skimpy arrangements, delicate flowers in too overpowering a vase and heavy flowers in a delicate one, are all errors we see from time to time and long to put right. So often it could easily be done with just a minor adjustment to a few stems.

The important thing to avoid is getting your flowers too crowded and stuffed into the vase; each particular item should show up well and all stems must flow from a centre point. Plenty of buds help to brighten the effect, and some flowers well recessed will help with the balance. Always get your outline flowers in first and then do not extend past them. Next position a few prominent leaves or flowers in the centre and work out from these. Balance should be both actual and visual, and a few stems going back away from the vase will help with this and also make the arrangement appear to be more all round, rather than a flat strictly facing group. This is a very common fault of many flower arrangers.

In floristry one can have fixed measurements

This magnificent arrangement was created by
Constance Spry herself. The big white flowers are
Paradise lilies (*Crinum moorei*), the fern is
Polystichum setiferum and the greenery an
ornamental kale.

An opulent arrangement in the finest Constance
Spry tradition. Ingredients include roses, gladioli,
seed heads of agapanthus *Vallota speciosa,*
sedum, actriplex and leaves of hosta and tree peonies.

Different colour forms of the Japanese anemone
make an unusual and striking arrangement for a
most unusual container – a Victoria silver and crystal
candleholder.

A high summer arrangement using roses,
carnations, tiger lilies, allium seed heads and reed
maces. Note the use of bergenia foliage to heighten
the effectiveness of the colours.

but in flower arranging one must keep an open mind, as so much depends on the materials being used. Light feathery materials can be used with much longer stems than some heavy blooms; if one stuck to a measure they would have to be the same.

A common fault is to get what one would call a 'surprised' look when all the stems seem to leap up out of the vase. Make use of your curved materials to go over the edge so linking up the flowers with the container. There should be no hard rim showing below upright stems. The use of colour to add 'weight' in the centre of the group can also make a difference to the visual balance. Do not dot your flower varieties about if only one or two of a particular variety are available. Try to keep them together, for this will make so much more of them. Overcrowding is such a common fault, especially in these days when competitions are popular. So many people worry about the judge looking for faults, they tend to stuff things in to stop any chance of netting showing. Netting, I agree, should not show, but a leaf here and there recessed can do such a lot without too much conglomeration.

At the Constance Spry School, instructors have never been in the habit of teaching fancy shapes for flower arrangements, and they hate the use of geometric names, such as 'a triangular arrange-

The shallow container used in the table decoration below is practically hidden by the floral materials used in the arrangement. The arrangement is twice as wide as it is tall – again, classic proportions – ideal for a stemless container.

ment'. Geometry immediately conjures up straight lines and rather set designs, which is just what one should try to avoid with flowers.

Basic designs one must have, such as the facing arrangement, when the flowers and foliage all flow from a point which is set three-quarters of the way back in the vase. This is suitable for use on a side table, or as a large group standing against a wall. If it is required to be seen from the side as well, more flowers must be used and placed in at the back of the vase. The flowers must all be free-flowing and of different lengths; make use of buds and flowers of different sizes together to make them look natural.

The shape of the arrangement will be determined by the position in which it stands, and also the type of vase in use. A modern cylindrical shape calls for a rather upright design, which is often called a 'vertical' arrangement. Set the flowers to the appropriate height for the size of the vase and then work within this imaginary outline. That the stems should be one and a half times the height of the vase is often heard, but so much depends on the materials being used, and it is nonsense when one considers the modern 'line' arrangements today, which are often done in a flat dish. In the latter instance an arrangement of six or seven times the height of the vase would be more in keeping with current practice.

For table arrangements, choose a vase to suit the occasion: usually long troughs, oval shallow dishes or round bowls, but never think of these in the terms of 'horizontal' lines, which is another favourite term used in show schedules.

Backgrounds are all-important and when arranging flowers remember always to choose colours and use a style that suits the furniture and wall-paper. This tall, triangular arrangement is related to both the plates and to the light above.

Flowers on a mantelpiece may well have to fit below a picture, and in this case, make something of an L-shaped arrangement to fit round the frame. It is also important to see that the flowers flow well over the edge of the shelf.

Hogarth curves (named after the eighteenth-century painter William Hogarth), and crescent shapes are the most difficult to do and generally should not be attempted. Many, when arranged, are so unnatural looking that the flowers are spoilt—especially as they are also often unable to reach the water.

Try to avoid over-arranging. The everyday flower from the garden should be arranged simply and not made into stylised shapes such as an 'L' or an 'S'. It is certain the painter Hogarth did not mean his particular style to be copied to the extent of mangling flowers into a 'Hogarth curve' which one sees done so often today. It is worth repeating that there should always be a sympathy between vase and flowers. How often does one see a delicate ornamental cherub holding up an arrangement that really a giant would have difficulty in supporting!

It is difficult to be logical about matters of taste. Choosing the right material and vase is important but only you can decide what these should be, having the setting in mind. It is far easier to arrange the group where it is intended to be displayed. Doing flowers in one room and then taking the completed arrangement to another room where it is to be displayed can lead to unexpected results. Remember that the background is part of your composition. By first getting a group of flowers in your mind, then choosing the vase and materials to go in it, you are creating a 'picture', but instead of using canvas and paints you are using a background, flowers and vase.

When doing an all-round arrangement first set five or seven points, all the same distance from the centre of the bowl, then set the height. A turntable on which to work will be most helpful. If you are using mixed flowers or mixed colours of one flower, group these but distribute across in swathes from one side of the vase to the other as may be seen from the colour pictures in this book. Do not build up blocks of flowers so that the arrangement becomes divided up in sections. However, in practice, it is best to work in sections, coming down from the highest point with stems of varying lengths and working out to the widest point. Keep doing this until the vase is full, looking at it from above and at a distance. See that you do not get a shelving effect or that the composition does not get a 'waist' shape. The first five or seven points should not stand out like spokes of a wheel.

Lighting is a very important factor in showing off the flowers to good advantage and should be from above the group, preferably shining down on to the front. Plinths with glass tops housing an electric light are quite useless. They only throw up light into a mass of stems where it is not wanted and, in many cases, heat up the water in the vase which helps encourage the development of bacteria in the water. An alcove in the corner of a room which is lit from above is quite excellent for housing a group of flowers, but do not make the mistake of using an alcove too small to house the correct-sized arrangement for the room. Flowers should fit in to the alcove, just as a group of flowers fits in to the background of a painting of flowers in a vase. It is a point one finds strange when judging a show which has in its schedule *A Flower Picture*. The exhibits in this class are often quite lovely, but many have to be disqualified because the flowers are coming out over the frame.

Containers

Vases made of pottery and glass, obviously the most commonly accepted containers to put flowers in, are not always the best to choose for everyday use. Inconvenient to store in any quantity, breakable and possibly difficult to replace, although not inexpensive in the first place, they have quite a few drawbacks. Nevertheless it is a pleasure to have them. So much pottery, glass and china is designed to hold flowers and is also ornamental in itself. There are, however, a lot of other things that one feels compelled to have. The magpie instinct is well-developed in most flower-arranging enthusiasts and, once the urge to collect sets in, it tends to get the upper hand of prudence; so, in building up a store of likely objects the question is where to draw the line.

In general, the simpler the container, the easier it is for flowers to look well in it. The range of things to use may be from cake tins (usually painted and cunningly concealed with foliage) to a golden chalice (which is worth showing off if you have one). Although a group of flowers may be put together intentionally to reveal the special quality of its container rather than the excellence of the arrangement, more often than not the main point is to make the two complement each other. Of course one wants to get the proportions right, not only so far as the height and width of the flowers in relation to their container are concerned, but so that in all senses there is no suggestion of one thing being awkwardly adjusted to the other, of the flowers being overwhelmed by whatever is chosen to hold them. If it is to show at all, a vase has to be selected with the thought in mind that the material of which it is made, as well as its shape, will fit the picture satisfactorily—that is to say to the satisfaction of oneself primarily, and only if necessary so as to conform to some arbitrary rule of stylised procedure.

A glass jam jar (or a stone one, if such is to be had now) full of primroses, for instance, can make an entirely acceptable flower decoration to all but the most exacting demands. Neither the container nor the flowers seem totally out of place with one another and the whole will happily light up some otherwise colourless spot in a room. An upright, elegant dark bronze urn filled with tall lilies is also something simple, a little grand perhaps, that provides an example of a complementary use of container and contents.

Emphasis has been put elsewhere in these pages on the part that colours, shapes, sizes and textures play in flower arrangements, and at this stage the same point can be made in discussing containers (see Colour; Composition). A perceptive grasp of what effect the shape and substance of a vase is going to have saves time and, possibly, will avoid disappointment in the final result. Let us say that one is buying glass: a clear glass vase is useful enough; on the other hand stems inevitably show up in it. Even though some stems are the better for being seen clearly (a rose's stem, maybe, with gem-like bubbles which cling to the stem under water), others are not so beautiful. A slightly patterned or fluted vase, such as a 'celery' glass, will help to obscure an untidy muddle of curling stems and, if one's preference is for neatness in this respect, may solve a minor problem in choosing the right thing on which to spend your money. Glass vases, so many of them being old-fashioned, are not plentiful now but are still to be found in sales and small secondhand shops. They have a scarcity value, just as pottery ones have, for production of both in this country has been intermittent for some considerable time and our output has been affected by competition from abroad. There is however a variety of modern pottery and glass, foreign or not, easily available from florists and other shops.

Potters fortunately have produced shapes and sizes of every sort imaginable; they have applied colours and glazes, matt and shiny ones, to suit all tastes. Incidentally, when buying earthenware vases, jugs, pots, cylinders, dishes or bowls for flowers, it is sensible to make sure that they are well glazed inside, otherwise the porous nature of the basic material, by soaking up moisture, may spoil the surfaces of tables, or other pieces of furniture on which they are placed.

The range of other things that can turn out to be just what is wanted for the flowers is a wide one, often unexpectedly so, and there is not room enough here to give an account of it in detail. It runs from odd, wooden needlework boxes which, with a small bowl inside, will comfortably set off small and delicate groups, to iron 'garden' urns. The latter, being low and wide-brimmed and firmly balanced (though heavy to move about) make sound bases for both tall and spreading arrangements. Silver, ormulu, copper, lead, alabaster and baskets all have marked characteristics of their own and a peculiar adaptability to flowers generally, and to some particularly.

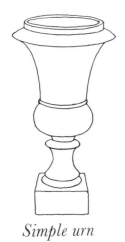

Simple urn

Cherub with scallop shell

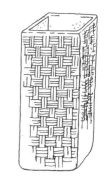

Modern ceramic basket

Tazza

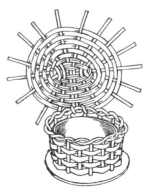

Hamper

Bevel-edged mirror trough

Shallow oval table centre

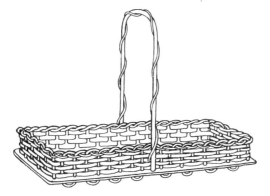

High-handle oblong basket

Oval tazza

Here the container, one of Constance Spry's innovations, a shallow bevel mirror trough, reflects the arrangement, and care has been taken not to hide it.

For example, if baskets can be considered to suit light spring flowers most readily, or generous handfuls of garden roses, then silver's characteristically suitable companion may be something more sophisticated, perhaps heavy purple and wine-coloured flowers and bold foliages.

The occasional 'bureaucrat' of floral art may dampen the spirit of the game, for example by inviting one to consider 'potential design force' in container material, or to study the effectiveness of 'analogous harmony' in colour, or the value of 'extended significant form' in groups, before setting out to arrange anything. Well, that is fine, if you have time for it. But as long as one is bent on doing the flowers for pleasure the less complicated one's ideas become, the better it is for the sake of everyone around. And, as the choice of containers is often fraught with indecision or the acquisition of them sometimes difficult, the direct approach is probably the least tiresome. In other words, if you have a good look round at what you have got already and make do with that, trouble is met half-way: the alternative is to go out and look for something you like, get it if you can, and then see how best you can make it and your flowers go together. Luckily there is a useful supply of paraphernalia to be drawn upon, which can be used to keep flowers in place in what may otherwise seem unmanageable containers. Various holders are manufactured in large quantities and are designed to allow the arranger to build up a group (much higher than the height of a single stem) or to stretch it sideways, so to speak, without appearing to force the issue unnecessarily and to make flowers stay where you want them to be in practically any circumstances. Under the heading of holders come pieces of wire netting, pin holders, tubes, candle-cups, sand, stones, plasticine and flower arrangers' putties which are of a singularly absorbent nature (see Basic Flower Arranging).

Wire netting is widely used as a practical holder because it can be cut and pulled and pushed into shapes to fit the majority of vases. Pinholders are spiky, compact sets of nails or pins set into a heavy base, usually a round one, on which the ends of stalks are impaled so that, if it cannot be done in any other way, an arrangement is transfixed, as it were, and almost forcibly rooted to the spot. Tubes are cone-shaped bits of metal which hold water (and stems, of course) and can be fixed to sticks or strong wires and then incorporated into an arrangement. They are one means of enlarging a group by providing an artificial extension of stems upwards. The use of cones requires some ingenuity in the art of concealment or camouflage. They and their sticks are apt to be obtrusive mechanical aids and, if they are not carefully hidden, their uncompromising outline catches the eye at once. As they are usually supplied already painted in a rather formidable green, they blend indifferently with other colours and, to say the least, are likely to upset any attempts one may be making to achieve 'analogous harmony'. Precise instructions on how to apply holders of any kind to their various uses are best obtained from a florist, but the pictorial illustration to this book, together with the illustration which shows the containers used, gives one a good idea of the mechanics.

Pewter mugs like this one can be difficult to use because the depth is so much greater than the opening at the top. The secret is not to try to push stems right down to the bottom of the container.

Convallaria/lily-of-the-valley

Flower/Leaf/Sp

These are hardy perennials natives of Europe, including Britain, have been cultivated since Elizabethan times and thrive in shady places in the garden, but can also be made to bloom in winter in the greenhouse or as indoor pot plants by keeping them under glass and bringing them indoors in late December. The leaves are like clean tulip leaves and the flowers appear as groups of tiny white 'bells', which make natural posies tied together inside a large leaf. There is a pink form known as *C. majalis* 'Rosea' and a double white form, *C. m.* 'Florepleno' which is longer lasting when picked. The garden-grown ones last well in water, but the florists' or greenhouse-grown flowers should be plunged in deep water and occasionally gently sprayed with an atomiser.

Convolvulus

Flower/Su

Attractive frail-looking, bell-shaped flowers in pinks, whites and blues. *C. cneorum*, which has pinkish-white flowers and silvery green leaves, is a shrubby plant suitable for cut flower arrangements. The trailing varieties produce flowers which will all too quickly fade in water. *C. mauritanicus*, which has trailing blue flowers, makes a good decoration in hanging baskets. See also Ipomoea.

Cordyline see House Plants (Pot Plants)

Coreopsis/tickseed

Flower/Su

The daisy-like flowers are mostly bright yellow, gold or yellow and crimson and are popular border perennials or annuals. The deep yellow flowers of *C. grandiflora* are very distinctive for flower arranging. Hammer the stems ends and the flowers will last well.

Corylopsis

Flower/Wi/Sp

A deciduous, frost-hardy shrub noted for its light-yellow, cup-shaped, drooping, deliciously scented flowers, which appear on the bare branches at the end of winter or in early spring. Hammer the end of the stem ends and remove about an inch of bark.

Cosmos

Flower/Leaf/Su

These are rather daisy-like flowers in white, pink, rose, purple, or crimson, that bloom continuously for months against a delicate tracery of fern-like leaves. The cut flowers should be newly in bloom, and they will last well. They mix well, and require additional foliage to their own.

Cotinus/smoke tree, wig tree, Venetian sumach

Flower/Leaf/Su

C. coggygria produces fluffy 'smoke-like' plumes which start reddish-pink and later change to grey. The foliage produces good autumn colour, some varieties turning reddish-purple or deep purple. See also Rhus.

Cotoneaster

Berry/Leaf/Flower/Sp

A group of deciduous and evergreen frost-hardy shrubs which mostly produce bright red berries in autumn. One of the most commonly seen species, *C. horizontalis*, has pinkish flowers (other species are generally white) and tiny, box-like leaves on branches in a herringbone pattern; but the berries of other cotoneasters tend to be more conspicuous. The deciduous species have

good autumnal leaf colour. Hammer stem ends and peel the bark slightly.

Crataegus/hawthorn, quick, may, thornapple

Berry/Flower/Leaf/Sp

There are many other more decorative sorts than the hedgerow hawthorn or thorn apple which adorns the wayside. Be that as it may, the hedgerow tree is a true source of plant material. The fresh green leaves will burst from their buds almost before winter is over if they are brought into the house. The delicate flowers too are lovely on bare twigs with the foliage removed, and the berries should be sprayed in autumn with a transparent cellulose varnish to make them shine and preserve them. Most species have red berries and white flowers and some have good autumnal leaves. See also Ilex and Trees (Crataegus).

Crocosmia/common montbretia

Flower/Leaf/Su

This bright yellow, orange or gold flower on gracefully branching stems is good for cutting in the late summer. The long, pointed leaves are also very decorative. It grows from a corm and is frost-hardy in most parts of the country: in the coldest areas it is wisest if the corms are brought indoors in November. The leaves may be pressed in sheets of blotting paper as they are approaching the sear.

Crocus

Flower/Au/Wi/Sp

Surprisingly, like daffodils and tulips, crocuses may be cut for indoor flower arrangements. That this is so rarely done is due to the diminutive size of the flowers. Nevertheless, when one considers that such treatment rescues them from the depradations of birds and provides colour in the house when there is so little else, it is a sensible procedure. By a careful selection of species it is possible to have crocuses in flower out of doors from November till April. The autumn-flowering crocuses should not be confused with colchicums which, though often confused with crocuses, are members of the lily family. See also Colchicum and House Plants (Bulbs).

Cryptanthus see House Plants (Pot Plants)

Curtonus

Flower/Su

A fairly frost-hardy South African flower which reaches four feet in height and produces, late in the year, bright orange blooms suitable for cut flower arrangement.

See also **Crocosmia**

Cutting and Conditioning

This also includes foliages, berries and all materials used in decorations.

The equipment you need is quite simple: a range of buckets and tins which are perfectly clean and will hold water to their full depth. Tap water is preferable to rainwater, because it is free from many bacteria. A pair of sharp scissors is important, also a good knife or secateurs. Use a wooden mallet to split stems which are very woody, and a block of wood or tree stump is excellent to hammer on. An area in a cool dark place is ideal in which to stand the cut flowers which are having a long preliminary drink before being arranged. If working with difficult materials, boiling water will also be necessary for sealing stems. Stiff, non-absorbent paper will also be useful for wrapping such flowers as tulips and roses to give the stems support during their first drink after cutting, especially if they are rather limp. Roll up the stems (12 to 24 per bundle), keeping the top of the paper just above the flowerhead so that the stems remain straight.

When picking in the country, it is a good idea to take with you a plastic bag with damp paper in the bottom. Each bloom or piece of foliage should be picked and placed straight away into the bag. Seal it up as soon as possible and keep it in the boot of the car away from bright sun. If cutting from the garden, take a bucket with you and cut straight into the bucket, treating the individual stems afterwards, as suggested under the sections devoted to them in this book. If the flowers appear limp, place each stem into warm water as you cut it.

The best time to cut flowers and foliage is in the early morning or late evening after the heat of the day has passed. Daisy-type flowers should have hard green centres with only a trace of pollen showing on the outside rim of the centre disc. Those with yellow centres covered in pollen have nearly finished their life cycle. Flowers must be cut at the correct stage of development. If the buds are too immature, they will not develop properly. In the same way, if flowers are too far advanced, they cannot be expected to last when cut. Some flowers are much longer lasting than others, and some, for example mimosa, are not really pretty until fully developed, that is when the flower is fluffy and covered in pollen which appears near to the end of the flower life cycle. A poppy should always be cut just as the calyx is bursting and the petals are showing colour. A gladiolus will develop in water if cut when the first flowers are showing colour, but the flowers of chrysanthemums and dahlias must be well out before cutting.

All flowers should have their stems carefully cut at an angle, leaving a few leaves at the base of the plant (but above water) to go on photosynthesising. No flower stems should be pulled because, in doing so, damage is done to the stem tissue and tearing down the plant by loosening it in the soil. Never cut a plant too hard, unless it is an annual and is at the end of its life. Once cut, some people break off a piece of the stem under water to stop any airlock forming (this is done with everything in Japan). Only one plant should have its flowers pulled, and that is the cyclamen, as this avoids leaving a short piece of stem to die back and so encourage Botrytis (mould) to form. Cut the end of the stem which has been pulled from the corm. Any stems which appear woody should be hammered lightly. All *unwanted* foliage should be stripped from the base of the stem; never remove more than is necessary. Flowers can be kept in a cold store, but the temperatures should not be below 45°F (7°C), and there should be good movement of air within the store. If flowers are kept below this temperature, they tend to go over quickly once brought into the warm air of a living room.

There is no need to change the water or recut stems each day unless something has gone wrong with the arrangement. Just keep the container topped up every day and remove any dead flowerheads as they occur. Any plant materials or flowers that have wilted may be brought back to life, providing they are caught in time, by re-cutting the stem and putting the tip in boiling water for up to 30 seconds, then plunging the whole stem into deep warm water for a long drink. Flowers should not be allowed to become dry, and at no time should they stand in a draught or full sunlight. For further information on treatment see also Water.

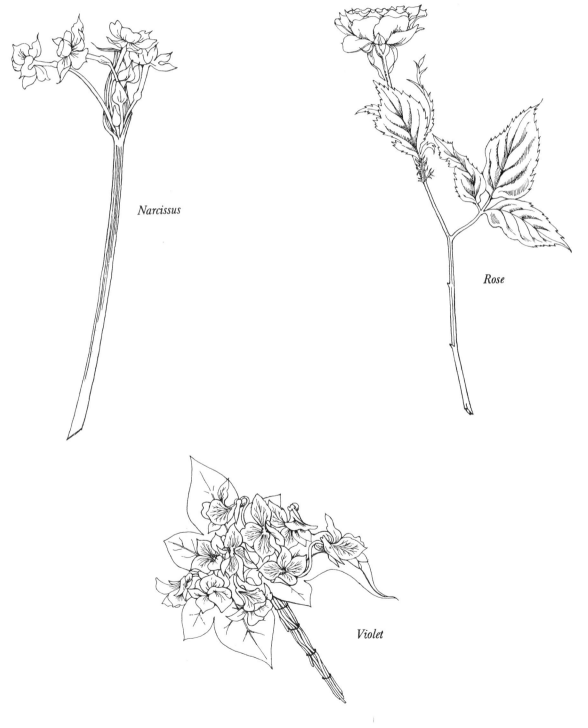

Narcissus

Rose

Violet

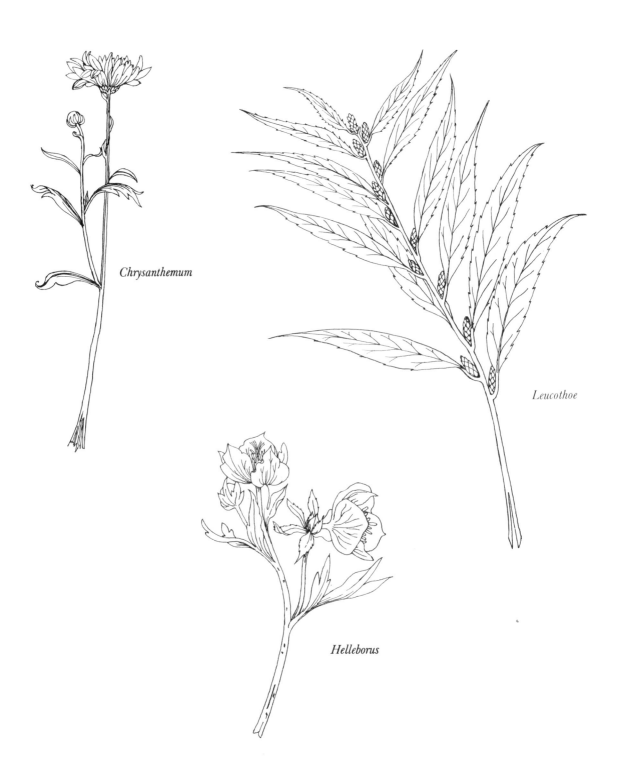

Chrysanthemum

Leucothoe

Helleborus

Treatment of stems

HARD WOODY STEMS Remove all unwanted leaves. Cut stems at an angle. Remove thick bark from the base of the stem and hammer or split the bottom half inch to break down fibres. Place into deep water for a long drink.

SOFT STEMS Cut at an angle with a sharp knife or scissors. Any stems which give off a sticky fluid, e.g. fresh daffodils, should be placed in a container on their own for a good drink, then after treatment they can be arranged with other flowers without causing any harm.

STEMS WHICH BLEED These must be cut and sealed straight away, by placing the tip either in boiling hot water or in a flame for 30 seconds before putting in water. Do this each time you cut the stem. Any leaf which falls will leave a scar, which should be sealed in a flame.

CARNATIONS Cut the stem at an angle between the leaf joints, and if very woody, hammer. Place in warm water.

TULIPS All tulips tend to flop over unless properly treated. Cut the stem at an angle, then tightly wrap up the whole stem by rolling the bunch in stiff paper. Give a good drink while the stems are supported.

ROSES Cut stems at an angle. Remove thorns. Wrap in stiff paper for a long drink. Split stems up at base.

CHRISTMAS ROSES Cut stems at an angle and put tips into boiling water. You can make a pinprick through the top of the stem just under the flower to help stop airlock. Also, some people score the stems with four to six fine pin lines.

WILD FLOWERS Cut and place in a large polythene bag containing damp newspaper. Keep airtight. Treat in normal way as soon as possible.

GENERAL All flowers should have a long drink in a cool place before being arranged. All containers should be kept perfectly clean, also the wire netting and all other mechanical aids.

The use of chemicals in the water should not be necessary. The addition of aspirin or copper has the effect of checking bacteria present in dirty water rather than doing anything to the flowers. Sugar and starch can be used, but if the treatment mentioned before is followed, nothing else should be needed. A spot of strong bleach or disinfectant will help keep the water sweet when such materials as the cabbage family are used in decoration. The really important details are clean water, clean vases and flower holders. Stems should be properly treated and free from foliage below the water line.

Cyclamen see House Plants (Pot Plants)

Cynara/artichoke, cardoon

Flower/Leaf/Seed/Su/Au

The large, divided leaves of *C. scolymus* (globe artichoke) arch beautifully and are best used as a foil to particularly bright flowers. They are handy in autumn when greenish foliage is getting short, but may be used at any time and go well with yellow foliage, such as golden privet.

When green the heads should be dried by hanging them upside down in a dry, airy room. When purple they are particularly attractive for arrangements and may be left standing in a dry vase to turn golden brown.

Before using the foliage, dip the stem ends in boiling hot water for a minute and then soak the leaves in cold water for some time. After arranging it helps to freshen the foliage with droplets from a water atomiser from time to time.

Cynara cardunculus (cardoon) belongs to the same family as the globe artichoke and is often liked by arrangers because it is a hardier plant and the heads are not wanted for food. The leaves should be well soaked. The thistle-like seedheads may be dried upside down. See also Ornamental Vegetables.

Cyperus see House Plants Pot Plants

Cytisus/broom

Flower/Sp/Su

Anyone who has seen the bright blooms of these hardy shrubs cannot fail to recognise their value for flower arranging. There are many species and varieties with colours ranging from yellow and cream to red and purple. *C. × praecox*, blooming in May with cream flowers, and *C. scoparius*, with varieties of red and lemon yellow, crimson and yellow, and yellow and primrose, are both popular. The flowers do not last well in water. Hammer the ends of the stems and give them plenty of water.

Dahlia

Flower/Su/Au

There is a wide variety of these flowers, varying

in shape (cactus, pom-pom, quilled, anemone-flowered, paeony-flowered, decorative, exhibition, etc.), and varying in colour from pinks, reds and purples to lavenders and creams. All are half-hardy tuberous plants, the tubers being lifted each year before the frost and kept in a dry warm shed throughout the winter. Types of dahlias often favoured for cutting are Charm and Collarette.

The florists' flowers seem to have even more exotic colours than the garden varieties. Dahlias do not last all that well as cut flowers. Make sure you remove all the leaves and flowers below the level of the water of the vase, dip the stem ends in boiling water and give them a long drink before arranging. You can try adding sugar to the water, or a little medicinal spirits.

Daphne
Flower/Leaf/Berry/Wi/Sp

This is a deciduous or evergreen shrub. Most species have beautifully scented flowers and red berries. The purple flowers of the popular *D. mezereum* bloom early in the new year, and you can gather the fragrant green flowers of the evergreen *D. laureola* (spurge laurel) in woods in warmer parts of the country in March and April. Hammer the stem ends and the flowers will last well in water.

Delphinium/larkspur
Flower/Seed/Sp/Su

The common name larkspur usually applies to the annual flowers. Both annuals and perennials have provided plant breeders with the opportunity of producing stately flowers growing on tall spikes in every imaginable colour apart from the characteristic blues so commonly seen in gardens. Some of the Giant Imperials (larkspurs) and Bella Donna varieties and all the Pacific Giants are well worth growing for cut flowers. To make them last fill the hollow stems with water and plug with cotton wool. Flowerheads can be dried when the buds are almost all open by hanging upside down. Dry the ripe seedheads in an upright position in a vase.

Deutzia
Flower/Sp

Two species of this deciduous shrub, *D. gracilis*

and the hybrid, *D. × candalabrum*, which is hardier than *D. gracilis*, produce delicate white flowers in June useful for early summer arrangements. Earlier blooms of *D. gracilis* can be forced under glass.

Dianthus/sweet William
Flower/Su

These gay annuals or perennials from Mediterranean countries are often seen in rock gardens. Most, but by no means all, are in the red section of the spectrum, some flowers having delicately fringed edges. There are some excellent varieties for cutting and for pot flowers, such as the variety 'Red Empress'. 'Giant Auricula-eyed Mixed' and 'Brilliant Fringed Mixed' are also good for cutting. For carnations and pinks, see the articles under these headings.

Dicentra/bleeding heart
Flower/Sp

Tiny rose-red pendants hanging on arching sprays make *D. spectabilis* one of the most popular plants with modern flower arrangers. It is a hardy perennial and will grow in any soil which is not too dry. It can also be grown or forced in pots.

Dictamnus/burning bush, dittany, fraxinella
Flower/Seed/Su

Tall spikes of white, pink, or purple flowers in June and July make this curious plant, which produces an inflammable gas, a good subject for cut flower arranging. It grows best from root cuttings in a sunny well-drained position.

Digitalis/foxglove
Flower/Su

Foxgloves can be had in variety with cream, yellow, pink or purple, sometimes spotted flowers, hanging like clusters of bells on tall spikes. The flowers of the modern 'Excelsior' hybrids do not droop and this is considered an improvement, though it seems that the older varieties are just as graceful, if not as colourful. The flowers like a long drink of water and you can dry the seedheads by hanging the stems upside down.

A Grecian urn makes a magnificent container for this
arrangement of foxgloves and roses. The roses are
Rosa gallica 'Complicata' and *Rosa virginiana*.

Dimorphotheca/cape marigold

Flower/Su

Daisy-like annual or perennial South African flowers which appear in bright colours of lemon, orange, blue, rose-lilac, etc. Results are a bit chancy for gardens in sun-doubtful Britain but are excellent in frost-free areas. The cut flowers last reasonably well but close up at night.

Dipsacus/teasel

Seed

The heads are easily dried. Pick them green and dry them upright, or dry them upside down when fully blown. They are marvellous in dried arrangements.

Doronicum/leopard's bane

Flower/Sp

Another daisy-like perennial flower which also lasts well in water. They mix well with other flowers and are very attractive in combination with lilacs.

Dracaena see House Plants (Palms)

Dried flowers see Preservation and Dried Arrangements (Flowers and Seedheads)

Dried leaves see Preservation and Dried Arrangements (Foliage)

Driftwood

The unusual shapes and textures of weather-beaten, sea-washed and even worm-eaten driftwood have the remarkable quality of matching easily with flowers and other plant material. Driftwood as its name implies is found on beaches where it has often been brought in by the tide. It is also often found by the shores of lakes and banks of rivers and streams. Florists sometimes stock fine pieces.

That found along the coasts is usually worn into a finished shape and only requires a base to be fitted. Other pieces may look better after branches or stumps have been trimmed. Small pieces of roots and twigs may be made to look effective in conjunction with larger pieces.

Sun-bleached driftwood should be cleaned in such a way as to avoid removing the polished white quality it has acquired. Household bleach can be used to whiten driftwood, by soaking it for a day or so in the solution.

Rubbing with sandpaper (starting with the coarse kind and proceeding through various grades until the wood responds to the finest grades) is the best means of producing a soft smooth finish. This finish is often the most effective, though a gleaming surface can be obtained by wax polishing, if so desired. Or the wood can be stained according to your fancy by using the wide range of wood staining solutions. It may then be waxed to restore its natural surface texture. Wood surfaces can also be varnished or dyed to match a particular arrangement. Choose a fast colour and one that will retain the appearance of the grain and texture of the wood.

Large heavy pieces of driftwood will require suitable bases. To make the bottom of the driftwood level before attaching a base, dip it in a bowl of water at the desired angle and mark the waterline with a pencil. It is then easy to saw it off level following the pencil line. The base of timber of the most suitable size, shape and appearance should be screwed on to the bottom of the piece of driftwood. The thickness and texture of the base will depend on the sort of arrangement you have in mind. It should be large enough to hold a container and any accessories required. A piece of cloth may be glued to the base to prevent it scratching polished surfaces.

A cement or adhesive can be used to mount a piece of driftwood on stone, which often makes an effective-looking base for driftwood. There are many beautiful effects which may be obtained with driftwood, but perhaps one of the best is for an austere winter arrangement.

Echeveria see House Plants (Cacti and Succulents)

Echinops/globe thistle

Flower/Leaf/Su

These distinctive prickly-looking flowers are almost perfectly globe-shaped and are usually various shades of blue. They are all perennials and natives of Europe or Asia, and will grow almost anywhere in the garden, though the very tall-growing type is to be avoided. *E. banniticus*, which has beautiful violet heads, comes from Hungary. This species has rather rough hairy leaves which, like the leaves of other types, will last well if pressed. It reaches 2 to 3 feet tall.

Echinops banaticus – a striking thistle ideal for flower arranging. The flower head is of a vivid metallic blue and is very long-lasting in water.

E. ritro reaches 3 to 4 feet high, and the flowers are a beautiful metallic blue. It is probably the best type for drying the heads. Stand them upright in a vase before they have come fully into flower. If you leave them longer you may find the petals drop off. The flowers of echinops last well in winter, but do not forget to hammer the stem ends.

Elaeagnus/silver berry

Leaf

This is a hardy shrub with deciduous, silver-backed leaves (*E. commutata*, silver berry), or with evergreen delightfully variegated gold and green-edged leaves (*E. pungens* 'Maculata'). There are several other species, including *E. glabra*, an evergreen with silver-gold backed leaves. The evergreen varieties are hardy for winter arrangements.

Emilia/tassel flower

Flower/Su

Small rather daisy-like flower of red, orange or yellow, which can be grown as a garden annual and reaches a height of one foot or more.

Enkianthus

Flower/Sp

A deciduous shrub which likes an acid soil and bears clusters of small bell-like flowers with delicate veins in cream, red or yellow. Hammer the stem ends and use in mixed arrangements.

Epimedium

Leaf/Flower/Sp

The leaves are decorative from spring to autumn of this hardy perennial rather low-growing plant. Shaped like shields they take on variegated tints of pink, green and yellow in spring, darkening towards autumn. The pale pink, yellow, white or violet flowers are not particularly long lasting, but dip the stem ends in boiling water.

Epiphyllum see House Plants (Cacti and Succulents)

Episcia

Leaf

These plants require a minimum winter temperature of 60°F (16°C), and provide decorative leaves in various colours. The trailing nature of the plants makes them suitable for hanging baskets.

Eranthis/winter aconite

Flower/Sp

Yellow, rather buttercup-like flowers on short stems, they bloom in February and March and will thrive in shade and ordinary soil. The leaves form frills round the flowers and the plants are tuberous.

Eremurus/foxtail lily, giant asphodel

Flower/Su/Au

Tall, rather lupin-like spikes of flowers may be peach, pink, rose, lemon, orange or white. Cut the flowers just before they bloom and they will last well. The plants thrive in sun and sandy loam.

Erica/heather

Flower/Leaf/Sp/Su/Au/Wi

This is a frost-hardy shrub with evergreen, feathery foliage and flowers of white, purple, pink or red. By using different varieties it is possible to have heathers in bloom almost all the year round. The purple-pink *E. carnea* flowers from November to March, and *E. × darleyensis* from November to April. All flower best when fully exposed to sun and frost. The foliage and flowers are attractively brown in colour when dried. Dry them in an upright position. See also Calluna; House Plants (Pot Plants)

Erigeron/fleabane

Flower/Su

Daisy-like flowers ranging in colour from pink to purple and blue to mauve and white, mostly hardy perennials that are suitable for cutting. They mix well in summer arrangements and are easy to grow.

Eryngium/sea holly

Flower/Leaf/Su

Thistle-like leaves and bluish teasel-like flowers distinguish many species of this plant so useful for dried winter arrangements. *E. giganteum* is one of the most attractive species with spiny ivory-coloured bracts surrounding the flowers. *E. maritimum* (sea holly) has pale blue rather rounded heads. *E. alpinum* has large delicate bracts of blue. They will last for months without deteriorating if just kept dry after cutting, or you can hang them upside down.

Escallonia

Flower/Leaf/Su

Rather tender shrubs with glossy, generally evergreen leaves. The flowers are mostly in shades of white and red which mix well with summer flowers such as carnations and roses. Hammer the stem ends before arranging and keep them as short as possible.

The shrubs do best out of doors when grown against a warm, sunny wall in well drained soil.

Eschscholtzia/Californian poppy

Flower/Leaf/Su

Brilliant orange, yellow, carmine or white flowers with delicate foliage are characteristic of this hardy annual which seems to yield new varieties every year. It is also a good garden flower. Lavish displays of mixed varieties are best for cut flower arrangements. Dip stem ends in boiling water.

Eucalyptus/eucalypt or gum tree

Leaf/Seed

The pale green or grey-green leaves of these trees are very useful for flower arrangements, particularly during winter. They last well and are often sold in florists' shops. Eucalypts produce two types of leaves, juvenile leaves, which are usually round, occasionally perfoliate, and very glaucous, and adult leaves which are usually sickle-shaped. It is the juvenile leaves that are most used in floral decorations. Plants can be made to produce juvenile leaves almost indefinitely by coppicing them: this involves cutting the shoots back to ground level each spring: alternatively a three or four foot trunk can be allowed to develop, and the shoots cut back to the top of this each year. *E. gunnii* is the species best-suited to the British climate, but in the U.S.A. a very wide variety of other species can be grown, many with spectacular flowers, also useful in flower arrangements. The seeds are produced in hard, wooden bottle-like capsules, often two inches long, and stems with clusters of these fruits on them are excellent in dried decorations.

Eucomis see House Plants (Bulbs)

Eucryphia

Flower/Su

Rose-like delicate white flowers distinguish this rather tender shrub, of which *E. glutinosa* and *E. × nymansensis* are among the hardiest species. The flowers appear in August and September and are useful for late summer arrangements.

Euonymus/spindle tree

Berry/Leaf

Only the deciduous species (useful for their bright pink or red berries and autumnal foliage) are known under the heading spindle tree. The ever-

Enonymus japonicus 'Variegata' – one of the most attractive of variegated plants for both garden and flower arranging. The leaves are green, gold and white.

Euphorbia wulfenii – one of the largest growing and most ornamental of spurges with green leaves and brilliant yellow-green flower heads. The white milky sap is exceedingly poisonous.

green varieties have interesting foliage, *E. fortunei* providing cultivated varieties with variegated foliage which lasts when cut if the stem ends are hammered well.

Euphorbia/spurge, poinsettia

Leaf/Flower

The best-known species is *E. pulcherrima* (poinsettia), a popular pot plant. See House Plants (Pot Plants). The colourful red bracts of the poinsettia, which appear at the top of the plant, resemble leaves but are often mistaken for flowers. The variety of form and shape of the *Euphorbia* genus is very great. For *Euphorbia splendens* see GREENHOUSES.

The arching sprays of orange flowers of *E. fulgens* are seen in florists' shops in January. A hardy species, *E. epithymoides* produces showy yellow bracts in April and is suitable for cutting. *E. cyparissias* (ploughman's mignonette) has rather glaucous foliage and greenish-yellow flowers and heart-shaped bracts in spring. Caper spurge (*E. lathyris*), a biennial, seeds itself freely in the garden and produces large green bracts. It is suitable for winter arrangements. *E. griffithii* has reddish-orange bracts in April and May. *E. veneta* (syn. *E. wulfenii*) is a rather shrubby

herbaceous plant having green and yellow bracts in spring or summer, and *E. marginata* (snow-on-the-mountain) has green and white bracts in summer. Dip the stem ends in boiling water and always keep in water to prevent the milky sap escaping.

European styles

There is no formalised, indigenous style of European flower arranging in the same sense as in the Oriental schools. Only in the last half century has flower arranging become an almost professional pursuit, largely through the efforts of individual flower arrangers.

In the past, and still to a considerable extent, flower arrangers took their cue from the artistic and design fashions of their period. For example, during the Baroque period of the seventeenth century, especially in France under the reign of Louis XIV, flowers were arranged in sweeping curves to ape the confident architectural style of the time.

Earlier, the monks, who kept flowers in their monastery gardens for medicinal purposes, also used them as subjects for illustrating illuminated manuscripts. Chapels and churches were decorated with flowers, and arrangements based on church adornment, often linked to the great festivals, may be thought of as a tradition going back beyond the Middle Ages to even pre-Christian times. With the festivals were associated the country garlands and other decorations celebrating the seasons. The vases of palm or pussy willow displayed in spring unceremoniously recall the approach of Easter. Church decoration is almost undoubtedly also reflected in arrangements seen in many ordinary houses. The artless simplicity of such home arrangements may be due as much to something handed down from mother to daughter as to lack of imagination.

A link with the East is shown in the symbolism of flowers and plants, which were the emblems of both religious and romantic ideas. In this context Ophelia's speech in Shakespeare's *Hamlet* shows how flowers were given meanings:

> *There's rosemary, that's for remembrance:*
> *pray, love, remember: and there is pansies,*
> *that's for thoughts. . . .*
> *There's fennel for you, and columbines:*
> *there's rue for you: and here's some for me:*
> *we may call it herb of grace o' Sundays. . . .*

The columbine is the flower of the Holy Spirit.

With the rise in power of the merchant classes a more worldly approach to plants became apparent. Pictures of arrangements of the time seem to show less austere reverence. The increasing scientific spirit led to paintings which show botanical as well as artistic interest. Flowers and plants became objects, beautiful, dynamic and living objects, but objects just the same. Something was gained and something was lost. Dutch paintings of the seventeenth and eighteenth centuries show bouquet arrangements full of feeling and reflecting artistic conventions of perspective, line and light, which are still used by modern flower arrangers.

With the nineteenth century came the introduction of exotic species and highly cultivated varieties which are now at the disposal of arrangers in really large numbers. Large decorative bouquets with flowers of all colours and foliage, fruit and nuts and ornate containers were fashionable and continued what could be called the nearest thing to a European style.

This style is still favoured for the right surroundings, but in the wake of modern design and art forms there is a tendency towards abstraction and simplicity. Modern rooms often lack space for the expansiveness of the past but by skilful arrangement a few flowers in a Danish vase can be seen to be just as exciting and far more suitable to the surroundings. The use of form and colour in an abstract way is encouraged by contemporary abstract art and is the direction in which European flower decoration will probably go.

Everlasting flowers

Invaluable for winter decoration, the so-called everlasting flowers are natives of South Africa. Where garden space allows, they should be grown for their indoor decorative value when cut and dried. Endowed by nature to withstand long periods of drought, the flowers will retain their beauty and colour when removed from the plant and dried.

They require an open, sunny situation away from the shade of the trees and they grow best in a soil devoid of manure. An ordinary well-drained loam will suit them well and they flourish in the sandy soil of a coastal garden. They are best raised from seed, sown in early April where the plants are to bloom, or under glass. They are only half-hardy and an earlier sowing should not be made outdoors. However, most will withstand transplanting, and in colder parts plants may be raised under glass and planted out towards the end of May when frost has departed.

To dry, cut the flowers when at their best, usually early in autumn, tie into small bunches and hang in an airy room for several weeks but away from the direct rays of the sun. Do not use a greenhouse unless very well ventilated, otherwise excessive humidity will tend to cause the flowers to be troubled with mildew.

For indoor decoration, the flowers may be used to make an attractive display of mixed everlastings or they may be used with lichen-covered twigs, grasses and berries. They are most attractive used in pewter mugs or in old wooden butter bowls if the stems are threaded into wire supports. To give an 'old-world cottage' look, use stems of lavender 'Lodden Pink' with its distinctive fragrance, with the pinky shades of *Helichrysum monstrosum*. Both may be harvested and dried together, early in September. Or as an alternative to *Helichrysum*, use *Xeranthemum annuum*, which bears its flowers of crimson, rose and pink singly on 20-inch stems. It is also harvested at the same time. See also the entries on Helipterum and Limonium.

Another attractive combination is to use purple

spikes of lavender with *Anaphalis nubigena*, which in early autumn covers itself in fluffy white flowers papery to the touch. It has bright silver-grey foliage which it retains through winter. The foliage makes a delightful contrast to sprigs of hips and haws with their brilliant red fruits and to the orange 'lanterns' of the Cape gooseberry, *Physalis alkekengi* (syn. *P. franchetti*), a perennial which may be grown in the border, like mint.

An attractive winter decoration of quite different colouring is provided by the almost hardy annual *Lonas inodora*, which bears its golden buttons on 15-inch stems. Use them with brown and yellow helichrysums and with dried grasses and beech leaves for a symphony in browns and yellows, real autumnal colours. The display will be enhanced by a few sprays of *Moluccella laevis*, bells of Ireland. This is not a true everlasting but dries perfectly, retaining its unusual lime-green colouring through winter. It is attractive used with various grasses and with the dried silvery 'pennies' of honesty or with the white and yellow flowers of *Ammobium alatum*. Two or three spikes of the chocolate-coloured false bulrush will add to the display. See also Preservation (Dried Groups).

Fabiana/false heath

Flower/Leaf/Sp

The white or lilac flowers and evergreen foliage of this rather tender shrub resemble heather, and the supple stems look graceful. Hammer the stem ends and give the flower stem a good long drink before arranging.

Fatshedera see House Plants (Palms)

Fatsia see House Plants (Palms)

Fennel

Flower/Leaf/Seed

The light, finely cut feathery foliage of *Foeniculum vulgare* (fennel), which is borne on long shiny stems, can be found on seaside cliffs and sometimes on wasteland. The leaves tend to turn greenish-blue towards autumn and the flowers appear in large umbels. There are variations of Florence fennel (*F. v. dulce*) which have red or black leaves excellent for arranging. The giant fennel (*Ferula communis*) grows up to 12 feet high and produces large orange-yellow seedheads,

which, like the seedheads of all the fennels, can be dried upside down and are suitable for large dried arrangements.

Ferns

Indoors or outdoors, most ferns like moist conditions and a position of partial shade. Because of this, they should be grown in the home on trays of moist sand or shingle and in a cool, sunless room. Or they may be grown in glass bell jars sealed down or in Wardian cases made of glass with a wood or metal frame, the plants being grown in pots and placed on trays of sand or shingle, or they may be planted into trays containing a suitable compost.

The Wardian case is named after Dr. N. B. Ward, a doctor in general practice in the East End of London, who died in 1868. During his lifetime, the Wardian case was to become the principal piece of furniture of the Victorian parlour.

When growing under glass in the home, it is necessary to admit air several times each week by removing the glass for an hour or so. This will allow excess moisture to dry off the foliage and prevent the appearance of mould. The glass is wiped dry and clean before being replaced. Keep the cases away from sunlight and make sure that when the covering is removed, the ferns are not subjected to cold, draughty conditions.

An excellent 'Wardian' case may be made from an indoor tropical fish container. The base is covered in crocks, over which is placed compost 2 inches deep, into which the ferns are planted. The case is lit from above and is most attractive, especially if silver and golden ferns are used.

The compost is made up of a mixture of 3 parts peat loam, 1 part silver sand and 1 part broken charcoal. It should be in an open friable condition but not too finely broken down. The ingredients must be free of pests, disease and weed spores.

If moorland soil is used (which may contain the roots of heather or bracken) it will be advisable to treat it with boiling water. It will then prove highly suitable for growing ferns. Or use coconut fibre instead of the soil or peat.

Ferns make attractive indoor pot plants grown in moist shingle without a glass covering. When growing in pots, ensure that the pot is large enough to hold the roots without cramping, for too small a pot would eventually cause the roots to decay at the centre through lack of adequate

food and moisture. Frequent division into quite small pieces and replanting into large pots will keep the plants healthy. When planting ferns, place the crown level with the rim of the pot and carefully spread out the roots, pressing the compost over them so that when planting is complete, the compost will be just below the rim of the pot to allow for watering. Water in after planting and stand the pots on a tray of shingle which should be kept moist, but whether growing in a case or not, do not keep the compost in a saturated condition which will cause the roots to decay. The moisture should be continually evaporating and more moisture should not be given until the compost shows signs of drying out or when the pot, upon tapping, gives a hollow ring.

Indoor ferns will benefit from being placed outdoors in summer, in a shady position where the foliage should be given frequent syringeings. Plants kept indoors will also benefit from a regular syringeing during the summer months.

Early April is the best time to repot or to make up the Wardian cases, for then the plants are beginning to make new growth.

Set the plants about 6 inches apart, using the most dwarf next to those which are taller growing, so that the Wardian case will be filled with their fronds but each will have room to develop. Plant also those ferns of dark green next to those with silver fronds.

Ferns may be grown in a lean-to greenhouse attached to the sunless wall of a courtyard or to the home, a wall facing north or east being suitable. The 'house' should be frost-proof, but artificial warmth in winter is not necessary for many ferns, except perhaps during the severest weather when a portable heater may be brought into use. The plants may be placed in their pots on narrow trays of shingle arranged on shelves constructed in tiers for maximum effect. As an alternative to shelves, the fernery may be constructed at the back or highest part of the 'house'. The use of tufa stone will give a natural effect to the display. Here, the most dainty and delicate of ferns may be grown and will delight with their fresh green colouring and their cleanliness all the year round. If, during summer, it is necessary to provide shade, this may be done by whitening the

Ferns may be used in floral arrangements or grown as house plants. (a) Maidenhair fern *Adiantum capillus-veneris*. (b) A variegated form of the Christmas fern *Polystichum setiferum*. (c) A crested form of a greenhouse Nephrolepsis species.

inside of the glass or by the use of venetian blinds on either the inside or the outside of the 'house'.

Once planted, ferns require the minimum of attention. Keep the compost comfortably moist and the plants free of dead fronds by cutting them away near the base with sharp scissors, taking care not to damage the young fronds.

When it is necessary for one to be away from home for extended periods during summer, the ferns may be kept supplied with moisture by capillary action. Stand the pots in a tray on a 1-inch thickness of sand which is kept moist by a glass-fibre wick, placed to draw water from an adjoining trough. This ensures that the compost in the pot is always comfortably moist.

Fern fronds may be used to lend an airy lightness to bowls of dahlias and spray chrysanthemums. The plants may also be used as the centrepiece to a bowl of early single tulips, especially of the Duc van Tol type, which have been forced into bloom for Christmas. A pleasing display can be made by planting several species of fern in a large bowl provided with satisfactory drainage. They are also charming where planted with winter-flowering ericas (heaths) of the *E. carnea* type. The evergreen maidenhair fern, *Adiantum capillus-veneris*, which grows only 7–8 inches tall, its fronds being irregularly divided into wedge-shaped leaflets, is particularly attractive. Another, *Pteris ternifolium*, has graceful narrow fronds, and *Asplenium trichomanes*, the maidenhair spleenwort, has a shining black midrib, on each side of which are deep green lobes regularly arranged.

A number of the most dwarf ferns may be used by themselves or with other plants in a bottle or carboy. Even an old brandy glass can be used quite enchantingly in this way for the centrepiece of a small dinner table. It should be filled with the tiny *Cryptogramma crispa*, which forms a dense clump only 3 inches tall, with its finely divided fronds of brilliant green, in appearance much like parsley. Or use one of the silver ferns such as *Pteris argentea* or *Gymnogramma tartarea*, the easiest to manage and with the underside of the fronds looking as if they were coated in purest silver.

Ficus see House Plants (Palms)

Floral Art

Constance Spry's ideas were very much in the tradition of English flower arrangement. She awakened people to what was—and is still—the beauty of the English countryside: the quiet warmth of the cottage gardens and a feeling for natural loveliness which goes with the English landscape garden tradition and the nature poetry of William Wordsworth.

When one gets away from her world of natural beauty and tries to create something more than a simple flower arrangement, then the dangers of bad taste and vulgarity become great. Not that one cannot create a piece of floral art following the lines that Constance Spry laid down. There is a great deal of wonderful work done which echoes her feeling for 'a natural, almost casual, look which is far from easy to achieve'. The difficulty of floral art is that one is more easily tempted into what is false and ugly, then when one is trying to arrange a few simple flowers. The use of accessories and all kinds of artificial aids may give one greater freedom but also tends to bring with it a dangerous ease.

If one can talk about an English school of flower arrangement then it can be said to rely on the intelligence of the eye rather than the mind. Floral art is often too much a matter for thinking about rather than looking at, and this is not a good thing. Christmas decorations, for instance, all too often rely on sentiment and all sensitivity is lost. Even the Japanese, consummate masters at arranging flowers and floral art, often seem at less than their best when attempting to suggest the theme of Christmas. The Japanese are world teachers when it comes to floral art. Their intuitive sense of fitness has been developed over many centuries and they have even been able to take modern developments in their stride. Far from being left behind and bound by rules from the past, Japanese have produced revolutionary ideas of decoration incorporating many of the ideas of modern art. Abstract shapes, artificial materials and sculpture-like containers are freely used in Japan to create contemporary effects. All this freedom is still based on artistic creativity and is not just the result of whimsy.

See also Shows.

Floristry

Floristry is a difficult skill which can only be learned by practice. In floristry, wiring or some mechanical aid is used to support and hold the flowers in position, whereas in flower arranging, the flowers are on their natural stems and are simply arranged in a vase or container, admittedly held in place by some moisture-retaining substance, wire netting or a pinholder, but in no way wired.

All good florists are capable of producing flowers in corsages and headdresses that would appear as fragile and delicate as good jewellery. Floristry is a profession that calls for great skill and ability to work fast with very fragile materials. Florists produce 'sympathy' flowers—wreaths and garlands—and flowers for every happy occasion from button-holes to bouquets. They must have a good knowledge of plant materials and with the demand for pot plants, a knowledge of general decorative horticulture is a great advantage.

Flower Cones

This is not a new idea but one which has come into its own since the introduction of new materials making these arrangements easy for everyone to do.

The old cone of flowers was made on a wire netting frame which was tightly packed with damp moss into which flower stems, previously wired, were placed. Today one has the choice of Oasis, Florapack or Mosy for use in its wet or dry state in which all materials can be easily pushed, in many cases even without wiring or mounting. Styrofoam can only be used with artificial or dried flowers and foliages because it is not water absorbent. Of course all these foundations are not necessarily cone shaped; they can be all manner of shaped to suit the occasion. Whatever the shape, they need lifting by placing on some form of a base, and a cone looks best stood on a small cake stand or bonbon dish with a foot.

For fresh flower cones, any short-stemmed flowers, berries, fruit and foliage can be used. The sizes should be graded to obtain a good point to the tip working down to a wide base. A set pattern can be followed or the pieces placed at random as long as a good even shape is obtained.

When finished the cone should be cone shaped. Both fruit and flowers can look most attractive done in this way.

For Christmas, holly, small baubles and small bows of red ribbon and mixed foliage can make a most attractive table centre or decoration for the mantelpiece. It should be remembered that the cones are highly inflammable.

Forcing

Forcing is the term used when plants are brought into bloom (or fruit) in artificial heat before their natural time. It is confined to those plants which will tolerate forcing conditions and is usually used for those periods when flowers (or fruits) are in short supply and are most expensive. A greenhouse, however small, is a necessity in obtaining sufficiently high temperatures to bring the plants into bloom several weeks before they would bloom under living room conditions, but it may be necessary to employ high temperatures for only short periods. Non-rusting tubular heating, thermostatically controlled to ensure correct temperatures and maximum economy in fuel consumption, is most efficient where a supply of electricity is available. The modern fan heaters, fitted with a built-in thermometer and a temperature control knob, will also provide the correct conditions. Where no electric supply is available, use a good paraffin oil heater, preferably one with a thermostatic valve which controls the flow of fuel and can be set to maintain quite high temperatures. Using either method of heating, many plants may be brought into bloom throughout the winter.

Artificial Lighting

Light and lighting will also play an important part in the selection of plants to be forced. Sweet peas and roses will require the maximum of daylight and a clear atmosphere, hence out of season supplies mostly reach the markets from districts away from the smoke-laden atmosphere of industrial areas. Artificial lighting is also important in the culture of a number of plants; pelargoniums and chrysanthemums, especially, respond to controlled lighting. If pelargoniums which have bloomed during summer are placed in a temperature of 50°F (10°C) in October and the electric light is switched on each day from 6 p.m. beginning early in November, new flower buds will form and by early December the plants will bloom as profusely as in summer. They should be given a rest period in early spring and be cut hard back before starting into new growth for the summer display.

By the use of artificial lighting, chrysanthemums may be made to bloom throughout the year. In general, the mid-season and late varieties form their buds when the days begin to shorten in autumn, and usually finish flowering by Christmas. Thus, to extend the season, more hours of daylight must be provided in autumn. The 100-watt tungsten filament lamps are spaced 6 feet apart and about 5 feet above the plants. To have chrysanthemums in bloom throughout the year, the plants will require two hours of artificial lighting per day in April and May; and again in August and September; 3 hours per day in October and March; 4 hours in November and February; and 5 hours per day in December and January. The period of darkness should be 7 to 8 hours daily, and a time switch is used to give alternating periods of darkness and light throughout the night.

To bring the plants into bloom in summer, black polythene sheeting is drawn over the plants at 6 p.m. each day and removed at 7.30 a.m.

Bulbs for forcing

It is necessary to plant 'prepared' bulbs. These are bulbs which have been kept in cold storage from the time of lifting and they should be planted in bulb fibre or some other suitable compost almost immediately they are received. But this does not mean they can be given forcing conditions at once. They will need fully eight weeks in

Florists have chrysanthemums in the shops all the year round. There is a wide variety of forms and colours; (a) incurved, (b) rayonnante, (c) tight incurved, (d) recurved.

d

b

a

c

which to form a strong rooting system which is even more necessary where they are to be grown in high temperatures.

For forcing always plant a top-size bulb.

HYACINTHS Use the 18–19 cm size and plant in bowls so that there is finger room between each bulb. Hyacinths are copious drinkers, especially when the flowering spike has formed. After two months in the plunge bed or in a cool, dark room, about mid-November place in a temperature of 50°–55°F (10–13°C), increasing to 60°F (15°C) after 2–3 weeks and keep the plants well supplied with moisture. To encourage a long flower spike, a paper dunce cap should be placed over each spike as soon as it is formed. It must be removed when the spike begins to show colour, about mid-December.

TULIPS These are forced by the million each year by commercial growers for sale as cut blooms or for moving to small bowls. The bulbs are planted about 1st September, into boxes 2 feet square, made of 1-inch thick timber and 6 inches deep. The compost, which is made up of loam, peat and sand in equal parts is placed 2 inches deep in the boxes and the bulbs are set so close as almost to touch each other. They are just covered with compost and placed outdoors under 6 inches of ashes. About the end of October, they are brought into a temperature of 50°–55°F (10–13°C) which is increased to 60°–65°F (16–18°C) after two weeks. During their first 10 days in heat the tulips should be covered with paper to exclude light.

Three types are chiefly grown for forcing: A The Duc van Tol varieties (e.g., 'Duc de Berlin'), single tulips which grow only 6–8 inches tall and are used for small bowls at Christmas time. 'Prince of Austria' (orange) and 'Prince Carnival' (yellow flaked with red) may be included here. B Double Early tulips are also suitable for pots and bowls and can be brought into bloom early in the year. Among the best are 'Dante', blood-red; 'Van der Hoff', yellow; 'Titian', crimson, edged yellow; and 'Peach Blossom', silvery pink. They grow 10 to 12 inches tall. C Darwins which grow 2 feet tall and are forced for cut flowers. In this section, 'Copeland's Favourite', rosy-lilac; 'Rose Copeland'; and 'Scarlet Sensation' can be brought into bloom before Christmas.

NARCISSUS These are not suitable for early forcing, apart from 'Paper White' and 'Soleil d'Or' which may be planted in pebbles and placed in the sunny window of a warm room without any time

in darkness. Daffodils require at least 10 weeks in darkness and if planted in bowls or pots in September, will not be ready for the greenhouse until the end of November. They should first be given a temperature of 50°F (10°C) which should not be exceeded. They will bloom late in January and in February, 4 to 6 weeks before those grown cool throughout. For forcing, plant double nose bulbs; among the best are 'Flower Record' and 'Pomona' in narcissi and 'Fortune', 'King Alfred', 'Unsurpassable' and 'Golden Harvest' in large and small trumpet daffodils.

As most bulbs tend to bear their flowers on a weaker stem when forced, the stems should be supported by wires or (for narcissi) with thin green stakes inserted into the compost about the foliage and around which green twine is looped. When once the bulbs come into bloom, they should be grown on as cool as possible. Bulbs will not force again but if planted out will bloom in their second year and will continue to do so each year afterwards.

Flowering shrubs for forcing

AZALEA One of the most popular of all plants for forcing, it is sold in thousands by nurserymen between early January and early May when a well grown plant will remain in bloom for eight weeks or more. Plants may be obtained from growers early in December when they are in bud. They are planted in pots in a lime-free soil containing plenty of peat and grown on in a temperature of 60°F (16°C), at all times keeping the roots well supplied with moisture and syringeing the foliage frequently.

It is the evergreen Japanese azaleas which are grown in pots. They grow only 18 inches tall and almost as wide and bear their flowers in clusters. 'Vuyk's Scarlet' bears large carmine-red flowers whilst 'Alice' bears salmon-red flowers. In pinks, 'Helena' and 'Blaauw's Pink' are outstanding, both bearing double flowers of brightest pink. When in bloom, azaleas should be grown on in a cool room and in partial shade.

LILAC 'Madame Lemoine' with its branches of pure white flower trusses is the variety most used for forcing in pots. The red and purple lilacs lose their colour in high temperatures. The plants are grown outdoors until autumn and then placed in a temperature of 80°F (27°C) until the flowers form, when the temperature is lowered to 60°F (16°C). They require a soil made up of fibrous loam, peat and decayed manure in equal parts and copious amounts of water when indoors.

GARDENIA With its glossy dark green foliage and wax-like flowers 3 inches across, the gardenia responds well to gentle forcing. The best bloom is from a plant 3 to 6 years old which will have reached a height of 3 feet. It requires a compost as recommended for lilac and, in a temperature of about 58°F (14°C), will need ample supplies of moisture at the roots.

The best form is the double white form of *G. jasminoides* Florida. The bloom should be cut just before the centre petals unfold. Handle with care for the flowers bruise easily.

FORSYTHIA This well-known garden shrub is readily flowered in pots in a temperature of no more than 52°F (11°C) when at Christmas its brown stems will be covered in delicate yellow jasmine-like blooms. Pot plants in early autumn using a compost as suggested for the lilac and place indoors. This plant requires a well-ventilated house but will not tolerate draughts. The best form is 'Beatrix Farrand' which bears large flowers of deep gold with orange markings in the throat.

BOUVARDIA This distinctive evergreen with its scarlet or pink flowers may be brought into bloom during the early winter months, given a temperature of 50°F (10°C).

ERICA The South African Cape heaths respond to gentle forcing and make excellent winter-flowering pot plants. They should be potted in early October using a compost made up of 3 parts peat and 1 part each sand and soil. The compost should be neither too dry nor too wet for long periods, otherwise the plants will lose their leaves and the flowers drop their petals. A temperature not exceeding 50°F (10°C) and partial shade should be provided.

ROSES A number of varieties will tolerate quite high temperatures provided they have plenty of light but plants should not be forced until their second year. Indoor roses bloom in flushes, like a crop of mushrooms, and should be retarded·or advanced in a similar way, beginning with the first flush of bloom late in November. Grow the plants in large pots and cut them hard back in mid-summer so that they will not bloom at that time. Then take them indoors in October and give frequent waterings, raising the temperature to 65°F (18°C). By late November the first blooms will appear and the flush will last for about three weeks; six plants providing about 2 dozen blooms

for cutting. Then reduce the temperature to 52°F (11°C) for three weeks and water sparingly before raising the temperature to 65°F (18°C) again and increasing moisture supplies. If the roses are cut so as to leave 2 to 3 buds at the base of each stem, new shoots will break from the buds and a continuous supply of bloom will appear throughout winter.

'Lady Sylvia' remains the best pink; 'Roselandia' is yellow and 'Baccara' an outstanding red, being more free flowering than 'Richmond'.

LILY OF THE VALLEY In a warm greenhouse it is possible to produce bloom all the year round by using retarded crown (roots). Upon receipt, the crowns should be placed in a temperature of 65°F (18°C), being packed closely together in boxes or pots in a sandy compost, and kept well watered. It is advisable to stand the pots in a bed of damp ashes beneath the greenhouse bench until the spikes are about 4 inches long. Then place in full light and reduce the temperature to 56°F (13°C). The crowns will come into bloom within a month of their planting and batches may be taken into the greenhouse for forcing at fortnightly intervals throughout the winter, shading them from direct sunlight. 'Fontin's Giant' with its large white bells is the best variety for forcing.

Forsythia/golden bells
Flower/Leaf/Sp

The bright yellow flowers of this frost-hardy shrub are among the first to be seen on the bare branches in spring. If you cut the branches early the flowers will bloom in a warm atmosphere long before outside. The foliage can be useful in the autumn when the leaves change to yellow and Indian red in colour.

Fothergilla/American wych hazel
Flower/Leaf/Sp

The whitish or yellow flower stamens which are like bottle brushes are quite striking. The leaves of this hardy, North American shrub are also ornamental, colouring well in autumn. Hammer the stem ends and give the flowers a good drink before arranging.

Fragrant plants

Fragrant plants are always welcome in any garden

or for cutting for a flower arrangement. The comment often heard today is that the colour is wonderful, the shape and size just perfect, but that it has no smell. This, of course, is often true, and with all the plant breeding going on today it does seem that in many cases the scent has been lost at the expense of other qualities. You must look to some of the old plants to give strong perfume, and these can be found both among perennials and annuals with the addition of greenhouse subjects, if a greenhouse is available.

Probably one appreciates scent most in early spring, when flowers are not so plentiful, and what could be better than winter sweet, *Chimonanthus fragrans*. This is best grown against a south or west wall and needs careful pruning straight after flowering in February. The wax-like petals of the flower make it a joy for the flower arranger and its perfume is superb. Another shrub to flower in the winter is *Jasminum nudiflorum* (winter jasmine); the bright yellow flowers covering long bare pendulous stems give colour for a long period during the winter months. The flowers are very fragrant and last well when cut. *Daphne mezereum* is another old shrub, often seen in the cottage garden. Its fragrant, waxy, lilac flowers appear before the foliage, and later these turn to red berries which readily seed. Very careful and restricted cutting is necessary, because this shrub does have the habit of suddenly dying back. A charming little evergreen shrub suitable for any position is the garland flower, *Daphne Cneorum*. It is indifferent as to soil, but does best on rockery, or at the front of the border where the roots may have a cool and moist run. Its pink flowers are produced in profusion and they have a wonderful scent. *Viburnum fragrans* is a useful small tree, but its blossom is so often damaged by frost. *Hamamelis mollis* (wych hazel) is more curious than showy, but a small tree well worth considering. Its bare branches carry the fragrant yellow flowers in January/February or earlier and its autumn colourings are excellent. The tree itself is very elegant in shape, and it just needs a little careful pruning to keep it under control.

Old-fashioned roses are full of scent, and as many as can be fitted in should be grown on walls and old trees. A few of the scented Hybrid Tea roses are worth including if there is a place for them. The Chinese shrub, *Osmanthus delavayi*, has a fragrant scent and again would be well worth considering. It flowers in April onwards and is evergreen. The blossom is made up of white tubular flowers, which last well when cut.

The lemon verbena is well worth the trouble and care it needs during the winter with protection of its roots. The lemon-peel scent of the foliage is so excellent during the summer months. There are many geraniums (pelargoniums) for growing in the cool greenhouse and the peppermint one has delicate scented leaves which are excellent in shape for special arrangements.

Night-scented stock, heliotrope and mignonette all provide summer scents, and a moist shady spot must be given to the lily of the valley. The old border carnations are worthy of a place, and some of the herbs, so necessary in the kitchen, are well worth adding to the borders.

Francoa/bridal wreath
Flower/Leaf/Su

Delicate spikes of white or pink flowers on wiry stems with evergreen leaves, which are scoop-shaped, hairy and quite decorative, characterise this plant. The flowers are popular for wedding decorations.

Freesia
Flower/Wi/Sp

These are favourite cut flowers for winter or spring arrangements, mixing well with other spring flowers. The plants are cormous and the flowers may be pink, yellow, orange, mauve or white. 'Snow Queen', 'White Madonna' and 'White Swan' are some of the white hybrids. Freesias are not frost-hardy and are popular florists' flowers.

Fritillaria/fritillary
Flower/Sp

Drooping bell-shaped flowers in shades of pink, bronze, red, purple or yellow are produced by these bulbous plants, which will also flower in pots after two or three years. *F. imperialis* (crown imperial) is a particularly tall-stemmed variety for large spring arrangements.

Fruits, nuts and vegetables

There are no rules and regulations with regard to what types of fruits and nuts or vegetables are used for decorations, but should you be working to a show schedule, great care must be taken to see that you are not breaking any rules. It is in this context that one has to consider whether certain items are classified 'fruits or vegetables' and what really is a berry, etc. Many beautiful displays have been disqualified as not being according to schedule.

The more interesting the shape, the better they look in unusual collections and the importance of colour cannot be underestimated. Just a collection of fresh fruit and nuts can be most attractive on a dining table and for special parties or harvest festivals. A complete mixture of fruits, nuts and vegetables, well arranged, will create much interest. In many instances, a few of the fruits have to be wired to help hold them in the container, and then, of course, they do not last so long, so try to keep this to the minimum.

Perhaps it is better not to have too wide a mixture of decorations in the home; a little subtle touch is needed, otherwise the arrangement gets too grand. If, for instance, you wished to use stems of blackberries with mature fruits, it would be good also to use sloes, wild clematis, perhaps stems of privet berries, some branches of silver-grey foliage, such as eucalyptus and a few metallic-coloured heads of hydrangea. A small group of black grapes grown outside in the garden would fit into this picture, whereas a bunch of hothouse 'Colmar' grapes would be quite out of keeping.

If using any fruits which stain, be careful not to arrange them over delicate fabrics, because as they ripen, they always tend to drop. Apples, oranges, lemons, can all be wired by putting two 22 gauge wires through the fruits and making a loop round the stem halfway down the bunch, the other end of the wire being secured to the handle on the stem of the bunch. Cherries are wired into clusters and many are just placed naturally among the other fruits. Green and red peppers and aubergine are excellent and are treated in the same way as apples and pears.

Wooden cocktail sticks make excellent picks, which can be used with such items as mushrooms. By placing the stick into the stem, you do not damage the vegetable, yet it makes it possible to stand each item in the position required. Fir cones are always useful in winter months, and these can be easily wired by threading a 22 gauge wire through the bottom scales and then securing on to the little piece of stalk.

Certain vegetables can give off an unpleasant smell after a time in water. Decorative kale is an example of this. It is a good idea to keep the stem

The fruits of many hardy ornamental shrubs are ideal for late autumn and early winter arrangements. Shown here are the fruits of *Rosa moyesii*.

in a polythene bag which contains a little water plus a small amount of disinfectant to check bacteria developing.

Fruits and flowers look well together, and one way to use paper white narcissi is with camellia foliage with small lemons or limes.

Fuchsia

Flower/Su

This beautiful flowering shrub with pendulous 'ballet-dancer' flowers of red and purple, which last well in water, is too often forgotten for flower arranging. There are a large number of varieties of many differing colour combinations. Some varieties make good pot plants given plenty of light. See also House Plants (Pot Plants).

Gaillardia/blanket flower

Flower/Su/Au

Cheerful-looking, daisy-like annual or perennial flowers in red and yellow, etc. The large-flowered hybrids are best for cutting and long-lasting in water. Dip the stems in boiling water.

Galanthus/snowdrop

Flower/Wi/Sp

Drooping white heads of snowdrops herald the spring long before winter has relaxed its grasp. The bulbs are excellent for growing indoors in pots. They also make nice tiny arrangements. See also House Plants (Bulbs).

Galega/goat's rue

Flower/Su/Au

White, mauve and pink flowers rather like sweet peas appear on long spikes. Some less common varieties have other but rather similar colours. The longish, pointed leaves are distinctively arranged in opposite pairs. The flowers tend to be rather untidy in the garden, but look excellent in arrangements. Dip the stem ends in boiling water and then give the flowers a good long drink.

Garden cultivation

A garden, when properly planned, can serve two purposes. It can make an attractive setting around the house. It can also be used to produce materials for cuttings for home decoration, but consideration has to be given to the amount of ground available and one has to decide what one really wants. It is quite obvious that there will not be room to grow all the materials required, so careful planning will be necessary.

Soil and site will have a bearing on what can be grown, also whether there is room to have a small greenhouse worked into the design, in which to extend the growing season of plants (see Greenhouses).

Perhaps it is sensible to grow mostly foliage plants, small trees and shrubs and then purchase the straightforward flowers from the florist. Certainly this is labour saving once the preparation and planting have been completed. Make use of any wall space and trees which can support climbing plants. Evergreen shrubs, silver-grey foliages and plants giving not only flowers but also autumn colour and perhaps berries are worth considering. It is essential to get as much from a given space as possible. When plenty of room is available, a good plan is to grow some plants in the flower border simply for garden decoration and then have others away from the general garden in nursery rows for cutting for use in the house.

Personal taste plays a big part in what to grow and some people go for a lot of colour and show, whereas others prefer shape and texture and would be happy with nothing but mixed green foliages, which are so important to the flower arranger.

When it comes to plants grown primarily for their flowers, it is probably wisest to concentrate on perennials and to these add the interesting annuals, biennials and bulbs when space is available. This gives the greatest variety and the longest flowering period possible. Careful planning can give colour and interest throughout the year. First make a plan on paper and remember that as plants grow they require a lot more room.

When planting a new garden, it is useless to economise on labour. The ground must be deeply dug, keeping the subsoil below the topsoil, but well opened up. During this operation, old manure or compost should be added. All old roots, rubbish and bad weeds should be removed. The ground should be allowed to settle prior to planting in the late autumn or spring, and only when it is in good condition should planting take place, seeing that everything is firmly bedded. Any trees should be staked straightaway to prevent them rocking and the roots becoming loose in the soil.

Cultivation should continue after planting to keep all weed growth down and a good tilth to the soil. This can be done by hoeing the ground at regular intervals.

Pruning may be necessary to keep the plants in good shape and this can be done when materials are needed in the house. Over-pruning should be guarded against, because then the natural habit of the plant or shrub is spoilt. Always cut back to a growing point, using sharp secateurs or knives to do the job. It will be necessary to tie in climbers to get the wall area or tree trunk covered quickly. A nylon framework on the wall area will help make a support. Stake plants before they fall over and remember to allow for the height and spread to which they will grow.

Once the garden is established it will provide useful material for house decoration. A good idea is to have a picture in your mind of the arrangement you want to make before going into the garden; then armed with a bucket of water and secateurs you can carefully cut your materials for each position in the vase, so saving on waste by over-picking.

No flower arranger's garden is complete without the following materials: rue, bergenia (megasea), hostas in their various shades of green: *Senecio greyi* with its pleasing silver-grey foliage, which can be used so well in floristry: alchemilla as well as providing excellent foliage for the decorator makes a good ground cover of green leaves and long stems of insignificant flowers of lime-green colouring during the June to August period. The beautifully shaped flowers of astrantia make it another plant which is useful to the decorator. If space allows, cardoon and fennel should be included, because these give excellent foliage during the summer and seedheads which dry for winter arrangements. The old fashioned roses are well worth including in the garden and on the walls. A fairly new 'old-fashioned' rose, 'Constance Spry', is excellent and will grow on a wall or as a hedge plant. It should not be pruned, other than by thinning out the oldest wood.

An area with acid soil should be planned so that you can grow ericaceous plants. A wide range of heathers are useful, giving flower almost throughout the year. Enkianthus, pieris, azalea and kalmia will all give interest and useful material.

Shady ground can be a problem, but if not too large an area, this is where some of the ferns will do well, also that fascinating plant *Arisarum proboscideum* (the mouse plant). Astilbe grows well in shade, providing there is plenty of moisture, and so is all the hellebore family, which is excellent for the flower arranger. One other plant good for ground cover is *Vinca major*, the periwinkle, and this is more interesting in its variegated form.

In the shrub and trees section, great use can be made from the following. They are good for their foliage and, in some cases, flowers and berries. Berberis comes in many varieties and although they have spiteful thorns, are well worth including. Skimmia is good, because it is evergreen and also carries berries late into the winter. Hydrangeas are excellent for the wide range of colours, and can be under-planted with bulbs. One or two of the *Acer* (maple) species are worth including — their beautiful shapes make them first-class specimen trees. Philadelphus (mock orange) and syringa (lilac) are both good including the new Preston Hybrid lilacs. If room permits, cornus, escallonia, hypericum, osmanthus and viburnum may be added to the shrubs.

Herbaceous plants are very numerous and a visit to a good garden centre or nursery will give you ideas. Wherever you can, choose plants that will flower well with the least amount of attention and also those which last well when cut. Leave space for the special annuals, bulbs, etc. which can be used when they become available.

Having listed all these plants, one must exercise great care in not over-planting. Try to allow some open space with either lawns or flag stones to set the plants off. Remember that everything should show up to good advantage. See also Fragrant Plants.

Gardenia/Cape jasmine

Flower/Sp/Su

The white, sweet-scented flowers of these evergreen shrubs are greatly valued for flower arrangements and bouquets because of their opulent quality. In continental Europe the species are usually greenhouse grown and forced, so that the blooms may be had in the florists' shops all the year round. The species most commonly used for floral decorations is *G. jasminoides*, which is certainly not frost hardy, though the rather similar *G. thunbergia* will survive mild winters out of doors in the milder parts of Britain and in the warm temperate regions of the U.S.A. Other species are more or less drought-hardy. The flowers are often found in wedding bouquets, but also look magnificent against the background of their own foliage in the house. Handle the flowers with care for the petals bruise easily.

Garrya/silk tassel bush

Leaf/Flower/Sp/Wi

Long droopy catkins from January to March and evergreen leaves of this Californian shrub make it a valuable addition to winter arrangements. *G. elliptica* is the best-known species of this hardy shrub, having catkins reaching up to a foot long. Hammer the stem ends.

Gaultheria

Leaf/Berry/Flower/Sp

The leaves are glossy green and useful for winter and spring arrangements. Unfortunately this evergreen shrub is rather tender in colder districts. The white or pink flowers are rather inconspicuous, but the blue, white, pink or red fruits are attractive in autumn. The leaves of one species contain natural aspirin.

Genista/broom

Flower/Sp/Su

Bearing bright, yellow pea-like flowers on tall or arching spikes, genistas give you something to make spring and summer arrangements richer and more exciting. Hammer the stem ends or strip the bark slightly before putting them in water. See also CYTISUS.

Gentiana/gentian

Flower/Sp/Su/Au

Beautiful, mostly clear blue, rather trumpet-shaped flowers which are borne on rather dwarf hardy perennial rock plants, gentians generally are not all that easy to cultivate. *G. acaulis* (gentianella), the most popular species, blooms in spring, a handsome species *G. septemfida* blooms around July, and *G. sino-ornata* has open deep blue flowers in September.

Geranium/crane's bill

Flower/Leaf/Sp/Su

Not to be confused with the greenhouse pelar-

Dark green gaultheria leaves act as a foil both to the gay colours of the carnations and to the brilliance of the brass container, which is only partially hidden by the arrangement.

goniums which are commonly misnamed geraniums. The flowers of crane's bill are generally pink, red, bluish-violet, blue or purple (sometimes veined). The plants are generally hardy border perennials. More modest than their greenhouse namesakes the plants are nevertheless delightfully free-flowering and useful for riots of summer colour.

Gerbera/Barberton daisy, Transvaal daisy

Flower/Sp/Su

Narrow-petalled, daisy-like flowers from South Africa are raised in gorgeous shades from salmon-red, pink and apricot to yellow and ivory. Unfortunately, they must be cultivated in a greenhouse in temperate climates where they are being grown in increasing quantities for florists. In warmer climates they make excellent garden plants. *G. jamesii* is the easiest to grow in a cool greenhouse. Dip the stem ends in boiling water for a few moments and give them plenty of cool water.

Geum/avens

Flower/Sp/Su

Handy for small arrangements (owing to the

tendency of the stems to bend), geums produce bright red, orange or yellow flowers with rather decorative loose-looking petals. Hybrids of *G. chiloense*, notably 'Mrs. Bradshaw', are popular with flower arrangers.

Gladiolus

Flower/Leaf/Sp/Su/Au

Sword-shaped leaves and large, well-shaped flowers on tall spikes in a wide variety of shades distinguish this cormous half-hardy plant. Symbolically the flower stands for the incarnation of Christ, and abundance and generosity.

Greenhouse cultivation makes it possible to have the flowers all the year round. To obtain the blooms from spring to autumn in the garden it is necessary to plant the corms in succession. Gladioli are most suitable for tall upright arrangements and are often seen in churches and at festivals, etc. Pick the flowers when they first open and plunge them in a bucket of water. Cut the stem ends daily. The leaves may be pressed for dried arrangements and the seedheads dried in an upright position.

Gloriosa/glory lily

Flower/Leaf

Showy reflexed petals in rich colours of red and yellow, purple and yellow-edged, crimson and purple, etc. The stamens are curiously pronounced. Hothouse tuberous climbing plants, they are a rare attraction.

Gloxinia

Flower/Leaf

A hothouse tuberous plant with velvety flowers in bright reds, pinks, blues and purples sometimes with differently coloured edges. A single cut bloom will often transform a flower display. The flowers last in water and the leaves are interesting, some having a tinge of red. See also Sinningia.

Godetia

Flower/Sp/Su/Au

Showy hardy annual flowers in rich shades of salmon-pink, orange, cherry red, etc. The blooms

a   b

Gladiolus flowers are always popular with flower arrangers but their spikiness, while it is one of their main assets, can also make them difficult to handle.

(a) a gladiolus primulinus hybrid, (b) a large flowered hybrid.

vary in height according to variety and blend well in summer arrangements. They last in water and can often be bought at florists' shops. Hammer the stem ends.

Gomphrena

Flower/Sp/Su/Au

A flower of papery quality which makes it suitable for dried arrangements. Hang it upside down to dry as soon as the flower has developed.

Grasses, ornamental

A large order of plants, usually tufted at the base with round or flattened simple or branched stems which are hollow between the swollen joints. The order includes the wheat, barley and other plants of economic importance and many ornamental grasses of great beauty for the garden and indoor decoration. In the border their foliage and graceful silvery spikelets will tone down the more brilliant colouring of the other flowering plants; or like *Deschampsia caespitosa* they may be planted by the side of a pond or stream. *Miscanthus sinensis*, its tall arching leaves having a central white strip, may be planted with other grasses in an island site on a lawn, and makes an excellent vertical effect in flower arrangements.

On the edge of the island site *Festuca ovina* (sheep's fescue) with its upright bluish leaves may be planted to supply unusual colour for foliage effects.

A number of grasses flourish in partial shade and may be planted about clearings in the wild garden. *Melica uniflora* with its leaves of brilliant green is most striking in filtered sunlight. The flower spikelets of many ornamental grasses are most decorative when dried and used indoors.

Hardy and easy to manage, most grasses are intolerant of shallow chalk soil. They require one of considerable depth, into which is incorporated some leaf mould and a little decayed manure. Plant in spring, allowing those species of vigorous habit ample space to develop. Mostly perennial, the grasses increase by stolons, and quickly make large tufts. To maintain them in a healthy condition lift and divide in spring every 4 or 5 years and replant into freshly prepared ground. During dry weather, keep them well watered at the roots. They will respond to a regular syringeing of the foliage which will take on a much richer colouring.

Ornamental grasses should be grown in abundance in every flower arranger's garden. The grass shown here is *Lagurus ovatus,* a native of Europe.

The annual grasses should be sown early in April where they are to grow. Scatter the seed thinly and rake into the top 1-inch layer of soil. Keep the ground moist and thin out if overcrowded. They will bloom in August and September. The hardy species may also be sown outdoors in September when they will begin to bloom early July.

The ornamental grasses are most attractive when used for indoor decoration, either together or with other flowers. The stems should be cut when the flowers are at their best, before they seed. They will then retain their beauty for twelve months or more and have a fairy elegance which makes them ideal for mixing with everlasting flowers and with the colourful hips and haws and other berried plants.

Cut the stems as long as possible and place them on sheets of brown paper in a dry, airy room but away from the direct rays of the sun. This is a more satisfactory method of drying than bunching the stems together and stringing them up to the rafters of a shed when the delicate flowering heads often become damaged. The stems may be cut to the required length when used in the floral display.

The alabaster container reflects the tonal values of
this arrangement, using fading autumn leaves and
autumn flowers.

Unusual containers such as this one demand
unusual arrangements. Here all the flowers are
different types of clematis. The seed heads come
from the yellow *Clematis tangutica*.

Shell-pink cyclamen in a large sea-shell. Note the
way the water reflects the flowers. The foliage,
though at first glance it looks like cyclamen foliage,
is in fact pepperonia leaves.

Eucomis and foliage make a striking
autumn arrangement. Additional interest is
created by the ornamental gourds which reflect the
green of the leaves and the white of the flowers.

Grasses, wild

Among the very many species of native grasses a number possess outstanding beauty and are highly desirable for indoor decoration. They must be dried and used with the ornamental or garden grasses or by themselves to form a pleasing group. They differ from the sedges in that their stems are round and hollow and the flowers are arranged in spikelets in opposite rows. The long, narrow leaves are also arranged alternatively and in two rows. The spikelets consist of 1–5 minute flowers, which have 3 stamens (male part) and 2 styles (part of the female structure) and are arranged in terminal heads, cylindrical as with the crested dogstail, or in sprays as with the meadow grasses.

Greenhouses

The possession of a greenhouse, however small, or of a garden room will enable you to grow out-of-season plants to provide flowers for the home during winter and spring. It will greatly increase your interest in gardening, and by careful planning a continuous supply of material for floral artistry will be available all the year.

The simplest type of structure is that made of rough timber enclosed by polythene sheeting. This may be fastened both on the outside and inside of the timber framework to give added protection, excluding draughts and giving better retention of heat. In such a structure may be grown all those ferns except the most exotic (which are those requiring artificial heat in winter). Here may be grown a wide variety of bulbous plants and especially those miniature bulbs which bloom outdoors when the weather is cold and windy, and which reveal their full beauty only where protected. These include a number of the crocus species such as *C. imperati*, which bears its sweetly scented fawn and violet flowers before Christmas, and *C. fleischeri* with its brilliant scarlet stigmata which shows through the transparent pure white petals like the yolk of an egg. Several of the tulip species which have long stems and are most desirable for floral art may be grown in this type of greenhouse including *T. eichleri*, which has grey foliage and bears its glowing scarlet bell-shaped flowers shaded with buff on 15-inch stems early in March. To follow is *T. acuminata* with its long thin, curled petals of golden yellow striped with red and *T. ostrowskiana*,

its scarlet flowers shaded with olive green. Pots of miniature daffodils and *Iris reticulata* will also be seen at their loveliest under such conditions, and may be taken into the home when they begin to bloom.

To plant in spring for summer flowering, there are freesias and babianas, ixias and nanus gladioli each of which will provide cut bloom for the home. The corms are planted 6 inches deep in boxes in a friable well-drained compost and they do not require any period in darkness. Keep the compost as dry as possible until they come into growth, then increase supplies of water as the sun increases in strength.

In a cold greenhouse, provided it is frost proof, lachenalias may be flowered in pots, planting them in September. They will bear their 12-inch spikes of tubular flowers in spring when they may be cut and used with other spring flowers such as the single early tulip 'Princess Irene' with its flowers of salmon and buff. The water-lily tulips bloom indoors at the same time, one of the best for cutting being 'Fritz Kreisler', its deep pink flowers flushed on the outside with apricot colouring.

An additional advantage of owning a cold greenhouse is that not only are the flowers protected from soot and heavy rain when they bloom during periods of wet weather, but one is able to grow many interesting varieties which are not generally available from florists, and which make flower arranging so much more interesting.

Many of the hardy and half-hardy annuals may be raised in a cold greenhouse and after planting out, will come earlier into bloom than from a sowing made directly into the open ground. Sweet peas if sown in August and wintered in a cold greenhouse to be planted out in early April will have formed sturdy plants which will begin to bloom at least a month earlier than if spring sown, and length of stem and quality of bloom will be greatly superior.

Sweet peas may be brought into bloom indoors in a temperature of 50°F (10°C) but they must have plenty of light. They will not grow well in industrial smog or in colder areas of the country. For early bloom, the winter-flowering varieties are grown and these are followed by those varieties which have proved successful under glass, for instance, 'Mrs. C. Kay' (lavender) and 'Reconnaissance' (cream, edged pink).

Sow seed in August in small pots and as soon as they sprout, place as close to the glass as possible.

No 'stopping' is done, for the plants are required to bloom early and are grown up canes on the single cordon system.

Early in January, the plants are moved to large pots placed on the greenhouse floor or they are planted in ground beds. They require a fibrous compost containing decayed manure and some lime rubble.

An even temperature of 50°F (10°C) and comfortably moist compost will ensure blooms of top quality with long sturdy stems. The plants will benefit from a daily syringe in spring when the sun becomes warmer and, during daytime, heating should be discontinued.

A number of annuals sown early in spring in a cold greenhouse may be grown on in pots and transferred to the home when in bloom. They will provide a welcome change from the cut flowers of summer. *Alonsoa warscewiczii* is a delightful pot plant for late summer flowering, bearing its scarlet blooms produced on 18-inch stems over several weeks. The schizanthus or poor man's orchid is also readily raised from seed sown in spring and if stopped twice will make a compact bushy plant covered with small flowers of orchid-like colouring. Ten-week stocks sown in April will come into bloom in August. The plants may be grown in pots and supported by small canes or grown in boxes and the bloom used for cutting to accompany scabious and dahlias.

Zinnias also do well in pots or boxes in a cold greenhouse. They grow best where protected from excessive wet and in the British Isles do well outdoors only in a dry summer. For cutting, plant 'Old Mexico' which grows 15 inches tall and bears mahogany-red flowers edged with gold. They look particularly striking when used with bronze leaves and the zinnia 'Green Envy' with its dahlia-like flowers of apple green.

Tuberous-rooted begonias for pots or hanging baskets may also be brought into bloom in a cool greenhouse. The tubers are planted about April 1st, in boxes of moist peat with the flat tops of the tubers level with the surface of the plant. When the sprouts are about 1 inch tall, move to small individual pots containing a richer compost and a month later to larger pots in which they will bloom. For a striking table decoration, a novel way is to plant the sprouting tubers around the side of a large bulb bowl, with a maidenhair fern at the centre. The flowering stems may be supported by wires as for bulbs.

Another pleasing display may be obtained from the pendulous begonias which grow in cascade fashion, by planting them in bowls which are placed over an inverted plant pot covered in black velvet. For table display, 'Yellow Sweetie' is charming with its small sweetly scented flowers of pale lemon-yellow. Equally lovely is 'Golden Shower', and 'Red Cascade' is striking against green drapery.

The large flowers of the exhibition begonias are most handsome if used like water-lilies for table decoration, four or five blooms being placed in a shallow bowl of water. The picotee-edged varieties such as 'Corona' and 'Harlequin' are most arresting under artificial light and will retain their beauty for at least a week.

Early winter-flowering chrysanthemums may be brought into bloom in an unheated greenhouse. Where no garden is available, the plants may be grown during summer in large pots or in deep boxes in a courtyard or on a verandah, placing them under cover towards the end of October. They require a buoyant atmosphere and should be watered only at the roots to guard against the leaves being troubled by mildew. The blooms may be cut or those plants of dwarf habit may be taken indoors in pots as soon as the buds show colour. For the flower arranger, the rayonnante varieties with their long thin-quilled petals are attractive. They bloom under cover during late autumn and may be disbudded or grown as sprays and are obtainable in bronze, pink, rose and yellow shades. Outstanding is 'Bendigo Bronze', its golden-bronze spider-like blooms having their petal points tipped with yellow. 'Johanna' has an almost grey appearance, the petals being tipped with chestnut-red.

Lilies are ideal subjects for a cool greenhouse where the blooms will be clean and the plants untroubled by winds. If planted in pots they may be taken into the home as they come into bloom or the blooms may be cut for floral arrangement. Plant the bulbs 4 inches deep in 8-inch pots in spring and stand the pots outside until growth commences; then move into the greenhouse, keeping the compost comfortably moist and staking if necessary.

Of the Asiatic hybrids which bloom in mid-summer, 'Corsage' is ideal for bouquets, bearing up to twelve outward-facing flowers to each stem, in a lovely shade of strawberry-pink shaded with green at the centre and with maroon markings. Striking too, are the hybrids of *L. regale* and *L. brownii*, bearing long elegant trumpets at the end of 3-foot stems; 'Green Dragon', of a unique shade of chartreuse-green, possesses extreme beauty.

Whereas a wide variety of flowering plants may be raised and brought into bloom in an un-heated greenhouse, where heat is available, the range may be greatly increased: the scented-leaf pelargoniums, so valuable for pot-pourris, may be grown as may other forms of pelargonium; perpetual flowering carnations; primulas; orchids and caladiums; crassula and euphorbia which when cut and placed in water will remain fresh for at least a month; sweet peas (previously described) and roses (see Forcing); asparagus fern and those ferns which are native of warmer parts in addition to many lovely house plants grown for the beauty of their foliage.

For winter floristry, *Crassula gillii* has dark-green leaves and bears white star-like blooms on long graceful stems, and *Euphorbia splendens* has blooms of intense scarlet; both may be grown in a temperature of 65°F (18°C). They are potted in summer and taken into the warm greenhouse in September where they are kept well supplied with moisture. They will bloom from November until February when their blooms are most welcome. They are then given a rest. As the stems 'bleed' when cut, this may be arrested by rubbing the ends with charcoal. When dry, place them in water.

Another winter-flowering succulent requiring similar culture is *Echeveria fulgens* (Syn. *E. retusa*) and its hybrids. From the fleshy grey-green rosettes arise arching stems 15 inches long, covered in orange bell-shaped flowers which will remain fresh in water in a cool room for at least six weeks.

For floral arrangement, one or two arrowhead shaped leaves of caladium, removed from the plant with their long footstalks, will give a tropical beauty and these aroids can be grown in a temperature of 65°–68°F (18–20°C). The tuberous roots are started into growth during the mid-winter months in a compost made up of turf loam, decayed manure, peat and sand in equal parts. Gentle sprinklings with water will soon bring them into growth when they should be shaded from direct sunlight. When in full leaf, the plants may be moved to a temperature of 60°F (16°C) and into the partial shade of a living room when the leaves will retain their beauty for many weeks. The variety 'Candidum' has white leaves and contrasting green veins, and 'Lord Derby' has rosy-pink leaves set off against an edge of brilliant green.

The flamingo plant, *Anthurium andreanum*, with its brilliant red spathe and yellow spadix, requires similar conditions. When in colour, it may be removed to the partial shade of a warm room where it will retain its beauty for many weeks, to be followed by other spathes. A small group of these easily managed plants arranged around a bowl of water will give the appearance of flamingos in a pool. The leaves are in shape similar of caladium and are held on footstalks often 2 feet in length.

In a warm humid atmosphere *Humea elegans* may be grown. It has brown feathery flowers like marsh bent grass, only larger, and which continually shake about. When cut, it lasts long in water and is most attractive when used with bronze and purple foliage and with flowers such as helenium and montbretia, which produce their orange and yellow flowers late in summer.

For a warm greenhouse, *Aechmea fasciata*, its huge strap-like leaves covered in farina and bearing spiky pink flowers; and the variegated pine-apple, *Ananas sativus* 'Variegatus', with its saw-edged leaves of dark green and wide golden margins may both be grown. They make up a pleasing table decoration used as quite small plants with bark from oak or ash trees.

To mix with carnations, sweet peas and other summer flowers, *Asparagus sprengeri* with its drooping feathery fronds and *A. plumosus* 'Nanus', a flat-leaved form, are cultivated by specialist growers in large quantities. One plant at the centre of an indoor hanging basket will create a most exotic effect surrounded by trailing ivy-leaf pelargoniums. Several plants may be grown in pots either to the front of the greenhouse bench to trail over the side, or at the back where the shoots are trained up the roof on wires. To maintain the fronds in the desirable brilliant green colouring, a temperature of 60°F (16°C) is necessary and the foliage should be syringed frequently, for in a dry atmosphere the tiny leaves will fall. Repot and divide the plants in alternate years. Frequent cutting of the fronds will stimulate the plants into continuous growth.

Another foliage plant of considerable beauty for a warm greenhouse is the coleus, the Rainbow hybrids raised in Japan having the most exciting colour range of any foliage plant. They may be grown as pot plants or the sprays may be cut and used for mixing with darker leaves. The scarlet-

A spring arrangement of Lenten roses *Helleborus orientalis*. Lenten roses come in a range of colours from white through creams and yellows to pinks and black-purples. The container is a china cornucopia.

A summer arrangement using water lilies, bergenia leaves and various foliage, in a wrought iron container. The stems of water lilies should be sealed with hot wax before arranging.

A winter arrangement using alder branches with last year's cones and next year's catkins and *Iris stylosa* in several colour forms. The blue-John container takes up the colours in the arrangement.

An autumn arrangement with larch, pressed oak leaves and chrysanthemums, using an antique Bible box as a container, against a background of stripped wood doors.

69

leaved 'Red Monarch' is excellent for cutting for it grows 2 feet tall; with it grow 'Salmon Flame', the salmon-pink leaves edged with brilliant green. The coleus is a plant of easy culture but requires warmth and humidity otherwise it will drop its leaves. It is grown from seed sown in a temperature of 68°F (20°C) and barely covered.

A similar temperature is recommended for *Grevillea robusta*, the Australian silky oak, which is really a tree but which makes an excellent pot plant. Its fern-like leaves are admirable for mixing. After germination, reduce the temperature which should be maintained at 55°F (13°C) during winter.

Perhaps the two easiest orchids for the amateur are those requiring a temperature of only 55°F (13°C) in which to bloom, namely the *Cymbidium* and *Odontoglossum*. They are plants of high altitudes and require only sufficient warmth to exclude frost and to keep the plants growing. Under such conditions they will require no yearly rest as do the really hot-house orchids.

Plant early in September. The large fleshy roots require room to develop so use a 5-inch pot containing a mixture of Osmunda fibre from Japan and turf loam, to which is added a small quantity of sphagnum moss. Plant so that the crown is just above the rim of the pot and the compost just below to allow for watering. Do not over-water, especially immediately after planting. Shading from strong sunlight is essential. In a temperature of 55°F (13°C) each plant will give at least six blooms during winter. Among the easiest to grow and bearing blooms of special value for the flower arranger are *Cymbidium giganteum* which bears its flowers of yellow and red in elegant sprays and *Odontoglossum pulchellum* which bears heavily scented flowers of purest white. *O. nobile* is most free flowering in spring, likewise *Cymbidium lowianum* which bears sprays of maroon and cream coloured flowers.

Perpetual-flowering carnations are capable of giving of their beauty under similar conditions but at all times require the maximum amount of sunlight and a clear atmosphere so that where growing in or near a town, the greenhouse glass should be washed down frequently.

Young plants obtained in spring should be twice 'stopped' (have their growing points removed), late in April and again a month later. In August, move to the pots in which they will bloom and in which they will remain for at least three years. Use a compost containing turf loam into which is mixed some wood ash, lime rubble and coarse sand. Do not plant too deeply and do not over-water. The plants should be grown 'hard' and the potash in the wood ash will assist in this respect. As the plants will grow 2–3 feet tall, they need supporting.

Two outstanding varieties for cutting are 'Dusty Sim', dusky pink; and 'Safari', silvery mauve, both of which work their best under artificial light.

In a temperature of 45°F (7°C), pelargoniums of all types may be grown and used in the home as pot plants, the scented-leaf varieties being especially attractive, for apart from the pungent scents which are released when the leaves are pressed, the leaves possess exceptional beauty, some being covered in short hairs to give them a greyish appearance, others being fern-like. Among the loveliest are *Pelargonium filicifolium* and *P. denticulatum* with its finely divided foliage of emerald green. *P. crispum* 'Citriodorum' has lemon-scented foliage edged with yellow, the tiny leaves being crinkled at the edges.

With their liking for partial shade, the variegated and scented-leaf geraniums may be used with other foliage plants requiring similar conditions, in bowls and indoor hanging baskets. One of the best of those with variegated leaves is 'Marechal McMahon', the leaves being almost symmetrical and of brightest green and gold.

Of the ivy-leaf type, none is more valuable than 'L'Elegante', with long graceful shoots which will trail over a pot or bowl or in an upwards direction to cover an indoor trellis. Its ivy-shaped leaves are of deepest green edged with gold, and of all indoor plants, this is the easiest to manage. It will flourish in almost complete shade when it takes on purple shading, and it will go for weeks without moisture. All it requires is a dry frost-free room.

The Zonal and Regal pelargoniums require more light and grow best in the sunny window of a room or in a greenhouse in full sun. They require a buoyant atmosphere and a temperature of around 50°F (10°C). One of the finest of the Regals is 'Carisbrooke' which bears large trusses of soft lilac-pink blooms with maroon markings at the base of the petals.

Pelargoniums require a compost made up of turf loam, decayed manure and coarse sand and containing a small quantity of lime rubble. They are not lovers of peat nor will they tolerate damp or humid conditions. To keep the plants continuously in bloom, remove the dead flowers as soon as they fade.

Grevillea

Leaf

Grown mainly for the decorative foliage effect of its delicate, silver-backed fern-like leaves. *G. robusta* is also a popular house plant (see House Plants). Dip the stem ends in boiling water. See Greenhouses (HOUSE PLANTS).

Gunnera

Leaf/Flower/Seed/Su

For most arrangers the attraction of this plant lies in the gigantic rhubarb-like leaves of *G. manicata*. Everything about this herbaceous perennial seems to be giant-like, because the flowers, though individually small, form enormous heads (up to 6 feet high). When using the leaves dip their stems in boiling water.

Gypsophila/chalk plant

Flower/Seed/Sp

Crowded white, pink or purplish-rose flowers often seen in cottage gardens distinguish this hardy annual or perennial border plant. The white flowers are much in demand for weddings, but if dried by hanging upside down they are also suitable for winter arrangements.

Haemanthus see House Plants (Bulbs)

Haworthia see House Plants (Cacti and Succulents)

Hebe

Flower/Leaf/Sp/Su/Au

Formerly included under the genus Veronica, hebes are a group of hardy or tender shrubs. Of the many varieties, which flower at various times from spring to autumn, the best known type has long spikes of pinkish flowers (sometimes violet or lavender). The stems tend to be rather untidy, though the leaf formation is symmetrical. Hammer the stem ends.

The 'whipcord' hebes with tiny conifer-like leaves are often found in rocky situations near the seaside and are useful for decorative foliage.

Hedera/ivy

Leaf/Berry

A climbing or trailing plant with evergreen foliage. Several modern hybrids make good house plants. See HOUSE PLANTS; Climbing Plants. A number of varieties have variegated leaves. *H. colchica* (Persian ivy) has enormous leaves with an interesting toothed shape. The trailing kinds are useful for hanging baskets and informal arrangements. Ivy symbolises immortality, a reference to its long-lasting qualities (it lasts well in water too). Its clinging quality suggests the symbolic links with faithfulness and memory. Preserve the berries of ivy in pure glycerine.

Helenium/sneezewort

Flower/Leaf/Su/Au

The sunny yellow or red petals are rather daisy-like in form, but the golden central ball is prominent and distinguishes this North American hardy perennial. The foliage of some of the modern hybrids is fern-like and delicate. They make excellent cut flowers, but hammer the stem ends before putting in water.

Helianthus/sunflower

A large single bloom of the annual sunflower in a wonderful focal point for a late summer arrangement. Strip the leaves and dip the stem ends in boiling water for a minute. The artist Van Gogh painted a vase of sunflowers in which the life and vitality of the sun seems to spring out of the canvas. The variety 'Autumn Beauty' has a coppery zone contrasting with the yellow. Though the flowers are smaller, like the Excelsior hybrids it is good for cutting, and the variety 'Italian White' has unusual white petals with a yellow zone.

Helichrysum/everlasting flower, immortelle

Flower/Su

The daisy-like flowers in white, pink, yellow and dark wine-red with their papery bracts are often seen in old-fashioned flower arrangements. The garden-grown annual flowers should be cut for drying as soon as the flowers have developed. Strip the leaves and hang the flowers upside down.

Helipterum

Flower/Su

White, bronze-copper, yellow, pink and red daisy-like Australian flowers which resemble helichrysums and make excellent everlasting flowers. The treatment for preserving is also the same as for helichrysums.

Helleborus/hellebore, Christmas rose, Lenten rose

Flower/Leaf/Wi/Sp

Useful flowers for winter arrangements, Christmas roses (*H. niger*) are white, perhaps tinged pink, rather saucer-shaped flowers with pronounced anthers. If the weather is mild they actually do bloom at Christmas, otherwise they must be forced with the help of cloches. The lenten rose, *H. orientalis*, has similarly formed purple, pink or nearly black flowers blooming from February till May. The green-flowered species include the stinking hellebore (*H. foetidus*) and also start to bloom in February. Dip the stem ends of all species in boiling water and give them a soaking in deep water. The fine-looking leathery leaves are useful foliage decoration.

Everlasting flowers are another group of plants that should be grown in every flower arranger's garden. The one shown here is *Helichrysum italicum*, another native of Europe.

Hepatica

Flower/Sp

Anemone-like blue, white or pink flowers on short stems make this a useful flower for March arrangements. The flower used to be included in the *Anemone* genus. It can sometimes be found growing wild in woods. Dip the stem ends in boiling hot water and then give them a good drink.

Hesperis/sweet rocket

Flower/Seed/Sp/Su

H. matronalis often seeds itself. There are variations in colour from violet to lilac, pale pink or white, and the fragrant flowers form heads on tall stems. They are not particularly spectacular, but last well in water and form a foil to other more exciting flowers.

Heuchera/alum root

Flower/Leaf/Su/Au

Red, rather delicate bell-like flowers are borne on stems of a foot or more long. They are hardy perennials providing useful cut flowers. The leaves appear at the base of the flower stems and are evergreen and quite ornamental. There are plenty of varieties to choose from in various colours, and the flowers last well in water.

Hibiscus/rose mallow

Flower/Su/Au

The flowers are not long-lasting but their deep mouths and bright petals of red, yellow, purple, pink, etc., make them very attractive. Mostly natives of the tropics, several species have to be grown in the greenhouse. The short-lived quality of the flowers makes them suitable for very special occasions only.

Hippeastrum see House Plants (Pot Plants)

Hippophaë/sea buckthorn

Berry/Leaf

H. rhamnoides is a hardy deciduous shrub and yields clusters of cheerful orange berries which last through the winter, and the narrow silvery foliage is also attractive. Hammer the stem ends and keep the stems in as deep water as possible.

History of flower arranging

Since earliest times flowers have been used in a decorative way, either on their own or to enhance the beauty of a work of art. Probably flowers were first used to adorn the human body, as an expression of delight in beauty. It is only through the work of artists, and later the engravers, that one is able to follow the progress and fashion of this gentle art.

Flower arranging is as old as civilisation, and civilisation began with man's first attempts to create an organised life of his own. The early Egyptians designed vases to hold flowers for their religious festivals and ceremonies, and special attention was given to the display of the blue water-lily of the Nile, which was held in such high esteem. The blue and white water-lilies (*Nymphaea*) were the 'lotus' flowers painted or sculpted by the Egyptians; the true lotus (*Nelumbium*) was never used by their artists. In China the lotus is linked with the Buddhist religion, and we may be sure the Chinese interest in flowers goes back to well before the time of Christ.

In Ancient Greece flowers played an important part in decoration, but although beautiful urns, tazzas (bowls) and vases were made by the Greeks, they were used principally for the storage of oil and other commodities used in the home.

During the period of the Roman Empire large quantities of flowers grown in Egypt were shipped to Rome, where the chief forms of decoration were wreaths, chaplets and garlands, the flowers used being Roman hyacinths, violets, roses, anemones, carnations, narcissi and lilies. Among the herbs and shrubs also used by the Romans were thyme, sage and myrtle.

Each Roman senator employed many people, whom today we would call florists, to make the wreaths and garlands used so extravagantly. The lavish use of flowers and petals strewn on marble floors would have helped to soften the austere look of Roman architecture. Even streets and lakes were at times scattered with them.

In the Vatican Museum can be seen a mosaic of the second century A.D. showing a plaited basket filled with easily distinguishable flowers: carnations, roses, Roman hyacinths, narcissus, morning glory and a large double anemone. The basket could be Victorian in its overall design. We may imagine it was copied by enthusiastic flower arrangers, and perhaps its style reached Britain during the Roman occupation.

There is little or no evidence of the use of flowers in Europe in the centuries following the end of the Roman Empire. With the spread of Christianity the monks pursued their peaceful occupations and cultivated herbs in the gardens of the monasteries for the making of potions and lotions to treat and heal the poor. Among the new arts practised during the medieval period was the illumination of bibles, psalters and Books of Hours. Flowers and foliage in both a stylised and natural form were used in designs for these works of art and devotion. Flowers no doubt found their way on festive occasions into the chapels of the monasteries and churches. England's King Henry VI (1422–61) left in his will a piece of ground in order that herbs and flowers could be grown for use in the chapel at Eton College, which he founded.

The Uffizi Gallery in Florence contains the Portinari altarpiece by the Dutch artist Hugo van der Goes (died 1482), which depicts at the base of the centre panel a majolica jar containing an iris and a lily dedicated to the Virgin. Standing beside this a glass container holds columbines, seven in all, representing the seven virtues of the Holy Ghost. Behind the vase, sheaves of wheat indicating fertility and a scattering of violets for humility complete the symbolic flower decoration of this magnificent picture. During the medieval period artists incorporated flower and plant motifs in both sculpture and wall paintings.

If one thinks of flower arranging as something relatively new, look at Botticelli's *Virgin and Child with St. John* in the Borghese Gallery at Rome. In the background are three carved stands piled high with roses (possibly *Rosa alba*), a worthy decoration for any church today. In the fifteenth century the maxim 'fitness to purpose' was as true as it is today.

A favourite Madonna and Child is by the fifteenth century painter Gerard David, which is often called *The Madonna of the Gruel*. It shows the Madonna feeding the infant child and at the same time distracting its attention by allowing the infant to hold a sprig of flowers. In the background, on a small table, stands a charming small arrangement, the tallest and most important flower being the iris (the flower of the Madonna before the introduction of the candidum lily to Europe). On the right is a group of columbines, and to complete the arrangement sweet rocket and heart's ease. This can be seen as the first true example of a Western European flower arrangement as such, it being a combination of both symbolism and artistry.

At the Brussels National Museum one can see the Madonna lily, *Lilium candidum*, used as the flower of the Madonna. *The Annunciation* by the Master of Flemalle shows a typical Dutch interior with the Madonna lily, thought by some to be the 'lily of the field' mentioned in the New Testament, growing, as it does, wild in Palestine. This simple but lovely lily is best known of all. It often succeeds well in the cottage garden, giving pleasure for a great number of years. Thus in the early seventeenth century the Madonna lily took pride of place with the crown imperial (*Fritillaria imperialis*). These two glorious flowers, with their charm and elegance, provide the focal point in many of the Dutch and Flemish flower paintings.

It is of interest to note that early in the seventeenth century Giovanni Ferrari of Sienna published a book in which instructions were given on the growing and care of flowers. Hints on arranging and subsequent care were also included, and a wide range of vases shown.

During the same period in England the famous gardener and botanist John Parkinson had published his *Paradisus Terrestris* to be followed by *Theatrum Botanicum*, books which showed interest in the decorative qualities of plants. A tremendous amount of excitement over plants and gardens was being shown. John Tradescant was laying out the gardens at Hatfield House in Hertfordshire, and making numerous journeys abroad for rare and unusual plants. What curiosity there must have been when these consignments arrived, and with what love and care they would have been planted. To quote John Parkinson: 'And I doe wish all gentlemen and gentlewomen whom it may concern to be as careful whom they trust with the planting and replanting of fine flowers as they would be with so many jewels.'

Before the seventeenth century, flowers had appeared as symbolic emblems in the paintings of religious subjects; now they were to be the subject of the magnificent Dutch and Flemish flower paintings. Some of the early paintings seem little more than a record of the then known flowers. These began to include flowers from many other parts of the world. Overland from the East had come the tulip, cyclamen, hyacinth, narcissus, lilac, fritillary and numerous other plants. These were soon to be followed by the sunflower, nasturtium, zinnia, begonia and petunia from South America. It is interesting to study these

beautiful and at times lavish paintings and to note when the newer additions were introduced.

The basis of flower arranging as we know it today can be traced to this Dutch and Flemish period. Artists with ability started to produce the exact colour and texture of flowers with a wonderful sense of design. Many of these glorious paintings were composed from studies of flowers done at different periods. A similar practice is still employed today, when an old-fashioned type of lily or rose will be used in various positions in an arrangement. Jan Breughel, Van Huysum, Nicholas van Veerendael, De Heem, to name but a few, captured great beauty in their flower paintings, and expressed the increasing interest in and love of flowers. In England the botanist John Gerard in his *Herball* of 1597 wrote: 'Who would looke dangerously up at planets that might safely looke downe at plants.' This seems all the more appropriate today.

In the past, the artistic life of a country centred around the court, and that of Louis XIV of France became the centre of all the arts. The landscape architect Le Nôtre (1613–1700) was employed to design the gardens at Versailles, and the painter Charles le Brun (1619–90) to decorate the interiors of the palace. Enormous quantities of flowers were raised and used for the decoration of Versailles and other royal residences. The Hall of Mirrors at Versailles must have looked magnificent with its thousand orange trees in silver tubs. On the Queen's stairway a *trompe l'oeil* by Belin de Fontenay shows an attendant arranging plants in one of the beautiful bronze urns used to decorate the palace. It is of interest to note that the handles of these urns were incorporated in the overall design of the arrangement. In the nineteenth century one sees this even more clearly in the truly magnificent paintings and coloured lithographs by Joseph Nigg (1782–1863), Viennese flower painter and porcelain artist. During the reigns of Louis XIV, XV, and XVI the art of flower arranging reached a peak. Enormous quantities of cut flowers and blossom were produced, much being grown in special beds heated by a system of hot pipes.

In 1632, at Oxford, the first greenhouse was built in Britain. Later, when the technique for the manufacture of sheet glass was perfected, greenhouses and conservatories were considered a necessity at most of the large houses in the country, thus bringing about an entirely different form of decoration. Where previously cut flowers had predominated pot plants now held sway. These were skilfully grown and graced many a grand stairway and hall.

A further change was yet to follow: a return to cut flowers as the principal form of decoration, but with a difference. In the past the more exotic flowers had been forced and used, now a new impetus and awareness of the beauty of the more simple flowers and foliage was being developed and closely studied.

Can one see in the style of the flower arrangements the social conditions prevailing at each particular period: the wild extravagances of the period leading to the French Revolution; the tight, rather prim posy of the Victorian period with its compact many-classed social system; the slightly freer Edwardian time when change was in the air? During the present period the greatest possible freedom is given to self-expression and the widest possible choice is available both from the point of view of style and plant material.

Home decoration

One cannot do better than quote the words of the late Constance Spry when she said: 'The art of using flowers to beautify a room is an important aspect of interior decoration. Some people contend that well-arranged groups of flowers, being beautiful in themselves, cannot look wrong. We believe, however, that for purposes of interior decoration the groups must fit happily into their surroundings. We still put it no higher than this for the moment, although there are times and occasions when flowers are made to play a more active part by enhancing the beauty of their setting. If you grow flowers in your own garden, bear the house in mind when ordering seeds and plants, particularly when you can reserve a plot for cut-flower growing—an excellent plan, which gives you freedom of choice and eliminates any argument as to what you may or may not pick. It is almost impossible, and certainly would be unwise, to "lay down a law" about the decorative aspect of flower arranging because it is simply a matter of taste.'

One should first decide on the personality of the room in which the flowers are to be placed and this will guide you as to what is best to use. There is a special feature in the room and this should help you to decide how to build your flower scheme. One room will call for red flowers, whereas another may be so heavily wallpaper-patterned in soft pink garlands of roses that the only sensible thing to do, when they are available, is to follow through the scheme with the same type of roses.

The position of flowers in the room is of the utmost importance and one can usually say it is better to concentrate on one or two large groups around the room rather than lots of little vases and pots on the window sills which is a stylistic relic of the Victorian era. If the decorations are to be for a party, then flowers are best on a mantelpiece and in a niche, where they are reasonably high up and out of harm's way. Remember when the room is full of people, so few of the flowers would show if they were down on low tables. All flowers last longer in a fairly cool room of even temperature, but, of course, this cannot always be arranged. By spraying them lightly from time to time you will help to keep them fresh—this, of course, must be done with the utmost care to prevent any fabrics close by being marked. Many flowers look at their best with a background, so an arrangement in a window with the light behind it can be disappointing. Flowers on a mantelshelf with a mirror background need arranging with care. Remember that the mirror will multiply the number of flowers in the vase and also show up the mechanics behind if these are not carefully hidden! Place your flowers which have been chosen in a certain colour near to the piece of furnishing fabric or picture which has the same colouring. A flower or foliage group should be part of the whole decoration and not stand out like a sore thumb.

Probably the most satisfactory way to decorate a room is to have one large group, then one or two special little things on one's desk or side table which are of special interest, perhaps the first iris of spring or the last garden rose, treasures which would not show up at all unless treated to the specimen vase or small antique container. The same principles apply to plants and one cannot do better than to have a plant table or tray on which all the pots are carefully arranged rather than scattered around the room. These need not be planted in a single trough. The pots can be placed together; some raised on other pots or tripods to give height, and the whole set-up on a little gravel which can be kept moist, so creating a good growing atmosphere. Each plant can then be treated on its own merits and no two need have the same amount of water, a great advantage when some need dry conditions during the winter months.

Home decoration. A useful asset in any flower arranger's home is an antique wall bracket like this wooden cupid. Such brackets lend themselves readily to a wide variety of arrangements.

If one wants to 'keep up with the Joneses', then a 'pot-et-fleur' may be considered necessary, and this can easily be arranged by placing a small water container holding cut flowers in among the pots. The sides of the pots and the areas between can be carefully disguised by one or two plants being placed on their sides, also by the addition of moss, bark and any other decorative materials. It is best to hide the ugly plastic pot which is produced today. To get the most from a group of plants grade them carefully for leaf, shape and colour so that as wide a range as possible is obtained. An open fireplace is not a suitable place for pot flowers or cut flowers, because it is far too subject to draughts. Make it attractive by just placing silver birch logs in it, and put your flowers and plants up where they can be seen when the room is full of people.

Wall vases are popular and show flowers off to good advantage but they must be used with the utmost care, because one leaf misplaced can act as a syphon causing water to run down. The wallpaper is then disfigured until the room is redecorated. Of course, they are economic to use because the flowers need little or no backing. Choose your materials carefully—a few elegant branches can make a perfect silhouette. Some rooms, because of their over-fussy wallpapers, do not really lend themselves to flowers and it is in these circumstances that one can use a special background of some plain fabric. It can be hung as a curtain or unrolled like a map from a special brass rod with ornamental ends. This type of wall ornament has now come back into fashion. The choice of various background colours can make it somewhat of a challenge as to what colour one can put into the rooms. These contrived backgrounds, however, must be used with discretion, because, as I have already stated, flowers always look best when they fit in naturally with the rest of the room.

It is only by trying different-shaped vases and colours of flowers that one can arrive at the best arrangements for a certain room. Again, one person's views are not always pleasing to another, so you do the arrangement as you like it; what a pity there are so many people today who are so bound down with rules and regulations. It is certainly restricting, and takes away from the fun of doing the flowers.

Table decorations are another point to be considered. It is generally thought that these should be low enough to allow a clear view across the table but this is not always so. Take a look at the flowers at a state banquet and you will see that this idea is not necessarily right for a big public occasion. I would suggest for the small, intimate dinner party a low bowl or oblong trough is ideal. For a more formal affair one can bring out the candelabra, and then the flowers are lifted up above table level and one can see through across the table under the small bowls fitted into the candleholders. The materials used in these small containers should be light and flowing and then nothing could be more pretty. So often one sees them over-decorated and stuffed, and then the whole effect is spoilt.

Fashions change from year to year and a vase in vogue today may well find itself useless in a year or so. Keep it if you can spare the room; the fashion will come round again. This is just what has happened to the epergne (a great favourite in Victorian times). It fell out of fashion, and many found their way into junk shops. A few years ago those that were left came back into the limelight and today a good specimen is worth a lot of money. They still lend themselves to very loose

▲ Home decoration. The problem here has been to fit an arrangement on a marble table top below an ornate gilt picture frame, against an elaborate floral wallpaper. Note that the highest point of the arrangement is off-centre in relation to the picture.

▼ Another problem arrangement. This time the problem was to shape the arrangement into the curve of the convex mirror. The slight asymmetry of the arrangement saves it from being boring.

A similar problem arises here where a tall, thin arrangement is used to reflect the floral design on the gilt picture frame.

and light flower collections rather than to many of the arrangements as we know them today. They are rather spreading in their design so they need large tables to be shown off to their best advantage, and trailing materials such as asparagus fern (*A. plumosus*) or *A. sprengeri*, lonicera and smilax (*Asparagus asparagoides*) look as well as anything in them with a few delicate flowers.

Finally, a few further words from Constance Spry are needed to put things clearly in perspective. She says: 'As in all other matters of decorations suitability should be the keynote—suitability to both place and occasion.' The flowers for the luncheon table should be simpler in their nature, and more simply arranged than those for the dinner table. Tables laid in the open, or in the verandah or a garden room will call for the simplest treatment, even on special occasions, because you are competing with plants growing naturally and an elaborate table always seems out of place in such surroundings.

The same would apply in the children's nursery; it is here the future flower decorator is born! Start off with the simplest of flowers gleaned from the hedgerow or field and place it in a home-made container, perhaps a biscuit tin covered with paper, a small sea-shell set up in plasticine, or a jam jar hidden among fungi and lichen glued together to make a base. This is certainly not the place for the glass mirror trough or the ormulu cake stand.

Hosta/plantain lily, funkia

Leaf/Flower/Seed/Su/Au

A hardy perennial plant for ornamental foliage often variegated with streaks or edges of green, cream or yellow. Both leaves and flowers last excellently in water. Every flower arranger with a garden will have these plants in borders preferably in moist soil or in tubs which can be conveniently watered. The variegated types like *H. albomarginata* (green with a white border), *H. fortunei* 'Albo-picta' (leaves at first yellow-white with a green border), or *H. undulata* (white central band and wavy edge) are very attractive. Some varieties have bluish green or grey leaves, such as *H. sieboldiana*. The leaves should be kept in water for some time before arranging or sprayed with an atomiser. Leaves left on the plant may be dried in the autumn by standing the stems in shallow water. The same may be done with the seedheads as soon as they ripen.

a)

b)

Hostas should be grown in every flower arranger's garden. The big, bold leaves are attractive throughout the growing season. (a) *Hosta decorata* 'Albo picta' with white margins to the leaves.

(b) *Hosta glauca* 'Elegans', has huge grey-green leaves and large lilac flowers followed by elegant seed heads which last throughout the winter.

House plants

The choice of foliage and flowering pot plants for the house is now so wide that to any gardener, certainly, and indeed to most people who like their homes to look as attractive as possible, there is an endless selection of plant material which can be grown as specimen plants and as groups. Because of the initiative of the nurserymen, many plants once thought to be suited only to greenhouses have been found to be quite happy in house conditions and, once it is understood that there are different types of plants requiring different sets of growing conditions, and what suits one will not suit another, success in cultivation will automatically follow. A collection of healthy, vigorous plants with shining, well-coloured leaves, sturdy stems and a profusion of flowers will be gained, giving the owner a great deal of personal satisfaction, as well as adding to the general decorativeness of the home. The trend towards growing more houseplants has been increasing steadily and there is no reason why it should not continue to do so. Today's style of building, which provides, among other things, large picture windows and a steady supply of warmth from central heating, has given greatly improved conditions of light and temperature, so making it very much easier to grow really healthy and attractive plants.

To some extent also, the increase in cultivation is due to those frustrated gardeners who are forced to live in flats, and have no other outlet for their green-finger instincts. Pot plants, window boxes, bottle gardens, 'pot-et-fleur', hanging baskets, and miniature gardens are all ways of growing and displaying plants which can be indulged in in various parts of flats and on outside window sills and outside walls.

Houses where the light is not very good or which are at best frost-proof only in some parts can, even so, provide conditions to the liking of some plants, but it is a rare home that does not have one well lit room.

There is no doubt that well-grown plants with green or coloured leaves, or flowering plants, make a great deal of difference to the appearance and decorativeness of a room; carefully placed they can highlight a piece of furniture, the grain of wood in a wall, the design of the curtains and the general colour scheme by contrast or emphasis. They can also be used to hide any ugly object, fill a dull corner, or make use of a wasted space.

Once only house plants which had plain-green leaves were seen, and the aspidistra is the classic example of this. But plants with leaves as brightly coloured as flowers can be grown now, such as the codiaeums and dracaenas, the variegated peperomias, and the zebra plant. There are many that flower, such as begonia, cyclamen, campanula, aechmea and hibicus. You can have climbing plants or trailers, perhaps for the side of the stairs, framing a window, or hanging from a trough of plants. There are some which grow straight up such as the rubber plant, mother-in-law's tongue and the silk oak. Others are shorter and bushy, to be used as a contrast, for instance maranta, coleus, fittonia, the sweet orange and the aluminium plant.

Indoor plants can be combined in all sorts of ways, perhaps in groups in which the shapes and foliage contrast. They can be planted in a single container, or kept in a trough either in pots or planted directly into it. It is interesting to have a mixture of flowering and foliage plants. Other ideas include bottle gardens and miniature gardens in the oriental style. Vertical stands with a mixture of trailing and bushy plants are charming, and such plants look fine as a collection hanging on the wall. The stag's-horn fern is particularly suitable used in this way as a focal point. A collection of plants by the window (the modern 'picture' windows are the most suitable) is an excellent way of displaying and growing house plants, and some that are specially good for this purpose are sweet orange, pelargonium, hibiscus, fuchsia, cytisus, solanum (the winter-flowering cherry), and all sorts of cactus. If you are lucky enough to have a home extension or garden room, a sort of modern form of conservatory, you can grow exotic things really well, like agapanthus, gloxinia, hibiscus and haemanthus.

The various possibilities for permanent decoration are endless: it is up to the owner to use imagination, and ornament each room with living material most suited to the conditions for growth and design in that room.

There is no doubt, however, that considerable skill is involved in growing plants in the home, and it is when plants die or look sick for no apparent reason, in spite of receiving a good deal of care and attention, that one begins to be discouraged and bored by house plants, and to think that cut flowers are preferable. You begin to ask, why bother with house plants at all? One positive

House plants look more decorative when grown together in the same container. These plants are still in their individual pots.

factor is the standard of plant health set by house-plant nurserymen which has now become very high, and one should be able to start with a strong plant. Unfortunately, some shops are still not very careful about looking after their pot plants. Therefore, when choosing a plant in the shop or garden centre, look for one with plenty of new shoots coming, with its leaves undamaged and a strong dark green or, if coloured, with the colour or variegation strongly pronounced. Make sure the main stem is not damaged, and that the growing points at the tips of the shoots have not been broken off. If a flowering plant, choose one with plenty of unopened flower buds, not one which is in full bloom. Look at the base of the pot or container—if roots are growing through the drainage holes, the plant is pot bound and will be less healthy. These troubles occur in transit, or because the plant has been standing too long before being sold. Try to buy a plant free from pests. Mealy bug, for instance, is often a trouble not noticed because it may be attacking at or below soil level.

For the journey from shop to house the plant should be completely wrapped and thus pro-tected from draught, cold weather or too hot sun-light. Once home, it should be regarded almost as a 'hospital' case for a few days, and placed away from a bright light, kept warm, and sprayed over-head frequently to keep the leaves moist. This should be kept up until it has settled down to the very different conditions in the home to the ones it was accustomed to in the nursery greenhouse.

House plants can grow very well, but it is im-portant to remember that they are living, like you or me. To make sure they go on living and growing well, they must have food and water. They do better if there is a slightly damp atmo-sphere and, very important, they must have the right soil, or compost, to grow in. The one condi-tion that they must have and that we can do with-out, is light, as they need this for making the green (the chlorophyll) parts of the plant. Plants in pots are *not* plastic dummies which will go on looking good without any attention.

Plants do not take their food in solid form as we do, but dissolved in water, in the form of minute mineral particles. The most important ones are those that supply the plants with nitrates, phosphates and potash, and in a good compost these will be present in the right quantities. The amounts required by each plant will vary, but modern composts are so carefully made up that they will suit the majority of plants. Besides these three foods, there are various others, called 'trace' elements, because only very tiny amounts of them are required. They are also very necessary and will be present in the composts. Sometimes, if the plant has been in the pot a long time or is flowering, it will have used up most of the food that was in the compost, and so has to be given a dose of a liquid fertiliser every so often. There are lots of proprietary brands and the rates and frequency of use will be given on the container.

As well as supplying food, you must also provide a slightly humid atmosphere. One which is really bone dry, as centrally heated ones so often are, is no good, and plants will dry up and wither, turn brown, drop their leaves and flower buds and become generally very unhappy. Spraying the plant with a fine spray of clear water every day is a great help, and if it is growing in a very warm place, two or three times a day is better still. You can also help create humidity by standing the pot in a shallow saucer of water, which has a layer of shingle in it. The shingle helps keep the base of the pot and the plant's roots from being waterlogged, but at the same time allows moisture to be evaporating all round the plant continuously. Another way to do this is to put the pot into a larger one, or one of the ornamental ones that can be bought, and tuck moist, granulated peat into the space between the walls of the two pots. Simpler still is to have a shallow tray containing water evaporating close to the plant.

House plants are potted in the nursery in special mixtures of soil, called composts, and the most widely used and best known of these are the John Innes composts. They are a mixture of peat, coarse silver sand, and loam, in set proportions, together with what is called a base fertiliser. This has the main foods in it mentioned earlier. There is a little bit of chalk, too, to prevent the mixture from becoming too acid. This mixture has been found by experiment to be well-drained (very important), and to suit most plants, except the specialist plants, of course, such as cactus or bromeliads, about which more will be said later.

The John Innes composts can be obtained as No. 1, No. 2 and No. 3, according to the amounts of fertiliser and chalk in them, and are used as the size of the plant and pot increases.

Besides these, there are some newer composts, the soil-less kind, which only have peat and sand in them, with some food but no loam. They are used for plants which do not have a great deal of top growth, for sowing seed and taking cuttings, and for plants which are to be grown for perhaps two months and then discarded or planted out of doors.

Pot plants will be sold growing in one of these composts, and if it is one containing loam, it will usually be J. I. No. 1. Plants in this may need repotting in one or two years, and if they are very squashed in their pots, should be put in one a size larger, with new compost. If there are not too many roots, and the plant is not showing signs of starvation, and is not wilting quickly after watering, then all that need be done is to top-dress it. This means scraping off the top $1\frac{1}{2}$ inches of compost carefully, so as not to damage the roots, and replacing it with new J. I. No. 1. Remember that there should always be a space between the compost surface and the top of the pot of about 1 inch, to allow for watering; if the pot is filled to the brim with compost, then any water given to the plant will just run over the sides, and only a little will actually soak into the compost.

Watering is the factor which causes an awful lot of trouble with pot plants. It has been overcome, to some extent, by the use of the John Innes composts, which include drainage materials, and even more by the use of soilless composts, which contain peat, sand and nutrient, but there is still a need to water according to experience and one's own judgement. If the compost surface is dry, and if a clay pot makes a high ringing noise when tapped with a long piece of wood, then it requires water, preferably at room temperature. The amount given should be sufficient to fill the space between the soil surface and the brim of the container, if poured on fairly fast, so that no time is allowed for it to soak in while watering. Any extra water will drain out of the bottom of the pot if the drainage is correct. The plant should not then be watered again until the soil surface once more becomes dry. The interval will vary according to the size of the plant, its rate of growth, the size of the container, the temperature of the room, the presence or absence of flowers, and the kind of compost used. It is not possible to say: 'Water every 7 days, or every 3rd day', since the needs of each plant vary, and each must be watched individually and watered when required. As one becomes more experienced the look of the plant and the feel of the leaves will decide whether water is necessary. In winter much less will be required, as most plants have a 'close' season then and may only need watering every 10–14 days as opposed to four or six days.

Plants growing in clay pots will react to watering slightly differently from those in plastic pots. The clay is porous and will absorb a good deal of water, and as a result in a moist atmosphere the compost dries out slowly and gradually. In a dry atmosphere though, the porous clay loses water through the sides by evaporation and thus tends to make watering necessary more often than would be the case with a plastic pot. As far as plastic pots are concerned, the compost remains moist for much longer, but then suddenly becomes very dry, so that a plant may be in urgent need of watering between one day and the next. There is a tendency when changing over from clay to plastic pots to over-water at first because of this.

The most important point about temperatures for house plants is that they should be steady. They need not necessarily be very high, but if the plant is alternately hot and cold, or is in a position where it has cold draughts blowing on it occasionally or frequently, it will not do well. It will grow slowly, drop its leaves, lose its flower or flowerbuds, and generally be very sad. A temperature of 50–65°F (10–18°C) during spring, summer and autumn is often all that is needed, with one not lower than 45°F (7°C) in winter, though there are, of course, exceptions, some plants in winter surviving 40°F (4°C), and others wanting 70°F (21°C) and over in summer. These are mentioned where relevant in the individual plant descriptions.

The final factor to remember for successful house plant growing is light. The intensity of light is important; some plants are happy in a darkish place. Some want a good light, but not sunlight, and others will not thrive without a good shot of sunlight every day, at least during the growing season. This is when it becomes important to find out what particular conditions plants like, and to make sure that you can give them these in your home. For instance, it is no good putting a plant with coloured and variegated leaves in a corner away from a window, for the leaves will lose their attractive colours and stop growing: they must have a window with plenty of light coming through it. Cactus are no good without sunlight in the summer, but African violets and fibrous-rooted begonias prefer only a good light, even a north-facing window, provided the temperature does not drop below 50°F (10°C).

House plants, and plants in pots, generally do not suffer from pests and fungus diseases, but there are a few that may occur. Greenfly are often found on the tips of shoots and young leaves; red spider mite will be found sometimes, particularly in hot dry atmospheres, another reason for keeping the air moist, as they do not thrive in humid atmospheres. The mites can barely be seen without a lens as they are very tiny, roundish and pale red. They collect on the undersides of leaves, near to the main vein, where they feed by sucking the sap from the leaf. This causes it to become mottled and greyish-green or yellowish-green, and it will eventually wither and drop off. Ivies are often attacked, also fuchsias, the shrimp plant, and azaleas. Spray the plants with malathion in aerosol form—this will also control greenfly—or water with a system insecticide, according to the maker's instructions.

Scale insects can be a nuisance, particularly on rather woody plants, such as sweet bay, the miniature orange or azaleas. They are brown, flat, and oval in shape, attached to leaves, both top and undersurface, and to the stems and bark of shoots. They can quite easily be missed, until there are a great many present, by which time they will be doing considerable damage, and will be difficult to eradicate. One of the first signs is the appearance of a black, soot-like covering to some of the leaves. This is a kind of fungus, called sooty mould, which grows on the honey dew excreted by the scale insects, and should be wiped off the leaves, otherwise the breathing pores will not be able to work properly.

Sometimes house plants are infested with mealy bug, a pest with a white woolly coating, which feeds on the young parts in the same way as greenfly. It is mostly found on bulbous plants, but can appear on other plants. Spraying hard with malathion or derris will help, and both these and scale insects can be lifted off and destroyed with the point of a knife.

Diseases are very few and far between; azaleas may get a greyish swelling on the leaves, which should be picked off and burnt. This is known as

a)

d)

c)

b)

House plants; cacti and succulents. All the cacti and succulents shown here are easily grown on a sunny windowsill. (a) An Echinocereus species; these are usually free flowering. (b) *Mammillaria spirosissima* var. 'Rubra' one of the ever popular cushion cacti. (c) *Mammillaria tolimensis,* another easy cushion cactus. (d) *Aloe dorothea,* one of the dwarf aloes suitable for growing as a pot plant. (e) *Haworthi;* an attractive 'zebra' plant for the house. (f) The Lampranthus make attractive pot plants indoors or may be grown in a sunny part of a rock garden.

f)

House plants; pot plants. (a) The house leek, *Sempervivum kosaninii* has pale green pads with bright red tips. (b) The Cobweb house leek, *Sempervivum arachnoidicum* looks as though spiders have spun webs over each of the rosettes. (c) Ferns make good pot plants for shady windowsills. The one shown here is a hardy Maidenhair fern, *Adiantum venustum.* (d) One of the florists' azaleas *(R. Simsii)* available in a vast range of colours. (e) Tradescantias make attractive house plants and will grow almost anywhere.

azalea leaf gall. Injured parts of a plant may be infected with grey mould, which is also best cut out as far as the healthy growth, just above a leaf joint. Occasionally mildew is seen, a whitish, powdery coating on leaves and sometimes stems. Cut out and spray the rest of the plant with dinocap.

The troubles that are the most nuisance are really cultivation troubles, or 'physiological disorders', and can only be remedied as one becomes more experienced in handling the plants. For instance, wilting leaves and shoots can be due to not enough water, but also, just as easily, to too much water, which drives the oxygen out of the soil, drowns the roots, and stops them from functioning and absorbing water, so that the top growth wilts from lack of water. If the bottom leaves turn yellow and drop off, this is frequently a sign of over-watering. If the top of the plant begins to turn pale green and then yellow, and this spreads back down the stem, then lack of nitrates is the reason, and the plant either needs repotting, or liquid feeding. Browning of leaf margins and tips, and dropping of flower buds, is usually because of lack of moisture in the air. Flower buds may also drop because of draughts or frequent changes of position and temperature. Brown spots on leaves may be, besides dry atmosphere or draughts, due to gas (where gas fires or gas stoves are used), too much food, sun shining through drops of water on the leaves, or too strong sun. If variegated or coloured leaves lose their colour or revert to green, they need more light. If the plant is growing slowly or not at all, this is quite normal, provided it is winter, but when this happens in spring or summer, it may be pot bound; or it may be short of water, or food, or both.

Sometimes one feels that it would be nice to increase the numbers of a certain plant, and the most common way of propagating them is to take cuttings. This means cutting off the top 3 or 4 inches of a new shoot, that is, one which was first produced in the spring, and putting the cut piece of stem, with the bottom leaves taken right off, into a sandy compost in a pot. Then put a polythene bag over it, fix it with a rubber band round the pot, and put the pot in a warm place until rooting has occurred. Once the cutting has produced roots it will start to grow, so in case of uncertainty it is a good idea to measure the cutting before rooting. If the pot can be put somewhere where the surface it is standing on is continuously warm, rooting will be much more certain, and quicker. Only a small pot is needed, about $3\frac{1}{2}$ inches in diameter, with the John Innes No. 1 compost with a little extra coarse sand added (not builder's sand) the cuttings being put round the sides of the pot. In each case, the cut should be made immediately below a leaf joint. Ivy roots very quickly in this way, jasmine can be rooted from cuttings with extra warmth, and so on.

Another way to increase your plants is by using offsets; these are small shoots produced at the base of plants, which have roots and can be detached from the plant and potted separately. The spider plant and mother-of-thousands produce tiny plants at the ends of long stems, and these can be tucked into a separate pot, and then detached when well rooted and growing. Some plants can be propagated from leaf cuttings, a little more difficult and calling for more experience in growing, and higher temperatures, and warmth for the compost is also necessary for success. The leaves are placed vertically in the compost or flat on the surface, pinned down, with cuts across the main veins, and covered with polythene. Begonias, African violets and peperomias can be treated like this.

Most house plants can be grown well if the advice just given is followed, but there is one group of plants which needs to be treated in a slightly different way. This is the bromeliad collection of plants which come from various parts of South America. Examples of these are the aechmeas and the earth-star (*Cryptanthus*) plants. They have very little in the way of roots, and these are really only for anchoring them wherever they are growing. Their food and water are absorbed through the 'funnel', a characteristic of bromeliads, which is a cup-shaped hollow in the centre of the plants, formed by the way the leaves grow. This should be kept filled with water, and when it needs renewing it should be at room temperature. They need a very peaty compost, and here the soilless composts would be best, or they can have a mixture of peat, leafmould, and rotted pine needles if they can be obtained, although they are not essential. Temperature needs vary, but roundabout 60°F (16°C) in summer and 45–50°F (7–10°C) in winter seems to be best. The correct temperature is generally indicated on the label. In summer they do best in a shaded position, in winter, full light is preferred.

The sections which follow deal with indoor plants in alphabetical order under the following headings: house plants, pot plants, climbing and trailing plants, bulbs, cacti and other succulents, and palms.

House plants

AECHMEA (urn plant) This is one of the bromeliad family, and so prefers to be grown in a peaty mixture. The strap-like leaves are grey-green with wide silver stripes, which are a kind of white, mealy coating. The leaves form a funnel, and from the centre the flower stem appears, through the water which is contained in the funnel. The flowerhead is cone-shaped, and bright rose-pink in the species *Aechmea rhodocyanea*; tiny, dark-blue flowers are produced from the pink bracts. The flowerhead lasts for several months, the flowers themselves for two weeks or so only. Give a good light in winter, light shade in summer, a temperature of 60°F (16°C), plus in summer, and a minimum of 45°F (7°C) in winter. Water through the funnel of leaves and occasionally water the compost so that it is kept moist. Offsets produced at the base of the plant after flowering can be left on it and then the parent plant should be cut right back to the base, or the offsets may be removed and potted separately. Flowers from offsets are more likely to be produced if given at least 70°F (21°C), or more during spring and summer; on the whole the plant does better at higher rather than lower temperatures.

AGAPANTHUS ORIENTALIS (blue lily of the Nile) An extremely handsome plant, with shiny, green strap-shaped leaves, and flower stems about 2 feet high, with a cluster of dark-blue flowers, each up to 2 inches long. Flowering time is in July and August. Compost should be fairly rich, J.I. potting compost No. 3, and tubs with plenty of crocks at the bottom for drainage are essential, Tubs should be at least 2 feet in diameter. Give the plant a light position in a garden room, and water freely in summer—it grows naturally close to water. Decrease watering as the flowers die down, and keep almost dry through the winter, and free from frost. Topdress in spring, and increase by dividing the old plants and separating the offsets.

APHELANDRA SQUARROSA LOUISAE (zebra plant) An upright plant with prominently white-veined, shiny green leaves, and a spiky head of bright yellow flowers and bracts. Flowering time is in

autumn and winter. Water freely when growing and flowering. They flag and wilt quickly when short of water. Give a temperature of 50°F (10°C) in winter, 65°F (18°C) and more in summer. A moist atmosphere is essential. but no draughts on any account. Good light, but not sunlight, is preferred. Wash the leaves frequently, with clear water, and feed when flowering. After flowering, the flower spike can be cut back to the first pair of leaves below it. Watering is reduced, but the soil kept just moist and the plant rested until spring. Then start into growth again, with warmth and additional water and cut back the main shoots to leave about two good buds from which strong new shoots will come. Once the new growth is about 2 inches long, repot, in new compost and a smaller pot, then move into a larger pot as the size of the plant increases, where it can flower.

ASPARAGUS PLUMOSUS NANUS (asparagus fern) An easily grown house plant providing feathery foliage for flower arrangements, or a background to flowering house plants. Sunlight or shady conditions will suit it, with plenty of water in summer and moderate temperatures. Give weak liquid feeds in spring and summer. Allow it to rest in winter, with little water, and cool conditions.

ASPIDISTRA ELATIOR (parlour palm, cast iron plant) The first house plant to become popular in Britain, introduced in early Victorian days. The large, glossy, dark green leaves are profusely produced, and its main attribute otherwise is that it will continue green and growing under all sorts of conditions, including downright neglect. It will endure light or deep shade, cold, dry atmosphere, gas, insufficient water, and so on. If watered freely in summer, given a good light, fed occasionally, and sprayed overhead to clean the leaves, it makes a handsome plant, and will even produce purple flowers close to the soil. It grows to 2 feet tall, and a variegated variety, *A. e. variegata*, has leaves striped cream. Increase by dividing in spring.

AZALEA The pot-grown azaleas are varieties of the species *Azalea indica*, and are not the kind which are hardy and grown out of doors in shrubberies and woodlands. In pots they are about 1½ feet high, and form small bushy plants with evergreen leaves, and double flowers in pink, rose, red and white. They flower during winter when they should have plenty of water. A steady temperature of about 60–65°F (16–18°C) is required, and a moist atmosphere; on no account should they be in a draught. Dry atmospheres, draughts and changes in temperature will make the flower buds drop before they open. If the plant becomes dry at the roots, the leaves will shrivel and drop. In this case give a thorough watering, by putting the pot in a container of tepid rainwater or soft water and allowing the water to soak up until the surface soil is damp. After flowering, remove the dead flowerheads, prune back the shoots a little, and decrease the quantity of water. When new shoots start to appear repot in fresh, lime-free compost, containing plenty of peat and sand. Remember that the ordinary J.I. compost should not be used, as it contains chalk. During the summer the plant can be plunged out of doors in a lightly shaded place, fed occasionally and sprayed overhead with clear water. In September it is brought inside, and as the flowerbuds appear watering is increased.

BEGONIA There are two kinds of begonia, those which are grown for their decorative leaves, and those for their flowers, notes about which will be found in the section on pot plants. The leafy begonias are called *Begonia rex* and there are all sorts with large leaves variegated with different patterns and colours. They are most attractive and easy to grow, provided they have a humid atmosphere and plenty of water. The leaves are generally purple to red, with silvery, light green or light magenta patterns on them. One particularly spectacular kind has a deep purple margin, a band of green, spotted with white, most of the central portion a reddish-plum colour, and purple outlining the central vein. Varieties of the *rex* begonias available are 'Hoar Frost' mostly silver; 'La Pasqual', so dark a purple as to be almost black with a silver band right round the leaf; 'Silver Queen'; 'Isolde', and many others. *Begonia masoniana*, also called the iron cross begonia, has a most unusual leaf; the colouring is a lightish green with a wide, deep purple marking following the main veins, so that it looks exactly like the German Iron Cross. The texture of the leaf is extraordinary, being rather moss-like, with bumps and bristle-like hairs all over the top surface.

BELOPERONE GUTTATA (shrimp plant) An attractive and easily grown house plant, the shrimp plant will 'shrimp' for most of the year, given sun and warmth. The name refers to the salmon-pink bracts produced in a short, fat cylinder, from which the white, purple-spotted flowers appear. Spray the plant overhead with clear water regularly, and feed in spring and summer. It is best to make it rest in winter, by keeping it cool and giving much less water. Prune back the shoots by about half in spring, to make it bushy and produce more flowers.

BILLBERGIA NUTANS This is a bromeliad and very easy to grow. It flowers freely, producing tubular, yellowish-green and blue flowers from deep pink bracts at the ends of arching stems. The stiff leaves are about 9 inches long and form a rosette, better not touched, as the leaf margins are spiny. Flowers appear in June and July, and the plant increases rapidly in size by producing many offsets. These can be detached, and will root quickly. It needs sun and a temperature of at least 65°F (18°C) to flower, and in winter it can be kept at about 45–50°F (7–10°C) and almost dry at the roots. It will tolerate dry atmospheres and a little gas.

CHLOROPHYTUM COMOSUM VARIEGATUM (spider plant) This is primarily grown for its leaves, which arch out in a large rosette, and are green with a central creamy-yellow portion. Long stems are produced from the centre of the rosette which will have tiny white flowers on the ends if grown in sunny conditions, otherwise they will produce young plants only, like strawberry runners, complete with embryo roots. If pegged down into compost, they will rapidly root, and can then be detached and grown as separate plants. The roots are fleshy and white, able to store a good deal of water, and so will withstand neglect quite well. The plants grow fast and need repotting in fresh compost once or twice during the growing

House plants. Chlorophytum is one of the most popular of house plants. Although a sub-tropical grass, it is very easily grown.

season. They are not particular as to temperature or light, except that they are a better colour in a good light. Dry air will result in brown leaf tips, and brown spotting.

CITRUS There is a miniature orange which can be grown as a house plant known as the calamondin, *Citrus mitis*, making a small shrubby plant, with leathery evergreen leaves. Very sweetly scented white flowers appear in spring, which in turn produce a mass of tiny oranges, about $1\frac{1}{2}$ inches round. Setting is encouraged by hand pollination, and flowers are produced if warm sunny conditions were provided in late summer and autumn of the previous year to ripen the shoots and buds. The shoots should be pruned back to keep the plant bushy in early winter. J.I. potting compost should be used, with plenty of water in summer and an occasional spraying overhead. Keep out of frost in winter and, better still, in a temperature of 45–50°F (7–10°C) with a moderate amount of watering. *C. taitensis*, the Chinese orange, is about the same size, but has a looser habit of growth, with scented white flowers, tinted pink. Its orange fruit makes good marmalade, and is about the same size as a tangerine. Another citrus, which really requires a garden room, is *C. limonia* 'Ponderosa'; it reaches about 8 feet, and should be grown in a really large pot or tub, with J.I. No. 3 compost. With plenty of water, and sun and warmth, the fragrant white flowers will produce large, round, yellow fruit, with thin skins, weighing up to 1 lb each. Hand pollination will help.

Other citrus fruit plants can be grown from the pips of oranges, lemons, and grapefruit, and will make handsome, evergreen shrubs with strongly aromatic foliage. Flowering of plants grown from pips is unusual.

CLIVIA (Kaffir lily) Natal is the native home of the Kaffir lily, *Clivia miniata*, and the lovely orange flowers are produced in a cluster at the end of a single stem in spring, sometimes earlier. It is a fleshy-rooted plant with shiny, thick, strap-like leaves. The temperature should be in the mid-sixties Fahrenheit in summer, and not below 45°F (7°C) in winter, rising in spring as flowering approaches. It needs a good light, but not sun, should be watered freely in summer, and very little in winter when it should be kept almost dry. Feed regularly while growing, but do not repot unless it is essential, as it does not take kindly to disturbance. Remove the flower stem when flowers have finished.

COLLIVIA ELEGANS (Syn. *Neanthe elegans*) (dwarf palm) Easily grown under room conditions, this small palm has frond-like leaves on delicate stems, with each frond perhaps 9 inches long. Its final height will be about 4 feet. It does not require a great deal of heat, but needs a moist atmosphere, otherwise the tips turn brown. Shade is preferable, and the leaves will look better if sponged occasionally. Feed it regularly. Repotting should not be done unless absolutely essential.

CORDYLINE The cordylines are grown for their gaily coloured leaves—they do not flower when grown in pots as they are trees of 25 feet in their native land. *Cordyline indivisa* has spiky narrowish leaves, rather a bronze colour with the central part a deep purple. *C. terminalis* is even more colourful, but correspondingly more expensive and less easy to manage. The leaves are large and oval, being green with irregular blotches and streaks of pink; there are several varieties which have varying combinations of purple, deep pink, red, cream, white and green, making them most exotic.

C. terminalis, however, requires at least 50°F (10°C) all the year, and a very good light to keep the variegation. Both should have their leaves sponged regularly, and should be fed during the growing season. Keep out of draughts and water freely in summer.

CRYPTANTHUS (earth-star) *Cryptanthus bivattatus* is a bromeliad, with five leaves radiating out from the centre lying flat on the soil. They are pink and cream in colour, or dark and light green if being grown in the shade; *C. zonatus* is green and a yellowish-brown; *C. tricolor* is cream, green and pink, and a bit bigger than the others, with leaves about 8 or 9 inches long. The earth-stars are not at all particular as to their surroundings, and are fairly tolerant of neglect. However, they should be given a peaty compost, as they are epiphytic plants, that is, they are 'perchers' and in their native country, South America, will grow on trees in rotted leafmould. A good light will bring out their colouring best, and a humid atmosphere is preferable. Do not overwater. Coolness in winter is possible, provided little water is given. They make good plants for bottle gardens.

CYCLAMEN The large-flowered cyclamen make beautiful flowering plants at Christmas and after, but cause some trouble in cultivation. For success in growing, keep in an even temperature of about 50°F (10°C), give a moist atmosphere at all times, preferably not smoky, and water only when required, but do not allow to dry out completely: only let the surface of the compost become dry. Yellowing leaves means over-watering, wilting leaves and flowers too little water, lack of flowers is due to insufficient ripening of the tuber the previous year. Draughts will also produce collapse of the plant. A good light, but not sunlight is required. After flowering, remove the flowers and gradually give less water until dried off. In late spring put the plant outside in a shady border, still in the pot, and leave until new leaves start to appear, in early or late August. Then repot in J.I. compost without lime in it, so that the tuber is partly above the surface, leave outdoors until mid-September and then bring into the house or garden room.

CYPERUS (umbrella plant) The common name could hardly be more appropriate, as the stems finish in a cluster of strap-like leaves which arch outwards and downwards from the centre. The stems are of varying heights, between 1 and $2\frac{1}{2}$ feet, so that there is a cluster of small 'umbrellas'. It likes plenty of water, will stand cool conditions, and should be kept in a water-filled saucer when actively growing. Some shade is required.

DRACAENA (dragon-tree) The dracaenas are tropical trees or shrubs with brilliantly coloured leaves, and grow 40 or 50 feet tall in their native countries. However, they do well as house plants, provided they are given quite high temperatures and moist air. The common name comes from the dye called dragon's blood, obtained from *Dracaena draco*. Their leaves are narrow and arching; they can be cream margined, or cream centred, and green; they may be golden down the midrib, or be heavily spotted with cream, on a dark green background. In summer water freely, but less so in winter; sponge the leaves with clear water occasionally and give a humid atmosphere, particularly in houses with central heating. *Dracaena sanderiana* will stand much lower temperatures, to $45°F$ ($7°C$). It has a different habit of growth, and narrow, green and cream marginal leaves. The light requirements of dracaenas are not exacting, though a good light is preferable.

FATSHEDERA (ivy tree) A plant which is that rare product, a cross between two genera, *Fatsia* and *Hedera*. The large glossy leaves vary in size between 4 and 10 inches across, and have fine lobes, so that they are palmately shaped and look rather like a very large ivy leaf. The habit is basically shrubby, with a tendency to climb, but if the tips of the main shoots are removed, it will bush out well. Some shade, and plenty of water in the growing season are important; high temperatures are not required but sponging of the leaves is advisable. Feed when growing.

FATSIA JAPONICA (false castor-oil plant, fig-leaf palm) This is hardy and will grow outside in a sheltered spot with some shade, so it will be understood that high temperatures in the house are not required. It may be a large plant to 5 feet and more, and needs plenty of room; the leaves may be 15 inches wide. They are handsome, being glossy, seven lobed, and rather leathery, and repay an occasional polish with milk and water. Taking out the growing tips will make the plant bush out further down. The variegated kind, *F. j. variegata*, has the tips of the lobes coloured cream.

FICUS Included in the *Ficus* genus are the rubber plant, *F. elastica* 'Decora', and the common fig *F. carica*. The ficus are mostly trees or shrubs, except *F. e.* 'Decora'. Under good management, it will reach the ceiling and either have to be trained along it, or decapitated and air-layered. *F. e.* 'Decora' has large, shiny, oval leaves produced alternately on the stem, very thick and leathery, and a reddish papery covering to the growing point. Successful care means no over-watering, as this results in the bottom leaves turning yellow and dropping, and particularly in winter they should be given little water, as they need rest at this time. Cleaning the leaves regularly is important; high or low temperatures and light or shade do not matter too much, although draughts are not advisable. *F. e.* 'Doescheri' has leaves margined with cream and tinted pink when young. *F. benjamina* is a small, graceful tree, with a drooping habit, and small pointed leaves quite unlike those of *F. e.* 'Decora'. Red spider mite may attack them all, particularly in dry conditions, so keep a watch for it.

GREVILLEA ROBUSTA (Australian silk oak) This is a charming and graceful plant, with fronds of light greyish-green leaves arching out from a central stem. It is easily and quickly grown, and prefers a cool, light place, with plenty of air. However, it does not like draughts. Unlike many house plants, it can be started from seed, in a J.I. seed compost. In Australia it reaches more than 103 feet in height, and has golden-yellow flowers, but not, unfortunately, in Britain.

HIBISCUS SINENSIS (Chinese rose) A shrubby, flowering house plant from China, this hibiscus has large, trumpet-shaped flowers, light red, deep pink or white, with a prominent column of stamens curving out and upwards from the centre of the flower. To encourage flowering, prune in early spring, cutting the shoots back by about half. Give a potash-high feed, and keep in a warm, well lit place. Make sure the air is moist all the time and keep out of draughts, spraying occasionally with clear water. Buds drop if the air is dry or the plant is much moved, or in a draught. In winter the temperature should be at least 50°F (10°C), but only moderate watering is necessary.

IMPATIENS (busy Lizzie, water fuchsia) Grown correctly, this can be a bushy plant covered in a mass of bright flowers in red, pink, magenta or orange-red; there is also a white variety. Cut the main shoots back by at least half to induce side shoots to grow, feed regularly, keep in a sunny position for good flowering and water freely in spring and summer. Make the plant rest in winter, by giving only a little water, and lowering the temperature slightly, otherwise it will exhaust itself. Flowers can be produced most of the year, but this is not advisable. *Impatiens holstii* has bright red flowers, *I. sultani* pink-red, and *I. petersiana* orange-red, with dark reddish-green leaves making an effective contrast. There are varieties of these, and there is a variegated version of *I. holstii* with leaves green and cream margined.

NEOREGELIA CAROLINAE TRICOLOR A bromeliad, with the familiar rosette of leaves forming a central funnel. The long, arching leaves are green on the outside, with a creamy slightly pink centre; the short internal leaves are bright red just before the flowers appear. There is no spike as with the other bromeliads, the flowers are simply produced just above the water in the funnel, and are light blue. Hence the plant is mainly grown for its foliage. It needs more careful handling than its relatives, with a higher temperature all the year, particularly in summer, to encourage the flowers, and more shade.

NERIUM OLEANDER (oleander) A tall house plant with pretty, pink, white or rosy flowers in summer; *Nerium odoratum* is very like it to look at, but has scented flowers. It is very important that it has plenty of sun in the spring and early summer, otherwise it will not flower very well, if at all, in the later part of the summer. Pruning need only consist of cutting back a little after flowering. The leaves, which are willow-like, should be sponged or sprayed frequently with clear water. The plant is rather prone to attacks by red spider mite, and dampness discourages the pest. The oleander needs plenty of water in summer and it can be kept at room temperature. During winter, it can be rested, but in a relatively warm temperature of 50°F (10°C) or more. One more important point is that every bit of the plant is poisonous, leaves, stems, flowers and roots, so it should be kept out of the reach of pets and children.

PELARGONIUM The pelargoniums contain a fascinating range of flowers, colours, leaf shapes and fragrance; it would be perfectly easy to grow these and nothing else in the house, particularly if you have a garden room to take the overflow. Pelargoniums include the plants known as geraniums, but which are really Zonal pelargoniums. They differ from the Regal varieties in that their leaf surfaces have a coloured ring or 'zone'. Pelargoniums come from a hot, dry climatic area, and grow in poor, well-drained soil; in the house they should have the sunniest windows and plenty of warmth in summer, and be grown in J.I. compost with an extra part of sand. Weekly liquid feeding when the flower buds appear is a good idea. When flowering has finished, cut the shoots back by about one third to half, otherwise they get too leggy the following year. In winter pelargoniums should be given cool conditions of 45°F (7°C) and very little water. The 'geraniums' have heads of smallish double or single flowers, in pink, magenta, brick red, orangey-red, and white; the Regal pelargoniums have trumpet-shaped, large flowers, usually with a dark blotch in the throat. Colours include pink, rosy, red, white, plum or nearly black. Miniature pelargoniums are particularly good for house-plant cultivation, needing only quite small pots. They make a gay show, particularly if coloured-leaved ones are used, with leaves variegated in yellow, purple, red and cream. There are also kinds with fragrant leaves, e.g. *P. crispum* 'Citriodorum', which has a greyish-green leaf, much crimped and folded, a creamy margin, and a strong perfume of lemon when rubbed. *P. tomentosum*, which is very hairy, has leaves with a strong smell of peppermint.

PEPEROMIA (pepper elder) The more recent introductions among house plants have included the peperomias, low bushy plants grown for their foliage, although one or two varieties do have white flower spikes which give them their alternative name of the rat-tail plants. *Peperomia caperata* has dark-green, much folded, rather heart-shaped leaves, with white flower spikes about 3–4 inches long in winter. *P. magnoliafolia* 'Variegata' has fleshy, shiny, smooth leaves with creamy margins, and a greyish-green central stripe; *P. sandersii*, more correctly *P. argyreia*, has most attractive, rather thick leaves with silver and green stripes fanning out and round the leaf from the point at which the leaf stalk joins the leaf on the undersurface. Nearly round in shape, they end in a slight point. The peperomias need careful handling to grow well, otherwise their leaves tend to rot off at the base of the stalk. A steady temperature of about 60°F (15°C) in summer, 50°F (10°C) in winter, no draughts, a good light, and occasional spraying with clear water are important. Watering should be carried out with water at room temperature, and should never be overdone; these plants do not need a great deal. Feeding during spring and summer is helpful.

PHILODENDRON Very good plants to grow if you have not much light available, as they prefer shade. There are both climbing and bushy kinds. *Philodendron bipinnatifidum* is one of the latter, and has very much cut and dissected, roughly triangular-shaped leaves, rather frond-like. They are large and can be as much as 2 feet long. Sponging them occasionally keeps them healthy and shiny. The plant prefers a temperature of about 50°F. Dry atmospheres are not very popular. *P. elegans* is technically a climbing plant, but is not very vigorous and usually makes a rather bushy plant with leaves about 1½ feet long, so deeply cut as to look like palm leaves. Much warmth is not required, and it is generally an easy plant to grow.

PILEA CADIEREI (aluminium plant) The common name comes from the metallic lustre of the silvery-white bands between the leaf veins, which makes the leaves very handsome. It is a bushy plant, and pinching out the tips will encourage the production of new shoots from the base of the plant and higher up the stems. It needs plenty of water when growing, and a moist atmosphere, otherwise it drops its leaves very rapidly. Feeding while growing is also important, to keep up the size of leaf and the metallic variegation. It is a satisfying plant to grow, and can easily be increased by leaf cuttings.

PLATYCERIUM ALCICORNE (stag's-horn fern) Once only grown in stove houses, it has now been found that this bizarre but handsome plant will grow perfectly well in the house, particularly the bathroom where the atmosphere is moist, not to say steamy, and often warm because the airing cupboard is there. It is a 'percher' living naturally on the bark of the trees where there is rotting vegetation so, if potted, needs a peaty compost. It is, however, better grown strapped on to a peat base on a piece of bark. The leaves are antler shaped, coming out of the centre of a round green sheath covering the base of the plant, and the top of the pot. A good light is preferable, and high up on the wall close to a window is a good place. Gentle spraying if the air is not damp is necessary; sponging should not be done or it will remove the thin covering of hairs on the leaf.

SAXIFRAGA STOLONIFERA (mother of thousands) An interesting house plant, as it produces runners which will trail over the side of the pot and end in small plants, hence its common name. The leaves are large, rather round, green and streaked silver down the veins, with a surface covering of bristly red hairs, also on the stems. It looks good in hanging baskets, on plant display stands, and in holders on walls, or by a staircase. It is not difficult to grow, and will survive neglect but looks its best if given a good light, plenty of moisture and a lowish temperature. White flowers with golden centres are produced in clusters at the ends of stems about 6 inches tall in summer. There is a variegated variety with red and cream as well as green leaves, not as easy to care for successfully, but very pretty. The young plants can be taken off and grown on.

SETCREASEA PURPUREA (purple heart) Distinctive purple leaves and stems are not often found in plants, but *Setcreasea* is one example. The colouring is actually in the leaves and masks the green part almost completely. In shape the leaves are narrow and pointed and the plant grows rather upright; it can be encouraged to bush by stopping, and this will overcome its tendency to get rather leggy. A good light and plenty of water when growing are also important. In summer it will produce magenta flowers, not a happy combination with the purple leaves.

SPARMANNIA AFRICANA (African hemp, house lime) The white flowers of the African hemp have a delicious perfume, and are produced in May, and through the summer. It is quite a large plant, being a shrub of 10–20 feet in its native South Africa. As a house plant its size can be restricted, however, by cutting back when flowering has ended. The large hairy leaves are heart shaped. It does not like draughts or dry atmospheres, but will stand gas. It needs a good light, and plenty of

House plants can be arranged just as flowers can be arranged. Here again the individual plants are in their own pots and can be interchanged.

water in summer; feeding is required, and the occasional spray with clear water will do wonders.

TOLMAIEA MENZIESII (pig-a-back plant) A foliage plant with heart-shaped leaves, lobed and toothed, the pig-a-back plant gives a bushy effect. Its main interest lies in the way in which it produces plantlets on the tops of the leaves in the summer, at the point where the leaf blade is attached to the leaf stalk. It does not require high temperatures and is in fact quite hardy; a good light but not sunlight is important. Summer feeding is necessary since the plant, with its many babies, makes rather heavy demands on the compost.

VRIESIA SPLENDENS A bromeliad with a rosette of strap-shaped leaves having brownish-plum coloured bands across them about an inch wide.

It is a very handsome, quite large plant, nearly 2 feet across when fully grown, with a bright red flower spike over a foot long on a stalk about 8 or 9 inches long; the fleeting flowers are yellow. It likes a good light, and warmth in winter, at least 50°F (10°C). It will stand central heating, but the leaves should be washed with clear water at intervals and watering carried out in the usual way, that is, through the central 'vase'; with this kind the compost should not be too moist.

Pot Plants

You will probably be wondering what the difference is between house plants and pot plants, as both are grown in pots and both are grown in the house. Since the vogue for growing plants in the house started, however, house plants have gradually come to be regarded as plants which have particularly attractive leaves either in shape or colour, or both, and they may also have flowers. Pot plants have as their only attraction their flowers. Once these have finished, they are no longer decorative. They have become popular as the price of cut flowers has risen, and besides, flowering pot plants will go on looking nice for weeks if not months, once you have the secrets of their care. Mostly they are the kind of plants which have had special treatment in the nursery to make them flower well at a time of the year when they do not normally flower, but when their flowering is over, it is often the case that they have to be discarded or planted outside in the garden. If you have very green fingers, however, and can give them the special conditions they require, it is possible to flower them again. One of the good things about pot plants is that they are mostly in flower during the winter when there is very little bloom in the garden. It is important, however, if you want to keep them to flower another year, that there should be a garden room, greenhouse or cold frame, which can be used for the period when they are resting, or building up reserves preparatory to flowering again. One or two cannot be grown indoors again. For instance, the artificially dwarfed chrysanthemums are treated with a chemical which makes them flower while their stems are only about 8 inches long; once they have flowered the effect of this chemical is finished. They will grow normally if planted outside in spring, to flower again out of doors in autumn on stems 4 or 5 feet high. Cinerarias are annuals and will die naturally after flowering;

coleus lose their colour in the poor light of winter, so are best grown afresh from cuttings each spring.

As with buying house plants, one should look for a plant with plenty of young growth coming on and with more buds than open flowers, so that it will be as pretty as possible for as long as possible. It is particularly important that the plant is kept wrapped and out of cold air and draughts on the way home, and when kept in the house. Draughts will make the plant shed its buds, and very rapidly too. Spraying it with clear water at room temperature as soon as unwrapped is a help, and making sure that the atmosphere round it is moist, too, with a tray of water, is essential in the dry atmosphere produced by central heating. Do not stand it immediately over a radiator, and if placed on a window ledge, bring it inside the curtains at night, so that it does not have to endure the nasty little pockets of cold, not to say frosty air, that get trapped there as the temperature outside falls at night. The general remarks on cultivation that were detailed under house plants apply also to pot plants, remembering that dry atmospheres, draughts, dryness at the roots and overwatering are particularly bad for them, as they lose their flowers quickly and then the plant will have been a waste of money, as it has little or no other ornamental value.

ASTILBE Once known as spiraeas, these plants have feathery plumes of flowers in white, rose, pink or a dull crimson, about 9 inches tall, above rather fern-like light green leaves. They are quite hardy and are usually grown out of doors in moist, slightly shaded positions by the side of pools and streams, flowering in June, July and August. As pot plants they will flower in early spring. They do not require high temperatures, and provided they have plenty of water, and moist air, will do well in a sunny position. Spraying overhead occasionally is a help and will deter red spider mites, which are rather fond of them. These are plants which have been treated by the nurserymen so that they flower much earlier than usual, and they are one of the few pot plants that are best transferred to the garden after flowering.

BEGONIA The leafy begonias have already been described in the section on house plants; the flowering begonias include those which flower in summer with large double flowers in yellow, orange, red, pink or white carried one on a stem, and the kind with fibrous roots, not tubers, and lots of tiny flowers which bloom in winter, sometimes called the Christmas begonia, or Gloire de Lorraine begonia.

Start the tuberous begonias into growth in March by putting them into moist peat and a little heat; when shoots appear pot the tubers into compost so that the surface of the tuber still shows above the compost. Give a light position, but not sunny, stake as they grow, and remove small, single side flowers. Feed while flowering. Ordinary summer temperatures are suitable. Dry off when the flowers have died, cut the stems right down when complete and withered and rest the tubers during late autumn and winter, with pots turned on their side. The fibrous-rooted or Lorraine begonias have a mass of tiny pink, red or white flowers with golden centres, which they go on producing in winter for two months or more. They need as much light as can be given in winter, regular liquid feeding, and plenty of water when flowering. A temperature of 55–60°F (13–15°C) is good and they like to be sprayed with clear water occasionally. After flowering they too are dried off until March. Although generally discarded, they can be grown again, and, after a rest in the greenhouse or garden room, will require potting in March into a larger pot with fresh compost. Cutting them back makes them bushier, and improves flowering.

CALCEOLARIA (slipper flower) The pot calceolarias have large, very curiously shaped flowers, the lower petals of which are fused together to form a pouch about 1 inch across. They produce a mass of flowers on a bushy plant masking the leaves almost completely. The flowers are red, yellow, orange, purple, magenta and all shades of these, and are often heavily spotted in orange, red and the other colours mentioned. They are most showy plants, and continue in flower for several weeks in spring or early summer. They need a lot of watering when flowering, and like a good light close to the window, but not direct sunlight. Close, hot atmospheres are not suitable, and they do better with plenty of air and coolish temperatures. As the plants make such heavy demands on the soil, a liquid feed every 10 days or so is a good idea. One or two stakes may be required for support. Unlike most indoor plants, they are very prone to greenfly invasions at the growing tips, and a close watch should be kept for these. If spraying is necessary, try to avoid the flowers, otherwise they may be marked. They are not plants which can be kept after flowering as they

deteriorate in flower size, and should be discarded.

CHRYSANTHEMUM Once known only as a cut flower, the chrysanthemum can now be grown as a flowering plant in a pot for the house without having to raise the ceiling to do so. This is because a chemical has been recently discovered which will, if watered on to the soil so that it is absorbed by the roots, make the plant produce flowers when the stems are only 8 inches or so tall. They are in effect mini-chrysanthemums, and will remain in flower for two months or so. Light and temperature are also much regulated, to induce the plants to flower at the required time of the year. Several cuttings are placed round the edge of a pot and rooted, so that the effect is of a single plant with a mass of flowers. Flowers may be pink, yellow, bronze, purple, orange, red or white, and they vary in shape between the incurved ball type, the reflexed, with petals curving outwards, and the pompons, small and completely globular. Coolness, good light, and air are important; smoky or hot dry atmospheres are very bad, and lead to red spider troubles, dropping petals, and short flowering. The soil dries out surprisingly rapidly, and a particularly careful eye should be kept on the water needs of these plants. They are another plant which can be severely damaged by greenfly, and should be sprayed accordingly. When flowering has finished the plants can be put outside when the weather is suitable, in spring, and will produce flowers again the following autumn the normal size. After this second flowering they can be cut down to form 'stools', and cuttings taken from them in the normal way. For greenhouse culture see GREENHOUSE.

COLEUS (flame nettle) This attractive foliage plant is included among the pot plants because it is difficult to keep through the winter. When the light is poor and the days are short, it tends to grow thin and spindly, and to lose its bright colours, so that it becomes a rather insipid brown, not at all like its common name. The flame nettles have leaves shaped very like the English stinging nettle, except that the teeth of the margins are blunt, not pointed. They are extremely colourful, as bright as any flower, and a good deal brighter than many. Colours and variegations include orange, red, purple, cream, yellow, beige, green and all sorts of combinations of these. They make bushy plants, if pinched back and there are named varieties such as 'Golden Ball', 'Paisley Shawl', 'Candidus', and many others. They need warmth and a good light, and plenty of water; draughts and dry air are bad for them. Feeding helps to maintain the colour.

CONVALLARIA MAJALIS (lily-of-the-valley) The delicate sweet fragrance of the lily-of-the-valley pervades the house for a month and more now, thanks to modern techniques of cultivation. The plants are specially treated by lifting the crowns, potting them, and keeping them in the dark in a high temperature until the flower stems begin to appear. Such flowers cannot be grown again as pot plants, and must be planted out of doors in spring. There are also 'retarded' plants, which are treated in the opposite way, and given a period of cold before being grown normally and these will flower at home quite quickly without any forcing. When in flower, the plants like a coolish temperature, spraying with clear water fairly frequently, or a humid atmosphere, and a well-drained compost. Feeding while flowering is a help, particularly if the plant is to be grown out of doors and not discarded.

CYTISUS CANARIENSIS (genista, broom) Yellow pea flowers massed above spiky green growths provide a patch of early spring sunshine, and the plant has a bonus in the perfume of the blooms. Normally hardy, quite happy out of doors, it needs cool conditions, moist air, and a good light. The soil must be well-drained, although it does like plenty of water while growing and flowering. Flowers will drop quickly in dry air. Once flowering has finished the shoots should be cut back to within about 2 inches of their bases, and the plant given a temperature of 50–55°F (10–13°C) to encourage the production of new shoots. When these are growing well the plant is repotted in fresh compost, and placed out of doors in a sunny place from June–September, giving plenty of water. It is then brought indoors and kept dryish and cool until February, when the temperature may be raised slightly and watering increased.

ERICA HYEMALIS (Cape heath) A South African hybrid heather, the Cape heath is a shrubby plant about 9–12 inches tall, with spikes of small purple, pink or white, tiny bell-shaped flowers set off by needle-like leaves. It looks most attractive and flowers from December until March, but it is very inclined to drop its flowers and leaves. The best way of preventing this is to provide a humid atmosphere round the plant, and as it is so sensitive to dryness, you will soon know whether your arrangements for dampening the air are successful. Dryness at the roots is also fatal, so give it

plenty of water, using rainwater or soft water at room temperature. High temperatures are not needed, and draughts should be avoided; this is one of the plants that really needs to be wrapped up well when bringing home from the shop. After flowering it should be potted, using a lime-free compost, and, like the cytisus, cut back hard after flowering and put outside in a sunny place from June to October. In late autumn and early winter keep cool, but just moist, gradually increasing watering as the time for flowering comes nearer.

EUPHORBIA PULCHERRIMA (poinsettia) Sometimes also called the Christmas flower, the poinsettia is a pot plant with what look like bright scarlet flowers. They are large pointed bracts which appear at the top of stems a foot or more tall. The tiny yellow flowers are in the centre. This is the typical poinsettia but there are now other kinds; for instance, with pink or white bracts and with cream variegated leaves. A strain of plants has been bred called the Middelsen varieties, which are much more tolerant to extreme changes in temperature; the original species would drop its leaves as soon as it was moved about in varying degrees of heat or cold, leaving only the 'petals' (coloured bracts) at the ends of bare stems. Flowering time is November–January, and poinsettias must have humidity, a good light, and occasional overhead spraying with tepid water. Smoky atmospheres, low temperatures, dryness, draughts and gas will all upset it. After flowering, cut off the flowerheads, leave the plant where it is, and give only just enough water to keep the compost barely damp. Then in April cut the stems right down to about 3 or 4 inches, water well, and put in a sunny place in the garden room, or your sunniest window sill. The shoots that then appear can be taken as cuttings, put in a sand/peat compost and a temperature of at least 70°F (21°C). If the ends of the cuttings produce a white fluid, this can be absorbed with powdered charcoal. Alternatively, the old plants can be grown on after cutting down hard, and repotting in May in new compost and a smaller pot, then transferring to a larger one as they grow. For both cuttings and old plants the temperature should be 60°F (15°C) and above, and if this is maintained flowers should be produced in December, or earlier. It is also important, from late September until late November, to keep the plants in the dark when it is naturally dark; if given artificial light they will not flower.

FUCHSIAS Fuchsias flower in the house in spring

Muted yellows through creams and pastel shades to
white combine to make a subtly pleasing
arrangement of freesias, alchemillea and lime
flowers in a quiet and restful key.

Chrysanthemums of several different types and
several varieties make a striking late autumn
arrangement. Such effects can easily be over-done.

An inverted meat dish cover on a wrought iron stand.
The arrangement is chiefly of foliage and seed heads.
The five yellow arum lilies give it great distinction.

A blue and green arrangement in a grey container.
This is a spring arrangement using hyacinths,
Spanish irises and the snowball tree. The grey
container complements the arrangement.

and summer and are one of the prettiest of pot plants. The dangling flowers at the ends of the arching shoots are so reminiscent of a ballerina in her *tutu*, with the outer red petals of the corolla forming the skirt, and the inner ones the frothy white petticoats. There is, in fact, a variety named 'Ballet Girl'. The long stamens, like legs, appearing below the white petals, add to the illusion. They are not 'miffy' plants, like poinsettias, and will endure some change in temperature, although they should not have their position changed when in bud. But, like all flowering pot plants, they need moist air, and plenty of water fairly regularly supplied. A light position and feeding when flowering are important. After flowering gradually dry off until just moist, and keep cool during winter, but free from frost, and prune back hard in February when growth may be started. Some particularly lovely varieties are: 'Abbé Farge', 'Alaska', 'Carmel Blue', Flying Cloud', 'Gruss an Bodethal', 'Marin Glow', 'Seashells' and 'Falling Stars'.

HYDRANGEA Strictly speaking, these are not pot plants suitable for permanent cultivation in the house, as they grow rather large. However, they are quite easily grown in a garden room or observatory, in a large pot or tub, filled with J.I. acid compost. They flower in spring and early summer, and have ball-like heads of flowers, in pink or white. In the house give them a good light, and plenty of water while flowering. This should be soft water or rainwater. Varieties which are naturally pink can be blued by adding a proprietary blueing compound to the soil as the instructions direct. After flowering, they can either be planted out or retained in pots. If the latter, the shoots which have flowered should be cut out, and the plant given a liquid feed occasionally and watered to encourage new shoots, on which will be next season's flowers. From autumn to the end of December they should be kept cool, but frostproof, and little water given, then the temperature can be raised to $55-65°F$ ($13-18°C$), and watering increased.

PRIMULA The primulas make beautiful pot plants in mid-winter and early spring. *Primula kewensis* has bright yellow, small flowers, and greyish-green leaves and stems, due to the mealy coating on them. It is also strongly scented. *P. obconica* has much larger flowers in pink, rose, or violet, and roundish leaves, and *P. sinensis* has similarly coloured flowers, but with the petal edges cut and frilled, and with lobed and serrated-edged leaves, so that they are more fern-like. *P. malacoides* grows much taller than the others, and the flowers are on 12 to 18-inch stems, rosy or lilac, with small delicately cut petals. They prefer cool conditions $45-55°F$, but *P. sinensis* is better in a slightly higher one, $50-55°F$ and plenty of light, but not sunlight. Greenfly and red spider mite have to be watched for. To keep them flowering, feed weekly with a liquid fertiliser. It is possible to keep them for a second season, but they are not so good, and it will usually be found that the offsets produced round the crown flower the best. These can be detached and potted up separately if required, keeping cool and shaded in summer, and bringing inside again in September if they have been plunged out of doors. Some people are allergic to primulas, and the ones that are particularly troublesome are *P. obconica* and *P. kewensis*. For those sensitive to them they may produce a skin rash, either on handling, or even as a result of being in the same room.

SENECIO (cineraria) Extremely ornamental, these daisy-type flowers come in the brightest shades of pink, magenta, plum, light blue, red and royal blue. The flowers are clustered in solid heads, almost hiding the leaves, and are really a striking mass of colour. They are unfortunately very greenfly-prone, and need constant watching to stop these pests building up into a bad infestation. While in flower, they must have a great deal of water, and in central heating especially spraying with clear water every day. Flowering will continue through January, February and March. Light should be good, but direct sunlight is not required, and they do best in cool, $45-55°F$ ($7-13°C$) conditions without draughts. This is a pot plant which is an annual and cannot be grown on, but it is easily grown from seed sown in May, in garden room or greenhouse conditions. During summer and early autumn the young plants need a lightly shaded place, out of the heat of the sun, but sheltered from cold or strong winds. They are brought inside in late September or early October.

SINNINGIA (gloxinia) Along with the aspidistra, the gloxinias are Victorians, now enjoying a renewed popularity. They are glorious plants, with velvety, trumpet-shaped flowers in red, purple, lilac, and pink with white throats, the throat sometimes spotted with similar colours. Some have much frilled and ruffled petals with veining in lilac, blue and purple, and some are spotted all over, on a ground colour of white.

They are tuberous-rooted plants needing warm temperatures, and flower in autumn and early winter. Humidity in the atmosphere is essential, but do not spray overhead, and water carefully so that drops do not splash on to leaves or flowers. Use only water at room temperature. When flowering has finished gradually dry off until the leaves have withered, and then keep dry in a temperature of about 50°F (10°C). They can be repotted from January–March, in fresh J.I. No. 1 compost, putting the tubers just below the surface of the compost, singly in 3-inch pots and transferring to larger 6-inch pots as they grow. Keep in a good light and warmth of about 70°F (21°C) during summer, and feed as the flower buds begin to show.

SOLANUM CAPSICASTRUM (winter cherry) The family of the potato and tomato contains many attractive plants, and the winter cherry is a pot plant grown for its bright red, or orange, cherry-like berries appearing on a bushy little evergreen plant in winter from late November. To prevent the berries dropping, the plant must be kept out of draughts, it must be well wrapped up when being carried from shop to house, and it must have a moist atmosphere, together with daily spraying with clear water at room temperature. It likes to be cool, but gas in the atmosphere will result in berry and leaf drop also. If all these points can be observed, the berries will remain on the plant through the winter until spring. After they have fallen the shoots should be pruned back so as to leave only 2 inches or so (they need really hard pruning). When new growth starts the plant should be repotted, kept warm and given a good light. White flowers are produced in summer, and spraying overhead will help pollination

Climbing and trailing plants

With the use of these plants another dimension can be added to one's rooms, enlisting the help of walls, ledges, shelves, pedestals, pillars and plant supports. There are some very decorative plants that will twine or adhere to posts and trellis work, that can be trained to frame a window, or will provide a room divider. They are particularly useful for the last named, enabling one to have (apparently) two rooms, and giving a light but effective screen, which can always be taken apart and used separately in other parts of the house. Canes, trellis work, wire mesh, hoops and circles of cane or wire provide a variety of ways in which climbers can be supported, securing them with raffia, fillis or sweet pea rings.

Often climbers will grow well in shady parts of the house, such as the ivies, cissus or philodendron, and so can be used in difficult places like the hall and staircase or corners remote from windows. Like house plants, climbers and trailers are grown for their leaves or flowers; there are some very attractive trailing and hanging plants such as columnea, ivy-leaved pelargoniums, the Italian bellflower and mother-of-thousands. Climbing and trailing plants fit in well in a group arrangement and give it a variation in line. They look equally good in the pedestal type of arrangement, arranged as a frame for a window or mirror, as part of a trough collection, or used in the garden room (if you are lucky enough to have one), where they can be trained on the back walls or around supports and staging. Hanging baskets come into their own with trailing plants and, for a change, so that their contents can be fully appreciated, they could be hung in the garden room at eye level rather than way above one's head. This would make watering easier too. Display shelves on the walls, whether of the house or garden room, are a good way of setting off a mixed arrangement of bushy house plants and climbers and trailers.

It is particularly important with this kind of plant that, if grown for their leaves, they should be kept well sprayed and clean; they have a much larger breathing surface, which can get clogged with dirt and chemicals from fumes and, if infected by scale insects or red spider mite, are much more difficult to free from these pests. Pinching out the tips of the shoots will help the production of side shoots lower down to make the plant bushier, and eventually much bigger and leafier; it helps to prevent shoots becoming rather thin and 'leggy' at the ends, and results in more flowers on plants which are grown for these rather than for the leaves. Taking out the tips has a side benefit in that they can be used as cuttings in a lot of cases, and with the right warmth and humidity will root and provide new plants. Make sure that, if supports are required, they are firmly anchored, and really sturdy; top growth of some plants becomes surprisingly heavy and a sudden collapse of a stake might mean irretrievable damage to plant and nearby ornaments. Attachments like rings, wire or twine should be tough and well fixed.

CAMPANULA ISOPHYLLA (Italian bellflower) The Canterbury bell family is a large and varied one and, besides having the familiar garden bell-like plants 2 or 3 feet tall, and the creeping or mound-like plants, covered in pale blue or purple bells, there is the slightly tender *Campanula isophylla*, which makes a good plant for the house where a rather light, airy trailing plant is required. The flowers are either pale blue or white, and are produced most in a place where there is plenty of light. The hanging stems have a mass of light green, heart-shaped leaves above which the flowers appear in July and August. The plant does not like high temperatures, but prefers to be on the cool side, with good ventilation, in well-drained compost. Feeding is important while flowering; when the flowers have finished they should be removed, unless seeds are definitely wanted, as their production means less vegetative growth. Cutting back after flowering will mean more flowers the following season. In winter, just enough water to keep the compost moist is all that is required.

CISSUS (kangaroo vine) A member of the same family as the grape vine, *Cissus antarctica* grows very fast, and has shiny, serrated leaves, rather like a large beech leaf, but a darker green and thicker in texture. It supports itself by tendrils which it wraps round the nearest convenient post or stake. It is very easy and needs a rich compost to support its rapid growth, and will grow in most conditions of shade, light, temperature and atmosphere, including gas. Greenfly may be a trouble (spray with malathion). Repotting will usually be needed every year, and be prepared for it to grow 6–8 feet tall if you are treating it well. *Cissus discolor* is another climber, but needing very much more care in the way of temperature, draughts and humidity. If, however, its rather exacting requirements can be met, it more than repays the trouble, as it has leaves which are attractive enough to put it, as one grower says, among the first dozen of house plants. They are large and similar in shape to the kangaroo vine, but in texture are velvety, and in colour are a superb mixture of white, purple, crimson and orange pink with a shimmering green background. It really is a lovely plant and excels many flowering plants. It must have a humid atmosphere at all times, and spraying overhead frequently; draughts are fatal, and the temperature in winter must be a steady 55°F (13°C) at least, with 65°F (18°C) and more in summer. Originally it was grown as a stove plant, which accounts for its exacting needs. If it drops its leaves in winter this is natural, and does not mean that it is being badly treated; it will grow new ones in the spring.

COBAEA SCANDENS (cup-and-saucer plant) A climbing plant with a light, graceful habit of growth, it extends its hold by tendrils and reaches 12 feet or more where happy. The 4-inch long leaves are a background for a frill of green sepals, hence the common name. It produces quantities of these flowers from July to September, and needs a good light and cool conditions to do so. The compost should be fairly rich with plenty of water in summer; after flowering in autumn cut back moderately hard, and keep the plant just moist during winter.

COLUMNEA The columneas are trailing plants from South America and when in full flower are like a waterfall of red and green. The blooms are tubular and produced on hanging stems in great profusion during early summer; when flowering is over the evergreen leaves provide a background for other plants. They have a tendency to produce flowers lower and lower down the stems so that the top of the stem has only leaves. To stop this happening, some of the stems should be cut right back to their base, so that new shoots take their place. The columneas must have a good light all the time, and a temperature of at least 60°F (16°C) in summer, if they are to grow and flower well. Humidity and plenty of water while flowering are essential, but less at other times.

HEDERA (ivy) Along with the aspidistra, this is one of the older kinds of plants to be grown in the house. The shape and colour of the leaves account for its charm as a climbing or trailing plant, particularly against a white background. Its popularity and ease of cultivation have resulted in the production of all sorts of new varieties with even more attractively shaped leaves, and with white, cream, grey, and deep yellow variations. *Hedera helix* is the common English ivy, and some varieties of this are: 'Glacier' with small greyish-green leaves, and a cream border, becoming larger as they age; 'Lutzii', also with small leaves, speckled and mottled with yellow; *H.h.* 'Cristata' has much curled leaves and crimped at the edges like parsley, rather round in shape and a plain light green; 'Little Diamond', small, greyish-green leaves, with a wide white border; 'Golden

Jubilee', small leaves with bright deep yellow, irregularly shaped centre, and a wide dark green margin—it has its best colour in a good light; 'Buttercup' has young leaves and bright-yellow shoot tips; *H.h.* 'Sagittaefolia' has small leaves with the centre lobe very much extended to give a spear-shaped and most attractive small leaf. *Hedera canariensis* 'Variegata', the Canary Islands ivy, has leaves bordered with cream, against a dark-green centre. The leaves are large, and roundish, and all are differently and irregularly variegated, on dark red stems. A fine species.

The ivies are easily grown, preferring cool conditions and a damp atmosphere, in which they will extend rapidly; they will grow in shade, but the variegated ones have their best colour in a good light. In hot, dry atmospheres the leaves turn brown and fall off, and they tend to get red spider mite badly. Most of them can easily be made to bush out by pinching back the tips, and as these tips root easily, a virtually inexhaustible supply of new plants is available. Feeding is appreciated.

HOYA CARNOSA (wax flower) A climbing plant, with thick evergreen leaves, the wax flower has clusters of tiny pink or white flowers in summer, looking rather unreal, as though they actually have been modelled out of wax. There is a variegated kind, with cream and green leaves, but it does not flower so profusely. It is a plant native to China and Australia and needs a good light and warmth in summer, together with a humid atmosphere. If you have a garden room, this is the best place for it. A well-drained compost is most important, preferably without chalk added to it, and watering with rainwater is advisable. It does not like a dry atmosphere. When the flower buds appear, give only a little water and stop feeding, but in full flower, normal watering and feeding can be carried on. When the flowers have died, remove the clusters, but carefully; the flower stalks can be removed, but there is a danger that the buds at their base, which will produce next season's flowers, will be removed at the same time, so it is probably best to leave the stalks on the plant, and cut off the flowerheads only. In winter give only a little water and a temperature of not lower than 45°F (7°C), preferably higher than this. If any pruning needs to be done, to shape or confine the plant, February is the time. If left to grow naturally, it will reach a height of 10–12 feet. Growth rate is moderate. Stems that trail down on to the compost will often root

House plants. One of the many variegated ivies useful for home decoration. This one is *Hedera canariensis,* a strong-growing ivy.

themselves, and layering is one of the recognised forms of propagating the plant.

JASMINUM OFFICINALE (jasmine) The strong sweet scent of jasmine is one of the most well-known and delightful of the flower perfumes but, surprisingly in view of its easy cultivation, is not as often grown as it might be. The small, white, starry flowers, pink in bud, cover the plant in summer, and it flowers from June till September or later, a remarkably long time. The plant will climb to about 20 feet, and provides a pleasant green background with its evergreen leaves, when not flowering. A good light, a little warmth in winter, with less water than in summer, and feeding during summer will ensure a healthy plant. Pruning is in February, cutting back the flowering shoots by about half to ensure good flowering in the coming season, and to keep the plant within bounds. Strong supports are required to accommodate the prolific growth.

MONSTERA The monsteras are really creeping plants in their native South America, rather than climbers, and have large leaves deeply cut, with large holes in them, which is why *Monstera deliciosa* is commonly called the Swiss Cheese Plant. This plant may have leaves up to 4 feet across, and is rather large for the average house but *M. pertusa* (syn. *M. deliciosa* 'Borgsigiana') has much smaller leaves, only about a foot in length, though still serrated and perforated eventually when fully grown. They need the right growing conditions to develop these curious leaves, warmth, humidity, no draughts (very important), and plenty of water and food in summer.

They will exist in low temperatures of about 45–50°F (7–10°C), but will not grow; with too much water, the leaves turn yellow. The stems have a habit of producing aerial roots, long, thin, brownish growths, and if these can be trained into the soil, the plant will grow better. Sponging the leaves occasionally with a milk and water solution is well repaid, as they are handsome leaves and the shine given to them in this way sets them off well.

PASSIFLORA CAERULEA (passion flower) A plant with a more curiously shaped flower would be hard to find; the blue, cream, yellow and pale green blooms are more or less round in outline, but with the stamens and styles at the end of a column projecting from the centre of the flower. The sepals and petals are white to pale green and inside these there is a circle of hairs, dark blue at the top, white in the middle and purple at the base; from the centre of these comes the pale green column with dark yellow stamens. The leaves are palmate with five or seven lobes deeply cut, and the plant attaches itself to its support by tendrils. It grows quickly during summer and spring, so should have plenty of water and food; it is a climber which lends itself particularly to

House plants. The Mexican bread-fruit plant is easily grown in almost any sunny room. In nature it climbs trees to a height of 80 ft. or more.

training round canes, formed into a circle, or a triangle, or a tripod, so that the flowers are displayed to their best advantage. Flowering is from July to October, and during spring and summer a sunny place should be provided; in winter a good light is sufficient, and a temperature of 45–50°F (7–10°C). If repotting is required in February, be careful when dealing with the roots as they are rather brittle. In early spring, cut back last year's growth hard to within a few inches of the base of the plant; with feeding, new compost, warmth and sun, it will grow fast. It does not like gas, and is one of the few plants that also objects to fires.

PELARGONIUM The trailing geraniums are the ivy-leaved types, with plain shiny green leaves and pink or red geranium-like flowers, or the ones with much smaller, greyish-green leaves, with a white margin, pink if watered only a little, and a mass of white flowers with purple spots. This kind look very attractive draped over the side of a trough, trailing from a hanging basket, or on a sunny wall. A good variety of this is 'L'Elegante'; 'Galilee' is another pretty one with rose-coloured double flowers, and 'La France' has purple and white veined petals above pale green leaves. They are trailing plants rather than climbers, but can be attached to upright supports with wire or fillis. They need a good light all the time, particularly in winter.

PHARBITIS TRICOLOR (morning glory) A fast growing annual, related to convolvulus, with trumpet-shaped flowers in white and bright blue changing to dark blue and finally to purple as they die. It climbs by twining, and although the gorgeous flowers only last a day, fresh ones unfold every morning. It needs a good light and, if you are propagating your own plants, a temperature of 65°F (18°C) to germinate the seeds. Plenty of water and liquid feeding is advisable when in full flower. The seeds are sown about three to a 3-inch pot, and will germinate more quickly if a shallow notch is made in them. When the young plants need moving on, the roots should be disturbed as little as possible.

PHILODENDRON P. scandens, the sweetheart vine, is a climber with markedly heart-shaped, rather large leaves, about 3 inches long. It will put up with dryness, and gas in the atmosphere, although it prefers humidity and plenty of water when growing. Cutting back the shoots to a convenient leaf joint will make it bushier if required. P. erubescens is another attractive climber, but with spearhead-shaped leaves, metallic dark green when adult, and tinged with rose when young. Its leaves are much larger than those of the sweetheart vine, being about 8 inches long. It likes the same kind of environment.

RHOICISSUS RHOMBOIDEA (grave ivy) Like *Philodendron scandens*, this is a climber, which will grow in shade; it clings by its tendrils rather than twining stems, and has 4-sided serrated leaves, which, if the plant is healthy, are shiny and gleaming. It grows very quickly and needs a lot of water, and liquid feeding in the spring and summer, with repotting at least every second spring. Bushiness can be encouraged by pinching out the tops of the shoots, and because it is so free-growing it can be trained to grow in all sorts of interesting shapes, up a tripod, up a single stem, in a circle and so on. Shoots allowed to trail down over the edge of the pot are attractive also. An occasional spraying gives very good results. Leaves will have brown spots and dry up and drop off in hot dry atmospheres.

SCINDAPSUS AUREUS (ivy arum, devil's ivy) This is a climber which twines, grown for its mottled yellow and green leaves. It likes the same sort of conditions as the philodendrons, but with a little more warmth in winter; its variegations are better, too, with a good light in winter. It is allergic to gas. If pinched back at the tips, it will be much bushier. Overwatering produces browning of the leaves, unlike most house plants the leaves of which usually turn yellow if this occurs.

TRADESCANTIA (wandering jew) Named after John Tradescant, a plant hunter and collector, and a gardener to Charles I, the tradescantias are trailing plants, extremely easy to grow and keep alive, but not so easy to grow well so that the variegations are strongly marked. *Tradescantia fluviatilis* (syn. *T. fluminensis*) is inclined to become leggy and small leaved, with browning at the tips of shoots and leaves. To avoid this grow it in a good light, so that the longitudinal white stripes on the leaves are well defined. In sun the plants tend to get a pink tinge, which is more pronounced if they are kept slightly dry and in an airy place. This is another plant which benefits from tip pinching, and is easily rooted from tip cuttings. If all-green shoots appear, they should be removed at once, to prevent the whole plant reverting. Cool conditions, and occasional overhead spraying are required. *T. blossfeldiana* has fleshy purple stems and leaves, which are purple underneath; the whole plant is covered in white hairs. It needs

higher temperatures than its relations. Both are quick growing.

ZEBRINA (wandering jew) The zebrinas are a little fleshier in leaf and stem than the tradescantias (they belong to the same family) and the leaves have a short stalk attaching them to the stem. *Zebrina pendula* has leaves striped in dark green, purple and pale greyish-green, and the whole has a glistening appearance, as though the upper surface of the leaf is wet. The under-leaf is purple. *Z. p. quadricolor* is very bright, with white, dark green, greyish-green and light purple on the upper side, and various shades of purple on the under surface. Both have better colours if kept slightly on the dry side, and both need a little more warmth and good light to maintain their variegation and growth. However, if *Z. pendula* has too much light, it turns brownish.

Bulbs

Bulbs must be the prime example in the plant world of instant packing. The flower, leaves and stem are all contained, more or less fully formed in a tidy round parcel, and only need water, moisture and warmth to bring them to life. They are convenient to handle and, once planted, can often be forgotten for two or three months, except for very occasional watering. By planting in the proper compost, and ripening off after flowering, they will continue to flower every year for several years. Even the bulbs forced for Christmas flowering, such as hyacinth or narcissus, will live to flower another year, if planted out in good soil after the flowers have died down.

There are all sorts of bulbous flowers, and if you choose the right ones, they will provide a succession of flowers all the year round. The spring-and-autumn-flowering bulbs which are grown in the garden make good pot plants; the greenhouse bulbs can, in many cases, be grown in the house or, if not, can be brought in from the greenhouse while flowering with no ill effect. There are bulbs which flower in winter too, either because they have been treated specially, or are the kind which flower naturally in winter.

Bulbous plants need, above all things, a well-drained compost; water hanging about in the soil finishes them off very quickly, producing rotting of the base of the bulb and its roots. Then mites and other pests start to feed on the rotting bulb, and complete the damage. So bulbs should have plenty of crocks at the bottom of the pot, and a little extra coarse sand in the compost. Do not sit them down too hard on the compost and do not pack the compost itself down too firmly, particularly with hyacinths, as the bulb roots tend to turn upwards and come out through the top of the compost or up through the outer skins of the bulbs.

Spring bulbs which are treated or forced for winter flowering from Christmas onwards must be kept in the dark and the cool for at least two months so that they can make a good enough root system in what is a rather confined space to support them through flowering. They can be brought into the light when the tips of the shoots are about 1 or 2 inches long, but the light should be only moderate and the temperature must not be high, about 45–50°F (7–10°C). When the flower buds have completely appeared the plants can then be given a higher temperature and as much light as possible. The summer-flowering greenhouse bulbs are usually started into growth in warm, e.g., 50–55°F (10–13°C), in February-early-March, by potting and watering, together with a good light. In some cases a window sill is sufficient, but it is often rather difficult to maintain the temperature in such a place and a gently heated greenhouse or a garden room may be necessary. See also FORCING (Bulbs for Forcing).

CROCUS It is probably not generally realised, but crocuses can be in flower from autumn, right through winter, to the end of March, if you pick the right species and varieties. The spring-flowering ones, which are the best known, start in early February; the winter-flowering kind begin in November and finish in late February; the autumn flowerers start in late August and go through, according to species, until January, but are mostly in flower in September and October. They are all generally purple, white and yellow, but blue, cream and a kind of rosy-lilac are available, with veining and feathering in various shades of purple. Shape, too, may vary from those with longish pointed petals to rather round globular flowers. The autumn crocus produce their flowers before the leaves.

Plant to about their own depth, in really well-drained soil, putting the spring flowering species in during October, and the autumn and winter flowering kinds in August–September. Those planted in October should be kept dark and cool until growth begins. After flowering, when the leaves have died down, they should be planted out of doors.

EUCOMIS (pineapple flower) An African bulb which flowers in late summer, eucomis has a curious, long, fat spike of greenish-yellow flowers, slightly scented, on top of which is a sort of hat of shiny green leaves in a rosette. The spike can be as much as 1 foot long, and the flower stem is unusually thick and fleshy. The bulbs are potted in October, and given a sandy, rich compost, putting one bulb in a 7-inch pot. This is not ideal as they need to be planted 5–6 inches deep, and in such a pot can only be put about 4 inches deep. What is really needed is a deep but narrow pot, which does not contain so much soil that there is a danger of the moisture becoming stagnant. Very little water is required until March, when it may be slightly increased, and from May onwards plenty should be given. A well-lit place with some sun is required.

FREESIA It is possible, but unlikely, that there is a more sweetly scented flower than the freesia. The perfume is elusive, but once met with, never forgotten. Looked at objectively, the flowers themselves are not outstandingly beautiful. There are plenty that are far ahead in beauty of colour and shape. Nevertheless they are undoubtedly pretty in their jewel-like colours and tubular flowers, six on each graceful, arching spike. Moreover, the flowers start to appear from December, and will be produced until the end of March as more corms come into production.

The corms are planted in early August in deep pots, and well-drained compost, 1 inch deep, and 2 inches apart. They are placed out of doors in a shady place and kept only just moist until the shoots start to appear, then watered normally. In late September, they are brought in to a well-lit, cool position, and by this time, will require supporting with about 1½-foot tall canes. Allow the foliage to die down after flowering, dry the corms off, clean, and place in a warm place to ripen. On no account, however, should the corms be left on a dry sunny bench for the summer. Seed can also be used, sown in April, 6 inches deep, and kept cool and shaded out of doors through the summer. If cool temperatures are provided, then flowering will start in October, and finish in early January.

GALANTHUS (snowdrop) The snowdrop flowers in January, often appearing through melting snow out of doors. They are a sign that spring really is on the way, even if sometimes it seems a little slow in coming. Indoors you can hurry the process a little more by growing them in pots, planting the bulbs about an inch deep in October, in shallow pans, preferably, though pots will do. As with other spring-flowering bulbs, they should be kept cool and dark until the first shoots appear; moderate watering only is required, and after the leaves have died down, the pots should be stood outside, and the bulbs planted in the garden in the autumn.

HAEMANTHUS (blood flower, blood lily, Cape tulip) Although one common name refers to the haemanthus as a lily, the flowers are most unlike a lily's, resembling more than anything a large, round, brilliant red or coral brush on a thick fleshy stem. The species *albiflos* has white bristles. In Britain flowering is in August and September. While growing and flowering they should be watered, but not too much, and then gradually dried off and kept dry when the leaves turn yellow, until repotting in spring. While resting they should be given a sunny position, preferably in a garden room or greenhouse. They like a sandy, well-drained compost and a really sunny position while growing; pot the bulbs into half their depth, and then give only a little water until they start to grow. Repotting is necessary about every four years; during winter the temperature should not fall below 55°F (13°C).

HIPPEASTRUM (amaryllis) Hippeastrums are those glorious plants with enormous trumpet-like flowers in red, coral, pink, white and rose. They usually flower in spring and summer, but prepared bulbs can be obtained which will flower in winter at Christmas and after. They need at least 55°F (13°C) in winter and a humid atmosphere; it helps also if they have a liquid feed occasionally. The prepared bulbs will not flower again until about 15 months later. For both prepared and normal bulbs plenty of water is needed while growing, but they should be kept dry after flowering has finished until growth begins again, usually in February. Topdressing each January is necessary, and complete repotting every four years, putting the bulb at two-thirds of its depth. Mealy bugs are very partial to hippeastrum, feeding between the leaves at the neck of the bulb particularly, and should be removed as soon as seen.

HYACINTHUS (hyacinth) The Roman hyacinths and the large-flowered hybrid can be flowered at Christmas and earlier, as well as in the early spring. The thickly flowered spikes and the per-

vasive perfume of the hybrids make them a difficult bulb to surpass for beauty, but the Roman hyacinths have an elusive charm which is all their own, with their loosely clustered bell-like flowers on arching spikes, and delicate scent. When grown for indoor winter flowering both kinds should be potted in September, for January flowering, and thereafter in succession as required. Time of flowering will vary according to variety, and good bulb catalogues will supply the dates. Do not firm the compost too much, and sit the bulb gently on it; too firm potting results in the roots coming to the surface or pushing the bulb out of the compost and growing up through the outer scales of the bulb. Leave in the dark and cool for at least two months, then bring into the light, and a little heat. Wait until the flower spike is well clear of the bulb, then give full light and more warmth. Remember to water occasionally while in the dark; both watering and a cool temperature are very important, otherwise the flowers appear with one or more buds brown and dead. After flowering, plant outside when there is no chance of frost, and allow to die down naturally. If given J.I. No. 2, when potted, they will flower again well.

Prepared bulbs for Christmas flowering are potted in late August, and the instructions given with them by the suppliers should be followed exactly. Some good varieties for indoor flowering are: 'King of the Blues', dark blue, February; 'L'Innocence', white, late January; 'Pink Pearl', early-to-mid-January; 'City of Haarlem', pale yellow, February; 'Myosotis', pale blue, late January; 'Madame du Barry', deep red, early January; 'Orange Charm', late January.

IRIS The irises which make good pot plants in winter are the species called *Iris reticulata*, with deep mauve-blue flowers and an orange-yellow beard on the petals known as the 'falls', the ones which are curved over and turn downwards. They are miniature iris, growing about 6 inches high, with small fragrant flowers. Potting is done in early August for flowering in late January, and the flowers will then last for about four to six weeks. They should be planted 3 inches deep and if brought indoors in late December, and given a little warmth only (they are quite hardy) and a good light, will flower in early to mid January. After the leaves have died down the bulbs should be lifted and ripened off in a warm place, selecting the largest ones for flowering the following season, and planting the smaller ones in a nursery bed, so that they can grow on to flowering size.

LACHENALIA (Cape cowslip) It is a great pity that these are not grown more often; the tubular flowers, about an inch long, grow in spikes, and are various shades of yellow and orange, sometimes with red. They are an unusual bulb, not difficult to grow, in cool conditions and a well-drained compost. Potting is in August-September, putting about six in a 5-inch pot and covering them with an inch of soil. They should be kept cool until November, then given a little heat, or if earlier flowering is required, given a higher temperature of 55–65°F (13–18°C) to flower in February. Drying off and resting is required from the time the leaves die until August, about two or three months. Greenfly are very partial to the broad, spotted leaves, and must be watched for.

LILIUM (lily) There are some kinds of lily which make very good pot plants, and it has been found that there are certain varieties which can be treated in the same way as chrysanthemums and made to flower while the stems are quite short, giving a cluster of flowers on one stem. Several of this kind of bulb planted in one pot give a beautiful and long lasting display. At present some which respond well to this treatment are varieties like 'Enchantment', orange-red, 'Destiny', bright yellow with brown spots and 'Cinnabar'. Some other kinds which grow well in pots without this treatment are *Lilium longiflorum*, with long white trumpets, having a yellow throat; *L. regale*, the Regal Lily, white strongly scented flowers, with prominent orange stamens; *L. candidum*, the Madonna Lily, which has large, white, bell-like flowers; the Tiger lilies, *L. tigrinum*, in yellow and orange, and many others.

The treated bulbs can be grown in the house with a good light, well-drained compost and plenty of water; high temperatures are not required, but a humid atmosphere is. After flowering has finished the bulbs can be planted out of doors, in well-drained soil, when they will flower about 18 months later.

The lilies grown in pots without treatment should again have well-drained soil. This is very important for lilies. Provide some peat or leaf-mould, potting in autumn and plunging out of doors in a border so that the compost is covered 2–3 inches deep or keeping in a cool dark shed. When the shoots start to appear, they can be brought indoors and gradually introduced to light and warmth, as with hyacinths; after

flowering, they are put in a sunny place and gradually dried off to be kept quite dry from October until February, except for *L. longiflorum* which only requires to be just moist for about six weeks, and then watered normally.

NARCISSUS The daffodils and narcissi, like the snowdrops, are symbols of spring and they are very suitable plants for pot cultivation, and for forcing. There is a bewildering number of varieties available, in all-white, white and yellow, yellow, orange and yellow, pink and white, and so on, and it is a matter of personal choice from specialist bulb catalogues which kinds are to be grown. Depth of planting is such that the tip or 'nose' of the bulb is just above the compost and, like hyacinths, they are potted in October, kept dark and cool for at least two months and then, when about 4 inches high with the flower bud well clear of the neck of the bulb, given more light and warmth. They particularly need as much light as possible, otherwise the stems and leaves become very leggy, and if given too much warmth too quickly, the same fault occurs. The narcissi 'Grand Soleil D'Or' gold and orange, and 'Paper White Grandiflora' can be forced, however, to flower at Christmas, and smell delicious. Both have several flowers in a cluster. Some good varieties of daffodils are: 'King Alfred', yellow; 'Celebrity', white and yellow; 'Beersheba', white; 'Fortune', yellow and orange-red; 'Sempre Avanti', white and orange; 'La Riante', white and red; 'Cheerfulness', double creamy-white; 'Texas', double, yellow and orange-red; 'Cragford', white and orange-red; 'Scarlet Gem', yellow and orange-scarlet.

The miniature daffodil species are a charming dwarf collection, which will flower from December to April, depending on species. The flowers vary in size from tiny ones $\frac{1}{2}$ inch across, to the comparative giants of $1\frac{1}{2}$ inches, and can be grown in a group of their own, or as part of a collection of plants in a miniature garden.

NERINE (Jersey or Guernsey Lily) Bulbous plants which will flower in autumn are rare, but the nerine will start in September, and continue until November. The petals are long and narrow, spraying out from the stem in a star-like manner, and are pink, white, coral, orangey-red to a pale purple or striped rose and purple. There are two kinds, *N. bowdenii* and *N. sarniensis;* the former is mostly various shades of pink only. Potting is between August and November in a very well drained rich compost, putting the bulbs at half their depth. Keep them cool and well lit until May, and then give them a sunny position and a higher temperature. Their water needs are unusual; moderate watering only until May, and then keep quite dry from May to September, as this is their resting time. Sunny conditions then will ensure the production of flowers in late autumn.

SCILLA (Squill) The squills are mountainous plants, mostly from Europe, often flowering as the snow melts, between January and March. They are in bright blue, of various shades, and occasionally in pink and white, with stems a few inches tall. The effect of a pan or two of these mixed with reticulate iris is most colourful. The small bulbs are planted about 1 inch deep in September–October, or in August for early January flowering, and kept in the dark until the flower buds are well clear of the soil. When the flowers open, feed occasionally, and after the leaves have died, the bulbs are gradually dried off and kept dry until repotting in autumn.

TULIPA (Tulip) The best kinds of tulips for flowering as pot plants are the single flowered early varieties, and the species tulips. Potting is in early-mid October, as they require a really long period of dark and cool to develop roots, at least 12 weeks. Depth of planting is such that the bulbs are barely covered. When brought into the light, it should be very little, to help the flower stems to lengthen from the 3 inches or so that they should have already produced, in the case of the varieties, and about $1\frac{1}{2}$ inches for the species kinds. The temperature should be at least 55°F (12°C). After about a fortnight of this treatment, they can then be given a good light gradually, and warmth.

By treating them in this way they should flower February to early March. Some good varieties are: 'Pink Perfection'; 'Couleur Cardinal', red to plum, 'de Wet', orange; 'Keizerskroon', red and gold; 'Proserpine', deep crimson; 'van der Neer', purple. The *kaufmanniana* and *greigii* hybrids are short, with water-lily-like flowers in early March, and have striped and mottled leaves in purple or dark brown, the flowers being various shades and combinations of red and yellow.

VALLOTA (Scarborough Lily) In spite of its common name, the vallota is a South African plant; bulbs from a wrecked ship were washed up on the beach at Scarborough, and it became known as the Scarborough lily. The bulbs are large and the flower stem and flowers in proportion, with the stem about 2 feet tall, and the funnel-shaped, bright red flowers 3–4 inches long, up to 10 on one stem. Late August and September is the flowering time, potting is in autumn or spring for first potting, and repotting in June and July. However, once potted they can be left alone for several years. They should be put at such a depth that the nose of the bulb is just below the surface of a sandy compost, and potted fairly firmly. June to September is the resting period, when they require sun and warmth, and the main growth time is March to June, when they need plenty of water. From September to March the temperature may be as low as 40–50°F 4–10°C), but higher, to 65°F (18°C) or slightly more until June.

Cacti and other succulents

To many people cacti and their relatives are simply bizarre, green plants which never seem to grow any bigger, and certainly never produce flowers. It is also believed that, because they are desert plants, they need not be watered except three or four times a year. Both beliefs are completely wrong, the former arising from the latter method of cultivation. Certainly, cacti need less water during the winter than most plants, and in most cases can be kept virtually dry but frostproof until spring. During spring and summer, however, they usually need water as frequently as ordinary plants, or else they may be watered less frequently, but with a very much greater quantity at any one watering. This is because they have evolved in such a way that they can store large quantities of water in the main body, and so resist prolonged periods of drought, at the same time making the most of the rare, very heavy rainfalls that occur in many desert areas. By correctly watering in this way, they will grow surprisingly rapidly, will produce masses of spines or the rather comical, hairy, wig-like growths that are characteristic of some species, will produce offsets, and will also flower most brilliantly during the summer. Some are easily flowered on a sunny windowsill, for instance the mammillarias, Christmas cactus, chamaecereus and epiphyllums.

The type of compost these plants require must, naturally, be well drained, and the J.I. seed compost with 1 part extra small shingle or brick chippings is suitable. Repotting should be carried out every spring. As much sun as possible in summer is essential, though not necessarily high temperatures, turning the plants occasionally, so that they do not 'lean' too much to the light, and in winter a good light is required and a temperature of about 50°F (10°C), but no frost on any account. Cold and winter damp will kill them very quickly indeed. Mealy bug is a pest which causes trouble most frequently on cacti, and they may be found on the lower part of the plant body or in the soil among the roots. Repotting in clean compost, dislodging as many of the pest as can be seen without harming the roots, and watering with malathion as soon as repotted, repeating about 14 days later, should put a stop to their activities. A warning however: the crassula family, kalanchoë and schlumbergera are harmed by malathion, and methylated spirits is safer, wiping the pests off with cottonwool soaked in it.

ALOE Although aloes are succulent plants they belong to the same plant family, surprisingly, as the lilies, but as they are inhabitants of the dry parts of South Africa and Abyssinia, they have adapted themselves so that they can store a great deal of water for a long period. They vary considerably in height, from trees to small plants only a few inches tall, but the one commonly grown as a house-plant is *Aloe variegata*, the partridge-breasted aloe. This has fleshy, dark green and white banded leaves, triangular in shape, and sheathed one within the other, in a rosette. It produces a stem about a foot tall in spring with a cluster of small red flowers on top, and prefers to be kept dry, in a good light; a sprinkling of sand on the compost surface helps to prevent rot round the base. Watering must be done extremely carefully. When happy, it will produce a lot of small side plants, or offsets.

APORACACTUS FLAGELLIFORMIS (rat's-tail cactus) This is a *bone fide* member of the cactus family, from South America. The trailing stems are fat and round, to a foot or more in length, and will hang over the side of a pot or hanging basket; in May rose-pink to crimson flowers are produced. It does best in a sunny place, and needs warmth, particularly in spring. Give it plenty of water in summer, and do not rest it too long in winter.

ECHEVERIA FULGENS Among the succulents, this echeveria is one of the easiest to grow, its clusters of bright red flowers being produced in spring on stems about 12 inches tall. The leaves are produced in loose rosettes, and are very fleshy and rounded, and a bluish-green in colour. They do not like dry atmospheres, or too much warmth, and can be grown in ordinary J.I. compost, either No. 1 or 2. There is no need to dry them

off in winter, though much less water is required at that season.

EPIPHYLLUM (orchid cactus) The name means, literally, 'upon the leaf', and refers to the way in which the beautiful flowers are produced directly from what was originally thought to be the margin of the leaf, but which it is now realised is the stem. The large, showy, rather tubular flowers come in various shades of red and pink, also white, and there are now one or two yellow ones; many hybrids have been bred, and epiphyllums are a cult in themselves, to which in America whole societies are devoted. Flowering is in the spring or summer, and J.I. potting compost No. 1 with an extra part of coarse sand will suit them. Sun and warmth are important while growing, and as much light as possible in winter. The temperature should not fall below 40°F (4°C) from September to November, and for the rest of the winter, should be above 50°F. Water as a normal house plant.

HAWORTHIA The haworthias are another genus which are masquerading under the cloak of succulents, being technically lilies, like the aloes. As a genus they vary very much in form, from having thin, leathery, overlapping leaves, to thick round ones in a rosette; pale or translucent green, or even almost transparent. They are easily grown, and are attractive small succulents, requiring cool conditions, and water all the year, though less in winter. Do not give them too much sun, as like you and I they are liable to sunburn.

KALANCHOË BLOSSFELDIANA Succulents of the *Crassulaceae* family, the kalanchoës come from all over the world, and will grow in a variety of conditions without needing a great deal of attention. Unlike most of their kind, they flower in winter, producing red, pink, white or coral flowers according to variety. They are easily grown from seed sown in a temperature of 70–75°F (21–24°C), in February, to flower the following winter. The adult plants should have the same compost as epiphyllums, and should be watered throughout the year. Lack of water results in the leaves dropping, but a thorough soaking will enable plants to grow new ones, if left in a warm sunny place, and not watered again until the leaves reappear. They do not like dry atmospheres, and should be sprayed overhead every day or given a humid atmosphere by providing damp peat or a shallow tray of water close by. *K. blossfeldiana* grows to about a foot tall, with bright red flowers, from November, variety 'Vulcan

Improved' has brilliant scarlet, large flowers, and 'Vulcan Yellow' is the same but for colour; *K. segatini* is a new one with cerise flowers, a colour break which has not occurred before in kalanchoës, 'Tom Thumb' has red flowers but is a small variety only a few inches tall. *K. fedtschenkoi variegata* has bluish-green, oval, fleshy leaves, with creamy, serrated margins, turning pink if kept dryish; it is very ornamental, and needs a good light and a steady temperature of 50°F (10°C) and more.

LITHOPS (pebble plants) Like stick insects, these tiny succulent plants are perfectly disguised to resemble parts of their environment; their resemblance to stones is almost supernatural. They consist of two leaves, which are fleshy and nearly round, joined more or less completely, with a crack in the centre, from which the yellow or white flowers are produced in autumn, without stems, usually larger than the main plant body. The pebble-like leaves are frequently the same colour as the stones among which they grow: pale brown, grey, pinkish, yellowish or greyish-green, or veined in these colours.

LOBIVIA The rounded, egg-like bodies of the lobivias are a familiar sight on the competition tables, which is proof enough of their ease of cultivation, and flowering. The large, many petalled, funnel-like flowers may be orange, pink, red, white or golden, and appear in late spring, opening and closing for several days in succession. Cultivation is easy, with moderate watering in summer, and very little in winter, when they are best kept almost dry and cool. Flowering from seed may occur within a year of sowing, but will in any case be fairly quick. Give them as good a light as possible when adult but not when seedlings as they tend to turn red.

MAMMILLARIA (pincushion cactus) Perhaps the most well known of cactus to the layman; the rounded, prickly humps sitting low on the soil seem unlikely to do anything but grow fatter and rounder as the years go by, as many of us do, but with the right management and watering will produce small flowers from among the spines in a circle round the top of the plant, so that it has a sort of bridesmaid's garland. Colours are mainly purple, pink or cream, but can also be yellow, red or brownish, and the flower will last several weeks from May onwards as flowers are produced successively and die. With luck and plenty of sun they may also produce fruit, red but sometimes pink or white, lasting for about a year. Sun at all times, particularly in winter, is important, but failing this give them as much light as possible. Between mid-November and March no water is required, if kept cool, or a little if the plant body shows shrivelling, and repot in spring each year, until about five years old, then only every fourth year or so.

SCHLUMBERGERA (Christmas cactus and Easter cactus) At one time the Christmas cactus was called *Zygocactus*, but botanists have now decided that it is truly the same genus as the Easter cactus; both are certainly similar, but time of flowering differs. They are rather drooping plants, with flat green stems in segments, from the margins of which erupt red and purple flowers, without stalks, like a fuchsia in shape, and often double, so that they appear to have one flower within another. Colours are red, purple and magenta mainly; in the new varieties they may be pink or white, but they are less easy to grow. The Christmas cactus varieties will start into flower in late November, and continue until February depending on variety; the Easter cactus flowers in March and April. Treatment follows the same basic principles, plenty of water while growing and flowering, with an occasional feed; much less afterwards. When there is no risk of frost they can be stood out of doors in a good light, but not too much as this turns the stems reddish. Compost is best if it is fairly peaty or contains plenty of leaf-mould, but should drain well. Repotting in late April suits the Christmas cactus, and in July for the Easter variety. Bud dropping, a common trouble, may be due to changes in temperature, too dry at the roots, draughts, change of position, gas, or dry atmospheres. Wrinkled stems and a generally limp condition may be the result of overwatering, or dryness; lack of flower may be because of too low a temperature three months or so before flowering time, or through keeping the plants in conditions which lengthen the daylight hours, in living rooms which are artificially lit.

SEMPERVIVUM (houseleek) The rosettes of triangular fleshy leaves of the houseleek growing together in clusters can often be seen on house-roofs and walls as well as the more conventional situation of paving and stony ground. Increasing rapidly in sunny or well lit conditions, with little water in summer, and practically none in winter, the sempervivums prefer stony, gritty, really poor soil. They flower readily, sending up a stem about 6–9 inches tall, and having flowers which may be pink, red, white, purple or yellow in a small, tight head. After flowering the rosette will die, but as it will already in most cases have produced a multitude of little ones, this does not matter. If the rosette is to be retained, the flower stem should be removed as soon as it appears. *Sempervivum arachnoideum* has a thick web of fine white hairs produced all over it from point to point of the leaves, and is called the cobweb houseleek; *S. × funckii* has bright green leaves, tipped purple, and purplish-pink flowers. Flowering time is July–August.

Palms

Palms are one of the most decorative types of indoor plants, and their varied size makes them useful in all sorts of situations. The small ones, such as *Syagrus weddeliana*, an elegant plant with fern-like leaves, make excellent table decorations, and the larger ones include the 30 foot giants, which have to be housed in big conservatories or palm houses. Palms can be purchased as small plants and should be potted in a compost of fibrous loam and silver sand or good quality peat and grit. Good drainage is essential. Potting is generally done in spring and early summer. Avoid injuring the roots and plant firmly. Palms do best in a restricted root space, so never put them in pots which are too large; but always repot when the roots become overcrowded. The base of the stem should coincide with the surface of the soil. Palms require plenty of water in summer, and must not dry out in winter. The leaves should be sponged preferably with warm rainwater. In spring and summer the leaves should, if possible, be syringed twice daily. In summer the leaves should be protected from strong sunlight. Warmth and moisture are both essential. Liquid manure may be used to feed the roots. Sulphate of iron will cure any tendency for the leaves to turn yellow.

Palms have two basic kinds of foliage—fan-leaved, in which the leaf veins fan out from the centre (palmate) and feather-veined, in which the leaves are divided into long, narrow segments rather like a feather. For some palms heat is necessary but *Areca* (betel-nut), *Chamaerops* (fan palm), *Howea* (curly palm), *Oreodoxa* (cabbage palm), and *Phoenix* (date palm) may easily be grown without heat.

The young plants of *Areca* (betel-nut) are good for table and house decoration. *Chamaerops humilis* (fan palm, European palm) has leaves which splay out like a fan and is very ornamental

and slow-growing. It is fairly hardy and may be grown outside in the south west. The Howeas (*H. belmoreana*, curly palm, *H. forsteriana*, flat or thatch leaf palm) are the most popular for house decorations. They are sometimes called Kentias. The drooping leaves splay out in the shape of a feather rather than a fan. *Oreodoxa granatensis* is another example of a palm which can be placed on the table when young. *Phoenix dactylifera* is the famous date palm which is lovely for potting when young with its arching, feathery, grey-green leaves providing decoration for several years. *P. loureiri* (syn. *P. roebelinii*) is another attractive pot plant, and *P. canariensis* and *P. rupicola* are both good but will grow out of all proportion after some years. *Livistona australis* and *L. chinensis*, which need to be kept warm, have fine crowns of leaves. *Verschaffeltia splendida* and *Washingtonia filifera* are other interesting species, with large leaves and reaching tree size after some years.

Hoya see House Plants (Trailing Plants)

Humea/incense plant

Flower/Leaf/Su/Au

The tiny feathery brownish-pink or red flowers and aromatic foliage are characteristic of *H. elegans*, a sub-shrub from Australia usually grown in the greenhouse in climates subject to frost. It may easily reach 6 feet. Its delicate flowers make it blend easily with other plant material. Hammer the stem ends and give the stems a good drink.

Humulus/hop

Leaf/Flower/Seed/Su

A vigorously climing perennial, the common species being grown for the making of beer rather than for decorative purposes. However, a variation of this plant, *H. lupulus* 'Aureus', has decorative golden leaves, and *H. japonicus* 'Variegatus' (Japanese hop) has leaves with white markings on them. The flowers retain their colour well when dried by hanging upside down and when fresh are also useful decoration.

Hyacinthus see House Plants (Pot Plants)

Hydrangea

Flower/Leaf/Seed/Su

Delightfully large heads of flowerets of shades from pink to blue or cream distinguish this

Hydrangeas in several different colours are the main interest in this arrangement. Note the elaborate gilt container, shaped like a crown.

generally deciduous shrub. Like peonies the flowers can stand on their own and go best in large groups. The leaves are also quite large and as the plant produces plenty it is possible to use them freely without despoiling the shrub. Only pick the *mature* flowers and dip their stem ends in boiling hot water for about a minute after stripping the foliage and hammering. Then totally immerse the flowerheads and stems in water for over an hour or spray with an atomiser at frequent intervals. If you wish to dry the heads leave them on the plant as long as possible and finish off the drying by standing them upright in shallow water. Hydrangea leaves can be preserved in glycerine. See also House Plants (Pot Plants).

Hydroponics

This is the art of growing plants without soil and is especially suitable for those living in city flats and dwellings which have no garden or where one's gardening is confined to a verandah or window box. To use indoors, soil is dirty, contains pests and diseases and is often difficult to obtain. However, the need for soil may be completely eliminated by using vermiculite, either by itself or mixed with the almost equally sterile peat or sand. Vermiculite will hold at least four times its weight of water which is given as a dilute chemical solution made up to a particular formula suitable for feeding the various plants.

Vermiculite is a form of mica heated to 2,000°F (1,093°C). The raw material is removed from the ground as wafer-thin layers which expand when heated to something like twelve times their original size and which have a sponge-like absorbency. It is sterile and so free from weed and disease spores, and it is light and clean to handle. Its structure is such that its use ensures correct aeration. The vermiculite is used as a support for plant growth, just as the casing soil on mushroom beds is used to support the mushrooms, and it may be used over and over again.

Self-feeding pots and trays are necessary where indoor plants are to be grown, and these include: ferns; foliage plants and bulbs; freesias and pelargoniums; African violets; begonias and many other plants. Such pots or trays contain a reservoir of nutrient solution which works by capillary action. This ensures that the plants receive a balanced diet throughout their life and enables them to go for long periods without attention. It is also now fully recognised that most plants prefer to take up their moisture requirements from the base and remain healthier and maintain a greater vigour when this is possible.

Almost any type of plant container may be used, metal, plastic, wood or earthenware. Pots must first be crocked in the usual way before adding the growing medium to within half an inch of the top. The Marmax self-watering camel pot is suitable. It is made from resin-bonded wood fibre and is unbreakable. It is so designed that the internal ridged surface permits the easing of pressure on delicate root formation. One pot fits inside another, the diameter of the outer pot which holds the nutrient solution being about 1 inch larger than that of the inner pot. Another type previously mentioned is a pot fitted with a lower container or reservoir containing the solution which is fed to the plant by means of a wick. With both types, the plants may be left unattended for several weeks.

Peperomias, caladiums placed in a sunny window where the light can shine through the

Hyacinths are fascinating plants to grow in glasses. Care must be taken that the bottom of the bulb never touches the water.

almost transparent leaves, fatshedera, and the maidenhair ferns are easily managed plants where grown without soil. The pots may be placed in wrought iron holders fastened to a wall or in jardinieres or pedestal stands. Oriental vases make attractive containers, the pots being raised on a wooden block so that the foliage of the plant may trail over the side.

A suitable plant food for indoor pot plants may be made to the following formula: nitrate of potash, superphosphate of lime, calcium sulphate, 4 ounces of each; magnesium sulphate. 3 ounces, sulphate of ammonia, 1 ounce. Mix thoroughly and add trace elements of ferrous ammonium citrate; manganese sulphate; boracic acid (20 gr. of each) and copper sulphate (2 gr.). A chemist will mix them. Then mix the whole together and use at the rate of 1 tablespoonful to each gallon of water. The solution used should always be as weak as possible so that the plant can readily utilise each ingredient and there will not be an accumulation of plant foods in excess of requirements.

Bulbs are especially adaptable to soilless culture and hyacinths may be grown in special glass jars of a size to hold a top-size bulb with a water compartment below. The base of the bulb should be just above the level of the water into which the roots will grow. The bulbs require a period in the dark while they form their roots just as if growing in soil or fibre.

Narcissus also do as well in vermiculite or pebbles and the 'Paper White' type of narcissus is the only bulb which may be placed directly in the window of a warm room immediately after planting. It is the most valuable of all bulbs for early forcing and may be planted in bowls containing only pebbles with the neck of the bulbs just above the surface. The pebbles should be kept covered with water.

Crocuses and snowdrops may be brought into bloom in acorn glasses. These glasses were at one time used by children to sprout acorns. They are made on the same lines as the bulb glasses but are much smaller. Both crocuses and snowdrops should be given a cool room and require several weeks in the dark before being introduced to the light.

When using bulb glasses it is important to ensure that the water is always within reach of the roots and occasional topping up may be necessary. Where obtainable, rainwater is better than tap water.

Hypericum/rose of Sharon, St. John's wort

Flower/Leaf/Berry/Sp/Su/Au

Masses of golden yellow flowers excellent for cutting are borne by this generally hardy shrub or sub-shrub. Different varieties flower at different times from spring to autumn. *H. polyphyllum* is a herbaceous garden flower for ground cover. The leaves on some species are particularly decorative in autumn when the fruits also appear. *H. calycinum* (rose of Sharon, Aaron's beard) produces flowers over 3 inches across and the small fruits form decorative clusters.

Hyssopus/hyssop

Flower/Seed/Su

Blue, red or white flowers on spikes 1 to 2 feet tall make hyssop a handsome herb plant with aromatic leaves. The effect is an informal one. The seedheads may be dried upside down.

Iberis/candytuft

Flower/Seed/Su

Small, delicate heads of white, pink or purple appear on the short stems. The perennials are generally found growing in the rock garden and the annuals in the border. Some of the modern annual hybrids are particularly colourful. The ripe seedheads may be hung upside down to dry.

Ilex/holly

Berry/Leaf

Evergreen shrubs and trees with glossy dark green leaves and generally red berries (drupes), they are well known for their use at Christmas. Like hawthorn, which it is considered unlucky to bring into the house at all (owing to its reputed use for Christ's crown of thorns), there are superstitions attached to holly. If you are superstitious about the holly, or 'holy' tree, remember it *is* lucky to bring sprigs into the house on Christmas Eve (not before) to be burnt on Twelfth Night.

The foliage helps to set off flower arrangements, but do not put the stems in the water as the leaves then seem to drop off more quickly. Instead spray them with transparent varnish (likewise the berries). There is a lovely type of holly with variegated leaves and another with yellow berries. See Trees (Ilex).

Iris innominata is one of the most delicate and beautiful iris species and of very variable colour, ranging from yellow through oranges and ambers to mauve, purple and blue.

Impatiens see (House Plants)

Incarvillea

Flower/Leaf/Sp/Su

Rosy-red or pink trumpet-shaped flowers borne proudly on thick, straight stems in May, June or July really look exotic, although the plant is a good hardy or almost hardy perennial. The leaves of *I. delavayi* are an attractive glossy green, and *I. olgae* has finely cut feathery foliage. In view of the long-lastingness of the flowers in water it is altogether a very useful plant.

Ipheion/spring star flower

Flower/Sp

Delicate blue or white star-like flowers appear on 6-inch stems. They last well in water. The bulbous plant was originally a native of the western hemisphere and grows well in a warm temperate climate. *Ipheion uniflorum* is sometimes known as *Brodiaea uniflora*.

Ipomoea/morning glory

Flower/Su

Although used in Japanese flower arrangement *I. hederacea* does not last well in water, but the well-known blue and white convolvulus-like flowers will grow well in pots.

Iris/flag

Flower/Leaf/Seed/Sp/Su/Au/Wi

Irises have often been likened to orchids, which their flowers somewhat resemble. Flower arrangers love their tall straight stems, showy elegant flowers and long, pointed leaves which mix so well with other foliage and flowers. The range of choice among these bulbous, tuberous or creeping-rooted perennials is vast and by using different varieties it is possible to have irises almost all the year round.

The most widely grown are the tall, 'bearded' types, flowering in May or June, sometimes called flag or German irises. There is a wide range of rich-looking modern hybrids including almost all colours and some reaching 3 feet in height.

For cut flowers the Dutch, English and Spanish

Irises. Many species provide attractive and long-lasting flowers for house decoration. This is a spring arrangement incorporating hyacinths and the gelder rose.

irises are very popular. These come into flower from May to July (earlier under glass) and are slightly more distinctive in colour and only a little shorter stemmed.

The short-lived usually lavender-blue or white flowers of *I. unguicularis* (syn. *I. stylosa*) are firm favourites partly because they flower in winter. In February and March comes the bulbous-rooted *I. danfordiae*, with its richly scented yellow flowers, *I. histrioides*, bearing distinctively light blue flowers, and *I. reticulata* in purple, violet and yellow. The snake's head iris, though not strictly speaking within the genus (it is *Hermodactylus tuberose* not *I. tuberosa*) is another lovely spring flower with enchanting green heads and velvety

black petals. The open clematis-flowered Japanese *I. kaempferi* comes in lilac, pink, blue and white in June and July.

There are also one or two varieties with distinctively variegated leaves. *I. foetidissima* (gladwyn iris) has the most exciting seed pods which break open to show bright orange seeds in winter. A little fixative varnish will stabilise them and make them even more glossy. The ripe seedheads of most species can be dried hanging upside down.

For cut flowers always remove any dead blooms as soon as they appear so that the buds on the same stem can open out. Pick the flowers when they are beginning to open and cut them diagonally over the white part at the base of the stem, plunging them immediately for a minute into water that is boiling hot. They then like plenty of cool water.

Isatis/woad

Flower/Leaf/Seed/Su

This is a herb known as dyer's weed (*I. tinctoria*) which was used by the Ancient Britons to make a blue pigment for painting their bodies. It has hazy heads of tiny bright yellow flowers. *I. glauca* has bluish-green leaves with a white central line. Dry the seedheads upside down and use the flowers and foliage for cut flower arrangements.

Ixia/African corn lily

Flower/Sp/Su

Lots of white, bright red, orange-yellow, purple-pink flowers distinguish this half-hardy cormous plant which is excellent for cut flowers. One species, *Ixia viridiflorus*, has unusual large electric green flowers in May and June. It is a good choice for the cut flower garden bed as the blooms last well and are produced in plenty.

Japanese flower arrangement

For the western flower arranger Japanese flower arranging styles can be an exciting discovery. They are inexpensive because even a single blossom and a minimum of foliage will provide you with enough material to create something extremely beautiful. You will find even your first attempt to arrange flowers in the Japanese manner will bring both enjoyment and artistic satisfaction, provided you have a sense of beauty and a love of flowers. There are many differing styles of Japanese flower arranging and thousands of schools teaching various modes. There are also many conventions, rules and variations. Do not let that discourage you: remember that even the profoundest master of the art has something still to learn.

In Japan, interest in the art of flower arranging began at least 1,400 years ago. *Ikebana*, the Japanese name for flower arranging means *living flowers*. It is supposed to have been started when the Buddhist religion was introduced from China in the sixth century A.D. A seventh-century scholar-priest, Ono-no-Inoko, is credited with formulating the earliest known rules of the art. He lived by a lake at Kyoto, and the style of arrangement named after him is called *ikenobo*, meaning *the priest-lodging by the lake*.

The most famous early style became prominent in the mid-fifteenth century. This is *rikka*, mean-

Ixias, African corn lilies. Early summer flowering plants in brilliant reds, oranges and yellows borne on thin, wiry stems and often more attractive picked than grown in the garden.

ing *standing flowers*. The rikka style was used for decorating religious shrines. Arrangements were generally over 6 feet high (a famous one reached 40 feet), and were constructed according to strict rules. The rikka style resembles the form of a tree with seven, nine or even eleven branches, each a different kind of tree branch, piece of shrub or flower. From the container, traditionally a bronze vase or urn, the bunched together branches rise vertically as a single trunk for a short distance, often fitted into pieces of bamboo tied with straw. Then the stems spread out spaciously from the tall central branch which forms the highest point of the design.

Tree branches, and then shrub branches, would be placed higher than flowers, illustrating a cardinal principle of traditional Japanese flower arrangement, which teaches the student to symbolise nature faithfully by grouping together and relating various kinds of plant material found growing together. Nature and art are combined in many of the styles. You can construct a small-scale rikka using straight material for a formal arrangement or increasingly curving or bending material according to whether the design is to be semi-formal or completely informal.

Around about the same time as the rikka style emerged, that is in the mid-15th century, the *heika* style, the forerunner of the *nageire* (meaning *thrown-in*) method of arrangement was evolving. This more casual-seeming way of arranging flowers was better adapted to the homes of the people, and it is associated with *chabana* (meaning *tea flower*) arrangement. A chabana is a simple affair, perhaps just a single flower in a vase. It became popular with the Japanese tea ceremony in the sixteenth century, and is still practised today.

The best known nageire designs may be said to consist of three main stems—long, middling and short—in a tall vase. The Japanese use pieces of stem inside the vase to keep the stems in position, but it is possible to achieve more or less the same effects using crumpled wire or by supporting a pinholder near the top of the vase. The plant material may be straight, curving or cascading. The length of the stems may be varied, but to begin with it is best to use the following rule of thumb. (All the lengths described refer to the length of the stem to be seen above or outside the container and you must therefore add on the length inside the container when preparing your material.) The tallest main stem, which is the first to be arranged, measures twice the combined total of the height and diameter of the vase. The second or mid-length stem is three-quarters of the length of the first, and the third or shortest stem is three-quarters the length of the second. These measurements apply to both straight or curved stems.

For an upright arrangement straight stems are used, and the longest stem is placed vertically or up to an angle of 15° to the left or right of the vertical. For a slanting arrangement the longest stem is placed at between 15° and 90° from the vertical (90° for a horizontal arrangement), and for a cascading arrangement it is over 90° from the vertical.

Continuing the upright arrangement: the second main stem might follow the direction of the longest stem but at a more inclined angle from the vertical, and the third main stem might be angled quite sharply to the line of the vase at a wide angle from the other two stems. Fillers, or assistant stems, may be added, which are slightly shorter than the main stem with which they are used. The subtle variations in the positions which the three main stems may occupy are virtually infinite, and in spite of the simplicity of the whole effect it requires great art.

The classical *shoka* style of flower arranging in Japan was developing towards the end of the seventeenth century and reached nearest to perfection in the following hundred years. It is highly stylised, and strict rules dictate the kinds of plant material used, etc., as in a rikka arrangement. The shoka style is known as *ten-chi-jin*, meaning *heaven, earth, man*. This is because the longest branch of a shoka is known as *shin* (heaven), the mid-length branch as *soe* (man), and the shortest as *hikae* (earth). This threefold principle dominates Japanese flower arrangement in its classical form, just as the philosophical *yin-yang* (dark and light) principle affects classical Chinese flower arrangement. In Japanese styles even when more than three branches are used an odd number is always the rule, so that the design can still be resolved into three main lines.

The Japanese fix a forked twig (*matagi*) inside the taller type of container and a cross-bar is used to hold the stems firmly wedged into the fork for a shoka. Pinholders are always used in shallow containers, even by the Japanese. If you cannot manage to rest the stems on the forked twig properly in the taller type of container, use a pinholder below. The main point is that the stems should come together at the base for a short distance before they enter the container. One can easily imagine a shoka arrangement being tried out by holding the various pieces of material in the hands first in order to get the right proportions. This is what the experts do, and it is a good way to start too. The visible length of the longest stem must be $1\frac{1}{2}$ times the height of the container, the mid-length stem is two-thirds the length of the longest stem, and the shortest stem is two-thirds the length of the mid-length stem. Shoka styles may be tall and straight—*shin* (formal, or heavenly); with gentle curves—*gyo* (semi-formal); or with more curving or bending stems in a shallow container—*so* (informal).

A formal shin-style arrangement might consist of one or two gladioli flowers.

The arrangement would be barely wider than the sides of the container, a medium-sized vase or urn. The gyo arrangement would extend beyond the sides of the container and the lines of the curves would be elliptical with a wonderful

Japanese flower arranging. Compare this picture with any other picture in the book and you will realise how highly formalised and artificial Japanese flower arranging has become.
[By courtesy of Meikof Kasuia (from: 'Introducing Ikebana')].

flowing feeling. The pinholder for the so-style arrangement is placed in the centre of the shallow container and might be covered with small pebbles to conceal it. The height of a so-style arrangement may be two or more times the width of the container. For both rikka and shoka styles a black or red lacquer base may be used to support the container.

Undoubtedly the most popular style of Japanese flower arrangement is that known as *moribana*, meaning *built-up flowers*, which was introduced by the Japanese master flower arranger Unshin Ohara in 1910. One moribana type of arrangement reflects a natural landscape and requires wide shallow containers which may contain 'mountains' and 'valleys', or a 'lake' with 'islands' or water plants, or an overhanging branch of spring blossoms. The plant material is generally placed to one side of the container to create an effect of space. Or the material may be divided between one side and an island centred at the other end of the container. A rock would suggest a mountain, and the plant material would be skilfully proportioned to symbolise woods, trees, shrubs and flowers, etc. Water is omitted from the container when making a seasonal winter arrangement, when the ground is assumed to be frozen, and the cup pinholder (*kenzan*) must

then be concealed with moss or stones, etc. In creating seasonal arrangements it is generally best to use only plant material found in nature at that time of year.

The conventional upright, slanting, horizontal and cascading styles are all used in moribana, the longest stem being equal to about $1\frac{1}{2}$ times the combined width and depth of the container, or it may be two or more times the container's width. The position of the arrangement in the narrow container may be varied, and unlike the classical style (at its strictest) it is not necessary that the bases of the three stems should be closely united. The stems may be sited next to each other on one pinholder, or divided between the edge of the container and an island site as in the landscape arrangements. Two containers may be used united by a base, or the container may be dispensed with altogether through the skilful use of the base, pinholder cups, moss, stones, etc.

For the basic upright moribana arrangement, place the longest flower stem or foliage branch vertically at the left front of the shallow container, but bed it in the rear of the pinholder. The mid-length stem should be further to the left and front and at a leftward angle of about 40° to the vertical and projecting slightly forward. The shortest stem is placed to the right and front of the longest stem and at a sharp rightward angle (60°) to the vertical and also projecting forward. Filler stems of flowers or foliage of the same kind of plant material may be added, remembering to keep the asymmetrical threefold design. One or two leaves should be sufficient to cover the pin-holder.

Naturally, for cascading arrangements taller containers are used, and in general the use of containers and material and the design are much freer than in the classical styles. Arrangers tend to use groups of colourful flowers on short stems accompanied by their own leaves. Plant material from anywhere in the world (provided it is reasonably adaptable for constructing the arrangement) may be used for moribana.

In the twentieth century Japanese flower arrangement became a form of Modern Art. The master Sofu Teshiguhara, who started the Sogetsu School in 1926, pioneered the use of non-floral material. Now, literally 'anything can be done with anything', provided it accords with artistic design. Driftwood, wrought iron, glass, wire, etc., are incorporated in abstract or geometric arrangements, which may not include any fresh plant material at all. Materials may also be 'upside down' or used in other non-naturalistic ways. The individual arranger or teacher is finally responsible for his own work, and it is through this ultra-modern or *avant garde* approach that perhaps ikebana has reached its most international style.

Some Japanese tips for preparing material

Always cut stems under water to prevent an air lock. When burning the stem ends of milky-stemmed plants wait till the stem is red hot and then immediately plunge it into cold water. Use damp newspaper or a towel to protect the rest of the stem when either burning or scalding stem ends. Salt helps to keep water in the stems. Put a small amount of salt in the boiling water when dipping the stem ends in boiling water.

Examples of traditional Japanese flower arrangement material

Apricot
Aspidistra
Astilbe
Azalea
Bamboo
Camellia
Canna
Cedar
Cherry
Chrysanthemum
Cockscomb (*Celosia cristata*)
Cryptomeria
Cupressus
Forsythia
Gardenia
Hemerocallis
Hosta
Hydrangea
Ipomaea
Iris
Juniperus
Lilium
Loquat
Lotus
Magnolia
Maple
Nandina
Orchids
Paeonia
Peach
Pear
Pine
Pinks
Plum
Podocarpus
Pomegranate
Poppy
Pussy willow
Quince
Water lily
Willow
Wisteria
Wych hazel
Yew

Examples of further material which may be used in modern arrangements

Amaranthus
Amaryllis
Arum lily
Barberry
Birch
Bittersweet
Box
Broom
Cacti and other succulents
Carnation
Cat-tail (*Typha*)
Cedar
Chaenomeles (*Japonica*)
Cineraria
Clematis
Cornflowers
Cosmos
Cyclamen
Daisies
Euonymous
Ferns
Freesia
Geranium
Grape vine
Grasses
Holly
Honeysuckle
Hydrangea
Ivy
Jasmine
Lilac
Mahonia
Mulberry
Mustard
Oak
Pelargonium
Philadelphus (mock orange)
Poplar
Privet
Rhododendron
Roses
Rushes
Spiraea
Strawberry
Thistles

Or alternatively rub the stem ends with salt. The boiling water treatment is best used for plant material which tends to deteriorate rapidly, such as the Chinese bellflower (*Platycodon grandiflorum*).

Prolong the life of anemones, asters, maple and wisteria foliage by dipping the stem ends in alcohol for over 15 minutes. Water may be pumped into water plants, such as water lilies, and the stems sealed with plugs of cotton wool or by dipping in melted sealing wax.

Jasminum/jasmine

Flower/Leaf/Sp/Su/Au/Wi

The yellow flowers on bare twigs of winter jasmine (*J. nudiflorum*) are a cheerful sight at any time from October to March, and the clusters of white, pink-flushed flowers of summer jasmine (*J. officinale*) are loved for their beautiful scent. The foliage of both winter and summer jasmine is a marvellous standby, the summer jasmine being almost evergreen and the deciduous winter jasmine proving useful in summer. Both are hardy.

J. mesnyi (*J. primulinum*) which has bright yellow flowers in winter is not so hardy. Other tender jasmines are worth having particularly for their scent and also for foliage and flowers. Dip the stem ends in boiling hot water for a minute and then give them plenty of cool water.

Kalanchoë see House Plants (Cacti and Succulents)

Kalmia/calico bush, sheeps laurel

Flower/Leaf/Su

The widely grown evergreen shrub *K. latifolia* has foliage rather like small laurel leaves. The bright pink flowers when fully open are like nothing so much as tiny delicate parasols. Strip some of the bark from the stem ends or hammer them and then provide plenty of water.

Kerria/Jew's mallow

Flower/Su

The popular double-flowered *K. japonica* 'Flore Pleno' is a deciduous shrub with yellow flowers. There is also a variegated leaf kerria. The flowers can be forced in the greenhouse and enhance early spring arrangements. Hammer the stem ends and give them a long drink in water.

Delicacy is the keynote of this arrangement of summer flowering jasmine. By using chicken wire at the top of the vase it has become unnecessary to have long stems, showing through the glass.

Kniphofia/red hot poker, torch lily

Flower/Su/Au

The hardy perennial plants producing the thick-stemmed spikes consisting of lots of tiny flowers of pure red or yellow, red and yellow, etc., are favourite garden subjects and a challenge to the flower arranger. It is simple enough to arrange them on their own either in a large vase or supported by a pinholder. In mixed groups, however, they need to be matched by equally brilliant flowers such as dahlias or zinnias. Cut the stems diagonally before placing them in deep water.

Kochia/belvedere, fire bush

Leaf

This half-hardy annual shrub-like plant is grown for its delicate bright green foliage which turns red in the autumn giving rise to the name fire bush. *K. scoparia* 'Trichophylla' (summer cypress) is the species generally grown. The plants can be kept in tubs in sunny positions or in the unheated greenhouse.

Lachenalia see House Plants (Pot Plants)

Lactuca

Flower/Leaf/Su

These plants are related to the lettuce, and the leaves as well as being quite ornamental can be eaten. The plants of *L. bourguei* reach 5 feet in height and bear purple flowers branching airily on long stems. They are very useful for large summer arrangements. Make sure you dip the stem ends in boiling hot water for a minute.

Lamium/dead nettle

Leaf/Flower/Su

The variegated leaves, which are green and edged white, of *Lamium* (now properly *Lamiastrum*) *galeobdolon* 'Variegatum', and the green leaves with a white central stripe of *L. maculatum* are often seen covering odd bits of the garden. Both the flowers and foliage can be used but they do not last all that well and tend to be too 'bitty' for large arrangements; they make a good replacement for moss to cover the 'mechanics'.

Lavandula/lavender

Flower/Leaf/Seed/Su

The purple spikes of common lavender are frequently found in old-fashioned gardens and both the flowers and the greyish-green leaves can be used for group flower arrangements. A mass of lavender flowers will set off brighter coloured ones such as daisies. The fragrant foliage will scent the house if you use it in little vases all over the place. This can also be a way of beginning the drying out process, for the heads will dry out naturally if left in a vase without water.

Lavatera

Flower/Leaf/Su/Au

Decorative pink, rose or purple mallow-like flowers are borne on shrubs or border plants. Though attractive as cut flowers they are not long lasting, so try hammering the stem ends or dip them for about a minute in boiling hot water.

Leaves, drying see Preservation and Dried Arrangements (Pressing Leaves)

Leaves, skeletonising see Preservation and Dried Arrangements (Skeletonising)

Leontopodium/edelweiss

Flower/Seed/Su

Yellow-centred flowers with white bracts extending out rather in the shape of starfish, the edelweiss is famous as the national flower of Switzerland. This is *L. alpinum*. The flowers do need a long drink, but make sure the water does not reach the flowerheads. Drying is done by hanging the heads upside down.

Leycesteria/flowering nutmeg

Flower/Berry/Su

Tassels of white, purple-speckled flowers with dark wine-red bracts hang down from the green branches of *L. formosa*, a deciduous shrub from the Himalayan region. They provide material for unusual, attractive arrangements. The purple or black berries follow the flowers in the autumn. The leafy-green stems remain attractive in winter. Strip a little of the bark of the stem ends and give the stems a good drink.

Liatris/blazing star

Flower/Su

The spikes of purple flowers on tall stems open from the top downwards—an exceptional feature of this easily cultivated hardy perennial from North America. It flowers in August when many other herbaceous flowers are finished, so it is very useful for late summer arrangements. There is a lovely white variety 'Snow White', but the flowers are generally in various shades of purple which blend well with the pastel colours of other summer flowers. Hammer the stem ends and strip at least half the leaves before arranging.

Lichens

Though they possess a wide variety of colour and form and may be used in many ways for indoor decoration, materials clothed in lichens are mostly neglected. It may be said that the lichens are the connecting link between the more primitive fungi and the green foliage plants, for they are composed of a fungus and an alga, the most primitive of green plants, growing in unison. Usually, the alga is contained in the main body of the fungus and supplies the lichen with its food requirements. Owing to its minute size, it forms little available nutriment and hence most lichens are slow growing.

Lichens grow only when wet and for this reason are found attached to the bark and twigs of trees and shrubs and to the stone of old walls in the cooler and damper parts of the country; they are often found growing as long drooping bodies attached to the branch or bark only at the base; or they may creep over the wood (or stones) to which they are attached by thread-like roots. They are removed by cutting away the twigs or pieces of bark to which the lichens are attached. They should be handled with care and placed in a box. If kept dry, they will retain their beauty of form and colour for years and may be used for mixing with teasels and with dried grasses and ferns.

They may also be used in Wardian cases where the lichens will continue to grow in the moist atmosphere but fresh air must be admitted frequently. Pieces of bark and stone on which the lichens are growing should be arranged as naturally as possible, using the stone at the base with ferns and club mosses planted near them whilst pieces of bark or branches may be used to form the background. The lichens and plants should be sprayed occasionally, being given just enough moisture to keep them growing.

Interesting collections of dried lichens may be built up and artistically arranged, using those attached to bark, twigs and stones and though they will not grow if kept dry, they will retain their beauty for years. They may be placed in shallow bowls lined with wire netting into which lichen-covered twigs are placed and held upright. The netting is concealed by pieces of bark and stone covered with lichens.

When removing lichens, do not attempt to separate them from the material on which they grow, for not only will they die if their thread-like roots are severed but in trying to remove them, the lichens will almost surely be damaged. They also need the bark or stone on which to continue growing, many pushing out at the edge by means of minute spores, like fungi, each of which contains a microscopic alga.

Few lichens will be found near industrialised parts for they are unable to flourish in a polluted atmosphere. They grow mostly in deciduous woodlands and on walls and stone tiles, also by the seashore and where the atmosphere is constantly moisture laden.

Of those most easily obtainable, one of the most striking is *Usnea comosa* which dangles its dense fern-like mass of greenish-grey from tree trunks. One of more upright growth and which is most attractive used for floral decoration is *Cetraria glauca*, also widespread and forming masses of silvery-green folded at the edges like paper. Another for use in floristry is *Parmeliopsis ambigua* which has the appearance of prostrate fronds of a maidenhair fern.

Physcia pulverulen and *P. grisea* are suitable for floristry, being grey-green in colour and silverer. They are found on twigs and branches as encrusted rosettes. *Candelariella vitellina* is also most handsome, forming an encrustation of mimosa-yellow on wood and stone.

Ligularia

Flower/Leaf/Su

The tall handsome feathery spikes of yellow flowers on purple stems and deeply indented leaves of *L. przewalskii* are a good example of the various types of ligularias. There are a number of modern hybrids in a variety of colours and foliage, some having round leaves, others heart-shaped ones. Hammer the stem ends and give the stems a good long drink before arranging.

Ligusticum/lovage

Leaf

The leaves of this perennial herb are quite decorative and the plant itself may reach 7 feet in height. It is best to hammer the stem ends when using the foliage.

Ligustrum/privet

Leaf/Flower/Su

So many privet bushes are closely cropped for

An alabaster container on the Chinese traditional pattern supports an exotic arrangement of lilies, gladioli, alstroemeria, carnations and peony-leaves.

hedging purposes that their flowers never appear and are forgotten. The clusters of small white or yellowish flowers are quite delicate and are good for varying your summer arrangements.

Unfortunately, too the plant most suitable for hedging (*L. ovalifolium*) produces not very exciting but rather nastily scented flowers. The common privet (*L. vulgare*) does have fragrant flowers. The foliage of most species lasts very well in water.

Lilium/lily

Flower/Leaf/Seed/Sp/Su

There are over 85 species of these bulbous-rooted plants in a wide range of colours and shapes (for arum lilies see Zantedeschia). One exotic-looking bloom will provide a focal point in a large group of varied flowers. The leaves are also excellent foliage material, setting off the flowers and providing interest of their own.

Lilies can be flowered under glass from March to December and are a main standby for florists' bouquets. If you want lilies for Christmas try *L. formosanum*, which is used by florists. There are several varieties including the pure white 'Wallace's Variety' and 'Wilson's Variety'. Lilies grown in pots may be brought inside to flower and some varieties are sold as pot plants to be kept inside permanently. See House Plants (Bulbs).

By no means all lilies respond to forcing. Among the lilies that may be flowered in gentle heat around Easter, the Japanese *L. auratum*, the golden-rayed mountain lily, is a favourite among flower arrangers. It is honey-scented and the wide-curving petals are divided by golden yellow rays and speckled crimson. Such a lily which may grow 7 feet high ought not to be used for any but large arrangements.

L. candidum is the well-known Madonna lily, which can be seen depicted in old paintings, and is the traditional Christian symbol linked with the Virgin Mary. The flower also signifies the mystical nature of divine marriage rites. The blooms are pure white with golden stamens.

L. longifolium, the Easter lily, is another good flower for arranging. Trumpet-shaped large snowy-white flowers generally appear in July, but can be obtained earlier by forcing. The long leaves are very decorative.

L. regale is an easily grown species with shorter leaves and with deep trumpet-shaped flowers reddening at the base. They open slowly in June and July. *L. regale* and *L. longifolium* mingle well.

When preparing lilies for arrangement cut the stems diagonally to stop them from curling. Dry the seedheads when they are still green by standing the stems in shallow water and giving the heads plenty of air circulating round them.

Limonium/statice, sea lavender

Flower/Su

The light feathery flowers growing in great profusion on branched spikes are easily dried and are used extensively for winter arrangements.

'Black Dragon,' one of the largest flowered of modern lily hybrids, provides stunning material for flower arrangements. It is apt to fall over under the sheer weight of the flowers when grown out of doors.

They come in shades of mauve or purple but may be yellow or white. They are quite frequently seen growing near the seaside, hence the common name of sea lavender. The more delicate-stemmed types help to lighten the effect of heavier-looking dried blooms and seedheads such as teasels, and may be used freely. The thicker-stemmed varieties provide flowers which when dried will blend well and can be used mixed with fresh-cut flowers.

Linaria/toadflax

Flower/Sp/Su/Au

The yellow-orange flowers of the wild toadflax are rather like tiny versions of the snapdragon flower and are found growing in the countryside in most places during a large part of the summer. The foliage is light and feathery in both wild and cultivated kinds. The garden varieties come in red-yellow, purple-yellow, white and cream. They are very free-flowering and will suit informal summer arrangements. Dip the stem ends in boiling hot water for less than a minute.

Linum/flax

Flower/Sp/Su

Common flax used for making linen has blue flowers, but for a sharper blue colour use *L. narbonense*. Not all flaxes are blue: there are modern hybrids which produce masses of flowers in red, yellow, white, etc. Dip the stem ends in boiling hot water and try arranging the flowers on their own or in mixed informal arrangements.

Lithops see House Plants (Cacti and Succulents)

Livingstonia see House Plants (Palms)

Lobelia

Flower/Leaf/Su/Au

Small flowers of blue, wine-red, scarlet and pale purple are typical of these generally half-hardy plants, the smaller varieties of which are often seen in the fronts of borders or in window boxes. The blue flowers of the trailing *L. tenuior* are popular in hanging baskets.

The perennial and taller-growing *L. cardinalis* (cardinal flower) is a more interesting subject for the flower arranger. Its rich tall spikes of scarlet

with long, pointed leaves go well with early autumn arrangements. *L. fulgens* is slightly smaller (about 3 feet) and *L. tupa* has reddish rather lupin-like spikes. Lobelias do well in pots which must be kept well watered, but need no heat.

Lobivia see House Plants (Cacti and Succulents)

Lonicera/honeysuckle

Flower/Leaf/Sp/Su/Au

Many of the flowers of this shrub or climbing plant have a sweet, almost sickly, scent. Different species come into flower at different times, generally in spring or summer, but *L. × purpusii* flowers in winter. Colours are varied: the common honeysuckle, or woodbine, may be yellow-white or purple, others are coppery yellow or yellow and pink, cream and pink, etc. The foliage of the trailing kinds is good for informal arrangements. A mass of honeysuckle in a large bowl with stems and leaves trailing over the sides is an excellent idea. Hammer the stem ends, or peel off about half an inch of bark from the bottom of the stem.

Lunaria/honesty

Flower/Seed/Sp/Su

Best known for the round parchment-like seed-head capsules which resemble the moon rounding towards the full (hence the name: *Lunaria*). After drying and removing their casings the seedheads may be painted with transparent cellulose varnish for use in dried arrangement and Christmas decorations. The seedheads appear after the white, purple or pink flowers have died. They are ornamental while still green, but if you wish to dry them stand them upright in a dry vase with plenty of space around the heads. The discs turn brown and then silver. When using the flowers, first dip the stem ends in boiling hot water and then immerse in deep water.

Lupinus/lupin

Flower/Seed/Su/Au

Tall spikes of flowers in fascinating colours of yellow, red, blue or purple, bloom according to variety from May to October. The lupin is a tenacious plant and perennial varieties will continue to flower for years without attention. In

Mahonia provides useful material for flower arranging throughout the whole year, the leaves in summer, the yellow flowers in winter, and the blue-black grape-like berries in late spring.

spite of this rugged quality, they are showy yet elegant in both shape and colour. The Russell hybrids are deservedly most popular. They are really too prominent *en masse* to mix with more modest flowers, but in ones and twos will add distinction to a mixed arrangement. They also match delphiniums and foxgloves.

After picking fill the hollow stems with water and plug with a tiny wad of wet cotton wool to keep the water in, or dip the stem ends in boiling hot water for a minute. The heads tend to bend in water and the petals drop easily. This bending quality is not so distracting in mixed informal arrangements. Steeping the flower overnight helps to prevent it.

To preserve the seedheads pick them as soon as formed and dry upside down.

Lychnis/campion

Flower/Leaf/Sp/Su

The red heads of *L. chalcedonica* appear in July and may be as much as five inches across. They are good for cutting and *L. coronaria*, magenta-red, and the shorter-stemmed border flowers of *L. fulgens* and *L. × haageana* are also good in this way. Dip the stem ends in boiling hot water.

Macleaya/plume poppy

Flower/Leaf/Su

The off-white flowers of *M. cordata* are very graceful: tiny petalless panicles on tall light stems which grace any arrangement. The sap oozes away easily and quickly, so dip the stem ends in boiling hot water. The large deeply-lobed leaves may be 8 inches across. They are white underneath and very decorative.

Mahonia

Flower/Leaf/Berry/Wi

The common ornamental shrub with leaves somewhat resembling holly, its chief interest for flower arrangers is its winter-flowering habit. *M. aquifolium*, *M. bealei* and *M. japonica* all produce fragrant yellow flowers in delicate sprays in winter. The leaves are also useful at this time as they are evergreen and the berries form bright bluish-black clusters which are decorative in small groups.

Malcolmia/Virginian stock

Flower/Sp/Su/Au

M. maritima, with its flowers of brighter violet to purple, white, red or yellow, is the easiest of all stocks to grow. By successional sowing from autumn onwards, it is possible to have flowers continuously from the following spring to autumn. It can also be grown in pots for window boxes and sunny window sills.

Mammillaria see House Plants (Cacti and Succulents)

Matthiola/Brompton, night-scented, ten-week stocks

Flower/Su

This genus of annuals and biennials includes some favourite florists' flowers because they are easily grown under glass and the tall spikes of pink, purple, mauve and white (often double) look particularly rich and impressive. Most stocks have a sweet scent and their pastel colours mix well with other flowers. Nearly all varieties are good for cutting. One exception is *M. bicornis* which is sown in patches in the garden for those who enjoy its evening scent.

Melissa/balm

Leaf/Flower/Su

This aromatic herb produces a tremendous amount of foliage and one species has variegated leaves. Lemon balm has a lovely lemon scent if the leaves are rubbed. Dip the stem ends in boiling hot water for a few seconds and keep them as short as possible.

Mentha/mint

Leaf/Flower/Su

The variegated variety *M. × gentilis* 'Variegata' has golden-veined leaves and *M. citrata* (bergamot mint) has reddish-purple flowers and bronze-green leaves. Dip the stem ends in boiling hot water.

Mesembryanthemum

Flower/Su

These are short-stemmed colourful summer bedding flowers with papery petals. They may also be grown in the greenhouse or in pots. The most popular species, *M. crinifolium* (which really belongs to another genus, *Dorotheanthus*) has the habit of shutting up at night. Still, the texture and colourfulness of the flowers make them well worth while in unusual arrangements.

Miniature arrangements

The same principles apply when arranging miniatures as when doing larger vases. All the flower stems should flow from a centre point and appear to sit happily in the container. The whole arrangement is simply just on a smaller scale.

The preparation of the container needs care, and damp sand or a tiny piece of Oasis will often hold the flowers satisfactorily. Wire netting is out of the question. A keen eye is needed to spot containers that will hold miniatures—silver snuff boxes, ink stands, small cruets, shells, thimbles, children's doll's house equipment and the gold top of a well-known whisky bottle can be used. The main points to consider are that it remains steady and upright, holds water and is in proportion to the chosen flowers. Anything fitting into a square 6 inches by 6 inches is considered miniature for show purposes. Some people find it easier to arrange miniatures by holding the plant materials in small tweezers. This is all right, but do not bruise the stems.

Flowers suitable for this type of arrangement include: roses—'Josephine Wheatcroft' and 'Cecile Brunner' are good examples; cyclamen— *C. neapolitanum* or *C. coum*; narcissus—(*N. jonquilla*); snowdrop, gentian, leontopodium,

muscari, erica, small pieces of shrub in flower and berry, tiny immature leaves, pieces of succulent sedum, etc. seedheads, wild grasses.

Try to get as many different shapes, colours and textures in your miniatures. Little mixed foliages, berries and seedheads can be so attractive. Tiny mixed border flowers are also pretty. Keep a good colour sense as you would with ordinary arrangements. Remember to top up frequently with water.

Many flowers can be used in miniatures. It is from the rock garden, alpine house, and the annual border that you will find your main supply, but miniature bulbs, the hedgerow and field will supply many items for use. For example, a small blade of grass can be used as one would use phormium (New Zealand flax) leaves. May blossom can be divided down into individual flowers, and the same thing can be done with many compound flowers, and these take the place of blooms in a large group. Side shoots and secondary shoots provide smaller flowers. The individual flowers of horse chestnut blossoms for instance look like miniature *Lilium auratum* blooms. As many of the pieces of material are small and immature, they need very careful preparation before use, as mentioned in the article on Water.

As the overall arrangements are small, they must be prominently displayed to make them show up. They look well in a glass china cabinet or in groups of two or three on a small table. Miniatures are extremely popular and appear in most show schedules, but are not so often found in the home.

Mimosa/Mimosa pudica

Although this term is often used to describe the yellow blossoms of *Acacia dealbata* the name properly refers to the sensitive plant *Mimosa pudica*, a pot plant for the greenhouse or for a warm, sunny window sill. It has pink flowers and delicate pale green leaves which close up at the touch of a finger, a propensity which always fascinates children. See also Acacia.

Moluccella/bells of Ireland

Flower/Seed/Su

M. laevis is a half-hardy annual and the spikes of tiny white flowers cupped in green, white-veined calyces are quite unique and excellent when freshly cut for green groups, or for winter arrangements when dried by hanging the flowers upside down (after removing the leaves).

Monarda/bergamot

Flower/Su

To be distinguished from bergamot mint, bergamot or sweet bergamot grows well in moist soils and has tufted mops of rich red flowers. Dip the stem ends in boiling hot water.

Monstera see House Plants

Morina/whorl flower

Flower/Leaf/Seed/Su

White and pink flowers in whorls surrounded by prickly bracts on tall spiny-edged, bluish-green leaves are to be seen on *M. longifolia*. The flowers are excellent for summer arrangements and the seedheads can be dried by hanging upside down.

Mosses

Sphagnum moss, which differs considerably in structure and appearance from other mosses is probably best known as the source of peat, formed from the accumulation of its old dead stems. It has many uses in flower arrangement: for lining hanging baskets; for covering pans of seeds which require darkness and moisture for their germination; for wrapping around the stems of cuttings, which are then placed in polythene bags to retain their freshness until ready to plant or before being packed and sent through the post; and for covering the compost in bowls of tulips and hyacinths, where it is held in place by hair pins and greatly improves the appearance of the display. Wire supports for floral arrangements can be hidden by moss, the flower stems being pressed through the moss into the wire which will hold them in place. Sphagnum moss is found in most woodlands and boggy moors; it may be kept moist and fresh for long periods if placed in a polythene bag.

The club mosses are extremely lovely. Their almost prostrate stems are clothed in tiny pointed leaves which gives them the appearance of dwarf heathers. They are divided into the two main groups, lycopodiums and selaginellas. The former have imbricated (overlapping) leaves, spirally arranged and of similar shape; selaginel-las have leaves of two sizes which differ in form. On careful inspection it will be noticed that between the noticeable leaves there are minute tooth-like leaves, resembling bracts.

The club mosses are charming if planted in pans. They are shallow rooting and require room to spread but they must have plenty of fresh air and ample supplies of moisture during summer. To keep them fresh, syringe them twice daily. They should also be shaded from the direct rays of the sun. To grow them successfully, they should be removed from wherever they are found growing, together with the rooting material attached to their roots, and they should be planted into a similar compost or one made up of

Narcissus triandus 'Albus' make a delicate arrangement very different from the type of arrangement usually achieved with narcissi.

leaf mould and sand in equal parts. Remove them with a trowel so as not to damage the roots and merely press them into the surface of the newly prepared compost, over which has been scattered a thin layer of sand. From then onwards keep them comfortably damp though they will require little artificial moisture during the winter months. The best time to remove the mosses is late in summer to allow them time to become re-established before winter. It should be said that quite small pieces may be removed from their natural habitat and when replanted will quickly form new roots. They are increased by lifting small pieces and dividing them before replanting 3 inches apart. Established plants will benefit from an occasional top dressing of leaf mould and peat. If the plants should become untidy cut them back. They will quickly come again and take on a new richness of colouring.

Of the lycopodiums, *L. selago* is a beauty. Known as the fir club moss, it makes a tufted plant with forked stems 3 inches tall. *L. annotinum* is equally fine with 5 inch stems clothed in emerald-green leaves, and it bears its tiny clubs, or spikes, or spore-carrying cones, at the ends of the shoots.

L. obscurum (syn. *L. dendroideum*) is an exquisite little plant. It is the ground pine of North America, in appearance like a tiny Christmas tree. It has an erect stem 6 inches high and clothed in brilliant green leaves which shine like those of the spruce fir. It requires the warmth of a fern case or a carboy to see it at its best. The stagshorn or common club moss, *L. clavatum* is interesting in that the cones are borne at the end of twin shoots which branch from near the end of the stems to give them the appearance of stag's-horns. Like most of the club mosses, it is mostly found in hilly country where the climate is mild and damp. Likewise the dainty lesser clubmoss, *Selaginella selaginoides*, which does well in bottle gardens. It grows only 1–2 inches tall with branched stems, at the ends of which appear tiny club-like cones.

The selaginellas are of more creeping habit than the lycopodiums, and of those which do well in bottles, *S. denticulata* has exceptional beauty. It forms a tuft of brilliant green, the stems being tipped with silver. *S. lepidophylla* has stems like tiny cedar trees, and *S. laevigata* has metallic-blue foliage and is of climbing habit, suitable for the fern case. *S. apoda* forms a plant of vivid green with dense moss-like growth. Like most of the

selaginella family it requires a warm humid atmosphere.

They may be used to plant with those ferns requiring similar conditions, when they will carpet the soil around them and beautify every spare inch which would otherwise be unused.

Muscari/grape hyacinth
Flower/Sp

Rather untidy bulbs in the garden, but the compact blue, rounded heads last quite well, and are good in small spring arrangements. They can be forced in pots for early flowering and grown in window boxes. Dry the seedheads standing upright in glasses.

Myosotis/forget-me-not
Flower/Sp/Su

Cheerful tiny blue flowers with yellow eyes on bushy little plants which are all too often forgotten. They are charming when seen in small china or porcelain containers. They are somehow associated with childhood either because of their diminutive size or because of their habit of materialising in remote parts of the garden where they are freely picked by children. There are many good modern varieties grown, such as 'Blue Bouquet', and one or two are winter-flowering.

Myrtus/myrtle
Flower/Leaf/Su

The link between marriage and the myrtle shrub is perhaps owing to its white flowers which often grace bridal bouquets. To get the flowers earlier in the year they are sometimes forced under glass. The attractive dark green leaves are fragrant if pinched. *M. communis* (common myrtle) is quite hardy in mild, sunny places. Hammer the stem ends when using the leaves for arrangements.

Narcissus/daffodil
Flower/Leaf/Wi/Sp

There are literally thousands of varieties of daffodils and some 500 are grown commercially. The trumpet-shaped yellow flowers are very popular, but it is the less well-known varieties, such as those known as tazettas, which are of

Hydrangea heads, achillea, teazles, acanthus seeds,
wheat, and the leaves and seed heads of lime and
beech preserved in glycerine make this a striking
autumn arrangement.

A china cupid supports a scallop shell containing
roses, anemones, freesias. Such arrangements must
be carefully proportioned so that they are neither too
large nor too small for the container.

A masterpiece of simplicity created by Constance
Spry herself. Here the deeper colourings of the
passion flowers are picked up by the cobea and the
velvet on the gilt Victorian hassock.

A simple but effective combination of daffodils, tulips, mimosa and pussy willows

Narcissus are among the most popular of spring flowers, being the true harbingers of spring. (a) 'King Alfred', one of the large flowered varieties. (b) Pheasant's eye narcissi are really more suitable for flower arranging.

a

b

greater interest to the flower arranger. Remember that though they are hardy in cold outdoor conditions, daffodils do not take well to the sudden change to warm room temperatures, especially if there are draughts. This is not to argue against using daffodils—there are no better flowers and the sight of golden yellow blooms standing proudly on the pinholder is unbeatable.

For early daffodils in the house it is a good plan to put a few bulbs in bulb fibre in a large pot and submerge it under earth or ashes about six inches deep in the garden in autumn. See HOUSE PLANTS (Pot Plants).

The hybrids of the 'wild' daffodil *N. poeticus* (pheasant's eye) type, which has white petals and a yellow eye, are excellent for mixing with other material and last well in water in cool conditions. Steep them overnight before arranging. The same applies to tazettas, such as 'Yellow Cheerfulness' and 'Bridal Crown' (a double white variety).

The large, trumpet-mouth yellow flowers, such as those of 'King Alfred' or 'Unsurpassable' need to be more carefully arranged. Forsythias, catkins and golden-variegated house plant foliage match them, and they look superb on their own with a few of their own leaves.

The miniature daffodils, such as *N. cyclamineus* and *N. triandus albus* ('Angel's Tears') are excellent in small arrangements.

Daffodils do not like deep water, but remember that if they are out of water for any length of time the stem ends will dry up and must be cut when reinserting in water.

Nemesia

Flower/Sp/Su

Bright, usually bicoloured flowers in cream and yellow, scarlet and orange, etc. appear on short stems. The iridescent colours attract far more attention than their size would lead one to expect. They are grown as half-hardy annuals, boxes of the young plants being sold by nurserymen in large quantities for window boxes and borders. As a cut flower, they are good in small arrangements. Dip the stem ends in boiling hot water.

Neoregelia see House Plants (Palms)

Nepeta/catmint, catnip

Flower/Sp/Su

Long-lasting in water, the bluish-grey flowers appear on long rather untidy spikes. Catmint is often seen in country gardens filling up gaps in borders and hedges. The rather quiet quality of the flowers makes them suitable for setting off other flowers such as pinks.

Nerine/Guernsey lily

Flower/Sp

Nerines have such rich flowers—bright rose-pink, crimson, white, or orange-scarlet, the petals splay out like curling woodshavings on large umbels. They are bulbous plants, generally grown in the cool greenhouse, and they make a vivid contrast to the somewhat more sombre autumnal colours. *N. bowdeuii*, and the selected forms 'Pink Triumph' and 'Pink Giant', as well as the white *N. flexuosa* 'Alba' are almost frost-hardy. They will also add colour to a bowl of white chrysanthemums and carnations. Dip the stem ends in boiling hot water.

Nerium see House Plants (Palms)

Nicotiana/tobacco plant

Flower/Su

Long-tubed flowers of red, white, or cream appearing on tall rather lax stems are the common types, but there are a number of modern cultivars with greenish-yellow flowers which are popular among flower-arrangers. They are good garden flowers—some species being fragrant at night and closing their flowers during the day, others remaining open during the day.

Nigella/love-in-a-mist

Flower/Leaf/Seed/Su

Bearing small blue flowers which appear against a delightful tracery of feathery foliage, the fennel flower (as it is sometimes called) has also given rise to crimson and white flowered varieties in recent years. Both the foliage and flowers help to create a hazy effect in summer flower arrangements, and when the seedheads are ripe, strip off the foliage and hang the stems upside down to get some of the most distinctive material for winter dried arrangements.

Nymphaea/water-lily

Flower/Su

Though the colours of the large, immaculate, pointed petals are gorgeous: pinks, oranges, reds, violets, as well as pure white, the tendency of the flowers to close up after picking is enough to exclude them from ordinary flower arrangements. They may stay open long enough to use for a table arrangement during a meal, and the Japanese apparently have a method of keeping the flowers open by filling the stems with pure alcohol. It is possible to plug the stem ends with sealing wax. The flowers can be persuaded to remain open when picked if tiny drops of hot wax are dropped into the centre of the flower.

Oenothera/evening primrose

Flower/Seed/Sp/Su

The strongly-scented pale yellow flowers of *O. biennis* give rise to the name of evening primrose because they open in the evening. There are also pink, red and white forms. They go well with other yellow and pink flowers, such as pyrethrum, and last well in water, though it is best to dip the stem ends in boiling hot water for about a minute. The seedheads are dried upside down after stripping the leaves.

Olearia/New Zealand daisy bush

Flower

Big clusters of white, daisy-like flowers are sometimes seen near the seaside where the milder climate suits these small evergreen trees or shrubs. Hammer the stem ends, or remove about an inch of bark from them.

Onopordon/cotton thistle, Scot's thistle

Flower/Leaf/Seed/Su

Giant thistles (*O. nervosum*, syn. *O. arabicum*, may grow to over 7 feet), the leaves and stems being covered with whitish hair, they are perennial or biennial. The Scot's thistle (*O. acanthium*) is more manageable in size and suitable for large gardens where it may reach over 4 feet in height. The grey spiny leaves are a deeper colour and more attractive in winter than the larger species, but are best used when young, their size when fully grown precluding them from use in any but large arrangements. The greyish-blue colours of the leaves mix well but the effect of the plant is perhaps rather sombre; it is regarded as a traditional symbol of the 'Fall of man', and for that reason the large heads and leaves are suitable for church decoration. The flowers are purple and the seedheads may be dried upside down.

Oreodoxa see House Plants (Palms)

Origanum/pot marjoram, sweet marjoram

Delicate purple or white heads of flowers with aromatic leaves (if rubbed) may be used for small arrangements. Singe or dip the stem ends in boiling hot water.

Ornamental vegetables

Rarely do we give much thought to the use of vegetables in flower arranging, yet a walk round the kitchen garden can be most rewarding in this respect. There may be seen the feathery fronds of asparagus fern, one or two sprays of which may be cut without it being detrimental to the future vigour of the plants; tree onions on their long slender stems which are so interesting where used with rushes and grasses; and purple kale to cut in early autumn to provide an admirable foil for the green-flowering *Moluccella laevis* (bells of Ireland), Zinnia 'Envy' and pale yellow dahlias. Nor is it necessary to have a garden to enjoy the ornamental vegetables.

Tree onions, a form of common onion, may be grown in pots or in boxes containing a 6-inch depth of soil and placed on a terrace or in the sunny corner of a courtyard; likewise the flowering cabbage which makes a most attractive pot plant. Swiss chards too, may be grown in pots when they will grace a sunny window with their handsome leaves and stems and colourings of ruby-red and purple.

Kohlrabi is not usually associated with flower arranging, but the apple-like 'bulbs' of brilliant purple which appear at the end of tall stems are admirable where used with globe artichokes with their ball-shaped heads of purple overlapping scales, all arranged with a base of rosy-mauve cabbages.

When better known, the brilliant golden beetroot, which also has golden chard-like stems, will be grown for its value in flower arrangements as well as for its own particular flavour. It does not 'bleed' like most red beets do and so keeps its bright guinea-gold colouring for many weeks. It makes an original table decoration used with 'Table Queen' or 'Acorn' marrow with its bright green channelled fruits, in size and shape like cocoa pods. They will retain their colour if dried slowly and may be pierced at the pointed end with a thin green stick, cut to any length required, when they will take on the appearance of green lanterns. 'Butternut' squash with its buff-yellow skin may be used with it. It forms a hard skin and retains its colour and form through the winter, its bottle-shaped fruits being most interesting.

The capsicum 'Yolo Wonder' forms a large fruit which changes in colour from deepest green to scarlet and provides a brilliant splash of colour for winter table decoration. The variety 'Chameleon' is equally striking, the conical fruits taking on almost every imaginable colour. The hot pepper known as 'Large Cherry' may be grown as a pot plant like the solanum or winter cherry (see main list), and equally attractive grown in this way is 'Long Red Cayenne' with its curled and twisted fruits of crimson-red which may be removed and dried and used for the base of a table decoration.

Almost all these vegetables are suitable for autumnal and winter decoration and they are valuable for floral arrangement because they are available when flowers are scarce. The long-keeping winter squashes should be grown in preference to the soft-skinned summer varieties and they should be harvested and stored with care. Likewise the root crops which if carelessly lifted will deteriorate quickly and will be unsightly in floral arrangement. The ornamental cabbages and kales are best grown in as cool conditions as possible, for their colours are richer where this is so. Most vegetable crops colour better in cooler temperatures, but allowance should be made for this when sowing seed.

Vegetables for flower arrangement

SWISS CHARD Also known as seakale beet, it is one of the most handsome of all vegetables both in the garden and where used for indoor decoration. The variety 'Ruby' has a rhubarb-like stem of bright ruby-red, the colouring extending into the veins of the dark green crumpled leaves. For contrast, 'Fordhook Giant' has pure white stems extending into the broad white mid-ribs of the silver-green leaves. The variety 'Rainbow' is even more striking, its leaves taking on various shades of orange, red, purple, pink and yellow. The outer stems may be removed and used for indoor decoration. They should be pulled away from just above the crown of the plant, almost at ground level, when new stems will appear.

Sow seed in April and thin to 12 inches apart to allow the leaves room to develop. Chards grow well in any soil but the young plants require copious amounts of moisture to produce thick succulent stems 18 inches tall. The first leaves and stems will be ready to remove towards the end of summer and there will be a continuous supply until late in the following summer when the plants usually run to seed; but by then plants from a fresh sowing will be ready to take their place. There will thus be a never-ending supply available for use.

ORNAMENTAL CABBAGE Originally raised for the flower arranger, the vivid red heads of some and the contrasting white of other varieties may be used as a strikingly colourful base, or they provide an unusual edging to a flower border. The two colours may also be used for summer bedding for the plants extend to 12 inches across and retain their form for many weeks, being at their best during autumn when the cooler weather intensifies their colouring.

The ornamental cabbage and variegated kales make up an attractive window box display for a position which does not face due south. Plant the cabbages (in alternate colours) at the front of the box 6 inches apart and the kales at the back. The flowering kales, which grow 20–24 inches tall, assume the same colourings and may also be used at the centre of a flower bed, surrounded with the flowering cabbages.

The seed should not be sown before April 1st, the young plants being set out late in May with other bedding plants. They will then not run to seed but will be at their best when the weather becomes cooler. They may also be grown on in pots, inserted into the ground to prevent excessive moisture evaporation and may be taken indoors in early September and placed in a sunny window. They will retain their colour until Christmas.

When cut and used indoors, it is necessary to place them in a cool room otherwise they will quickly deteriorate.

GOLDEN BEET It is delicious when boiled or pickled in malt vinegar, and most striking for floral decoration. The globular roots which attain the size of a grapefruit (though for culinary purposes they should be lifted when much smaller) are of brilliant golden-yellow, the colour extending into the ribs and veins of the leaves in the manner of Swiss chard, a closely related plant which may be used in a similar way. Where using for decorative purposes, the colourful leaves are best left on the roots; upon lifting, scrape away the fibres and clean with a damp cloth. If the globular roots are then wiped with a cloth soaked in olive oil, they will take on an additional brilliance which will be retained for many weeks.

Sow the seed in drills 1 inch deep in a sandy soil late in April and thin out the seedlings to 3 inches apart, later removing alternate plants as the roots continue to swell. Keep moist during summer and lift the first roots in July when of tennis-ball size. Lift as required but not later than early October and store in boxes of dry sand until wanted.

ROOT CROPS The long tapering roots of carrots, the parsnip and salsify may be used for decorative purposes, likewise the pencil-like roots of scorzonera. Long straight roots are required and this means sowing in a well-prepared soil. Lift with care and scrub clean before using.

GLOBE ARTICHOKE Besides being a great delicacy, it is perhaps the most handsome of all vegetables and with its globular heads of purple (or green) overlapping segments (like a lily bulb) and large fern-like leaves of silvery-green, it makes a handsome indoor decoration. For this purpose, the stems should be cut (almost to the base) when the heads are quite small for then the leaves will be at their best. They make a beautiful indoor display when used with sea holly (*Eryngium maritimum*) and globe thistles (*Echinops ritro*) for both have similar spiny leaves of silvery-purple colouring. Together they make a striking display in a large earthenware jar and may be used like everlasting flowers, entirely without water, when they will retain their beauty for many weeks. They may also be grown together in the border for they require similar conditions, i.e. a sandy soil and an open, sunny situation, being native of the sandy shores of north Africa.

Globe artichokes are best grown from suckers which are potted and placed in a frame to winter, or they may be planted directly into the

Ornamental gourds in yellows, oranges and many shades of green make a vivid contrast with the sprays of pure white snowberries.

border, protecting them during winter with bracken or conifer branches. Keep them well supplied with moisture during summer.

TREE ONION (*Allium cepa* 'Aggregatum') Producing little clusters of bulbs at the end of stems which, if grown against a trellis, attain a height of 5 feet or more, they are completely hardy and may be used throughout the year both for culinary purposes and for indoor decoration. The terminal clusters of dark brown onions, each measuring less than 1 inch across, make an arresting display in late autumn and winter mixed with hips and haws and sprays of berries.

The tree onion grows in any well-drained soil. To propagate, remove the clumps of bulbs late in summer and plant them as they are, after first making the surface of the soil level and compact and merely pressing them in like shallots. Plant 12–15 inches apart.

SPROUTING BROCCOLI 'Curtis's Perennial White-sprouting' and 'Christmas Purple-sprouting' are not only invaluable as winter 'greens' but will provide material for indoor display at a time of year when it is most scarce. As both forms grow 3 feet in height, the 'flowers' may be cut with long stems. They should be used only in a very cool room when they will remain fresh for a considerable time; they quickly deteriorate in a warm atmosphere.

MARROWS, GOURDS AND SQUASHES Those grown for winter use have hard skins which enable them to be stored until ready to use as table decoration or for culinary purposes. The fruits must remain on the plant until matured but must be removed before the frosts and late autumn rains. Remove with an inch of stem attached and handle carefully so as not to bruise. Store on trays or shelves in a temperature of 45–50°F (7–10°C).

The highly colourful 'Turk's Turban' squash is a globular fruit about 9 inches across. At the stem end is a large 'button' from which radiate stripes of scarlet or orange and which show up brightly against the dark green skin which later changes to orange and is spotted with cream or white. The 'Buttercup' squash is almost as

Tree peonies have the largest flowers of any hardy shrub, often the size of dinner plates, and come in a wide range of brilliant colours.

striking, the turban-shaped fruits being about 6 inches across with a dark green skin and radiating silver stripes. 'Gold Nugget' makes a small round fruit of brilliant orange. The 'Acorn' squash has deeply channelled fruits like cocoa pods of darkest green. The skin of 'Royal Acorn' turns orange in storage while that of the 'Butternut' squash with its peculiar bottle-shaped fruits turns from cream to a rich buff or straw colour with keeping.

The squashes may be used for grouping around the base of a display or ornamental grasses and corn tied in small sheaves and they are most colourful used in groups perhaps as a display for the dinner table.

See also Fruits, Nuts and Vegetables.

Ornithogalum/star of Bethlehem

Flower/Sp/Su

Star-like white flowers are typical of this greenhouse or hardy bulb. The dense spikes of white chincherinchee flowers (*O. thyrsoides*) are often sold in florists' shops at Christmas and last particularly well as cut flowers. Such flowers are generally imported, for they must be greenhouse grown to flower at Christmas. The star of Bethlehem (*O. umbellatum*) is hardy and tends to grow prolifically. It produces its flowers on umbels in May. *O. nutans* is another fine species with whitish-green flowers in June.

Osmanthus/fragrant olive

Flower/Leaf/Sp/Su/Au

Rather holly-like leaves and small, strongly scented white flowers in clusters are typical of this evergreen shrub or small tree. *O. delavayi* (also known as *Siphonosmanthus*) is particularly noted for its strongly scented flowers which are useful in spring arrangements. Different species bloom at different times and are mostly hardy. Hammer the stem ends.

Paeonia/peony

Flower/Seed/Sp

These large, often showy flowers are rather like opulent roses appearing in May. They have decorative long leaves and the flowers appear in many different shades from rich golden yellow to plum red, pink and white. Nothing can be better in spring than a bowl of the dark red

134

flowers with their own foliage and perhaps a few flowers of chives or marguerites. Among the first to flower is the tree peony (*P. suffruticosa*), which is hardy in sheltered positions. Tree peonies have woody stems, may reach over 6 feet in height and can produce 300 or more flowers each season when mature. The individual blooms can be more than 18 inches across. The original species has rose-pink to white flowers with maroon blotches, and there are hybrids in many other colours.

Among the sub-shrubby kinds *P. delavayi* grows over 4 feet and bears smallish, velvety-crimson flowers which go well with elder blossom, etc.

The large-flowered herbaceous varieties of peony have been derived from *P. lactiflora* and the common peony, *P. officinalis*. They are difficult to arrange because the heads tend to hang down and it may be necessary to prop up the stems. The more woody parts of the stem will serve for this, the props being hidden by the large flowers and foliage. Among the best double varieties grown for cut flowers, *P. lactiflora* 'Edulis Superba', has rose-pink flowers with silvery margins. 'Alice Harding', another double-flowered variety, has very pale-pink, fragrant flowers with creamy centres and finely formed foliage. An early variety with flowers with long-lasting properties, the fragrant 'Mons. Jules Élie', has lilac-rose flowers good for cutting. 'Sarah Bernhardt' with large apple blossom pink flowers has long stems and is very decorative. 'Duchesse de Nemours' has almost rose-scented incurved flowers which are in subtle shades of white and creamy yellow.

Of the single-flowered varieties 'Eva' has fine rose-pink blooms and *P. lactiflora* 'Whitleyi Major' has blush-white flowers and good foliage. When picking herbacious peonies, first strip the leaves and then dip the stem ends in boiling hot water. Hammer the stem ends of the woody varieties and give both as long a drink as possible. You can dry the flowers in a borax box when they start to come into full bloom.

Palms see (House Plants): Palms

Pansy

Flower/Sp/Su/Au/Wi

It seems a shame to pick these flowers which look so cheerful in the garden in late winter and early spring, but you will find that picking them only seems to make the plants produce more and more flowers. Pansies belong to the same family as violas. They are grown as summer bedding plants and many strains have been produced by crossing *Viola tricolor*, obtaining some outstandingly colourful varieties. The seeds are sown at different times according to the periods they are required to flower. The main difficulty with pansies is to stop them flagging after arranging. It is a good idea to steep the heads in cold water or spray regularly with a water atomiser after a good drink. See also Viola.

Papaver/poppy

Flower/Seed/Sp/Su

There are several kinds of poppies (there are 100 species of annuals and perennials) and all make good cut flowers provided the leaves are stripped and the stem ends are singed or dipped in boiling water to prevent the milky sap from escaping. Follow this by giving the stems a good drink of cold water.

In June the petals of the perennial Oriental poppies (*P. orientale*) look like delicate shot silk, and their colours are generally smoky shades of white or red with dark blotches at the bases of the flowers. These are followed by the annuals, corn poppies (*P. rhoeas*), especially Shirley poppies, lighter in tone and with many varied colours, and *P. somniferum*, the Opium poppy, which includes the peony-flowered and carnation-flowered kinds.

The perennial Iceland poppies (*P. nudicaule*) make excellent cut flowers in orange, yellow, white, etc., including some with picotee edges. Like all the poppies it is best to pick them early in the day and well before they are fully in flower as petal fall is all too soon even after taking the above-mentioned precautions. It is best to dry the seedheads by standing them upright in a vase when green.

Parthenocissus/Virginia creeper

Leaf/Au

Although the leaves are decorative in autumn, looking rather like maple leaves, turning into shades of golden-red, yellow and orange, they tend to curl after being picked. The only way to ensure this does not happen is to press them between several sheets of paper under a pile of books for a day or so.

Party arrangements

The word party gives one an immediate impulse to arrange flowers in a special way and the style of the flowers should be suited to the occasion. It could be that the party is for children, for a small luncheon, or for a very large gathering of people, but whatever the reason for holding a party, the same amount of care and planning will be necessary. The flowers should help to add gaiety to the occasion, and should act as a talking point and make an impression immediately you enter the room.

They should fit into the general decoration of the surrounding features and not stand out like a sore thumb. Over decorating will spoil the whole effect. Incongruous arrangements will jar.

For children the theme should be gay and simple, the table flowers and novelties should be arranged in some way that perhaps each child on leaving can take a little part of the overall setting home. I can think straightaway of a

Party arrangements. Freesias and variegated hosta leaves together with lumps of rough glass make an unusual table centre arrangement.
Party arrangements. This is a table centrepiece in the grand manner. The arrangement has been created in two meat dishes, with the lids removed and used for decoration.

Pedestal arrangement. Arrangements placed in corners, particularly when there is a strong diagonal line behind them, are particularly difficult. Here the problems have been overcome superbly well.

maypole in the centre of the table, or a low basket filled with simple flowers and from this ribbons to each place; sitting at the end of each ribbon could be a tiny basket of flowers. Perhaps for Christmas, a tree of small baubles and crackers in the centre of the table and again ribbons across the table with a cracker for each person at the end.

It is better to have one or two large arrangements than lots of small things about the room. The mantelshelf is ideal because it is up high and flowers cannot easily get knocked over. The arrangement should be kept low, flowers should flow well over the front of the vase. Pick up the colour of some special feature in the room, perhaps the curtains or maybe the picture above it. Another excellent place is an alcove in the corner of the room should one be available. The flowers will still show up when the room is full of people. Table flowers should be kept in keeping with the occasion and a polished table always gives a more pleasing effect than a white tablecloth which tends to kill the effect of flowers. For summer parties or parties in the garden a gaily coloured cloth can be most pleasing with a contrasting colour to the flowers. There is no end to the scope of this type of display but time is necessary to plan it well.

Pedestal arrangements

First see that the pedestal is firm and standing level, then set the vase on it. An urn-shaped vase or large bowl is excellent for pedestal arrangements. Secure the wire netting (2-inch mesh for choice) to the vase, by tying it in and clipping some pieces over the container. If your material is on the short side, it will be necessary to use flower tubes or cones. These are made of metal, shaped like an ice-cream cornet and painted; 8-inch and 10-inch are the best sizes. They should be fixed to long pieces of stick (not bamboo or metal stakes, because these slip round in the netting). Wire them firmly, painting the wood green to match the tubes. A little netting in each tube may be useful. Build up a framework of tubes; three to five may be necessary in a large arrangement. They should not show when the vase is well arranged.

Next get your foliage for the background and make an outline with it. The type used will depend on the background and also the flowers to go with it. Camellia, beech, eucalyptus and stripped lime are four favourites. This foliage should all flow from a centre point, making the flowers, when finished, all appear to sit well in the vase. After fixing the height, fix the width. For a large facing arrangement, go three-quarters of the way back in the vase with the foliage. Make use of good interestingly shaped pieces of foliage and those flowering in the correct way for use over the edges. It may be necessary to prune and thin it a little.

There are no set rules on how one should continue. It is best to set the centre of the vase, coming well over the front edge. It is important to break the line between vase and flowers and have flowers flowing downwards, giving the vase a good chest. Group your colours and shapes, tending to keep the larger and darker ones to the centre, as these appear to look heavier. Use good large leaves for the centre to clean it up. All flowers should be seen clearly. So do not overcrowd. Watch your colour groupings and do not form blocks of them, but bring them through in sweeps of colour. Watch that stems do not cross, but continue to flow from the centre. Some trails of foliage, such as ivy, are very useful and can be placed over the edge of the vase. If the vase has to look more than just a facing arrangement, put a few of the flowers at the back flowing outwards: this makes it appear to be all round. For lightness, set the flowers at different depths. Make use of buds. After finishing the arrangement, fill up the tubes to overflowing, then top up the vase. Check the water regularly, because flower tubes do not hold much. Watch out for any siphoning, which can easily occur when a leaf is at water level. The leaf draws up the water and continually lets it drip. A fine spray with water will help to make everything look very fresh when arranged.

Pelargonium/geranium

Flower/Leaf/Su

These bright clean-looking flowers of scarlet, crimson, pink, lilac and white, bloom all the summer long in small pots, in the garden, on window sills or, if they are the trailing kind, from hanging baskets. They require hardly any attention and the minimum watering. They are propagated easily by cuttings and the only bugbear is keeping them in winter, when they rot if over-watered or die if allowed to get too cold. Cuttings taken of Zonal pelargoniums in the spring will bloom under glass in the winter.

Although the petals tend to drop off in water they last better than is often realised, especially if the flowers are not disturbed and the dead petals are removed to allow the dormant buds to open. The Zonal and ivy-leaved pelargoniums have particularly attractive foliage. Both flowers and foliage blend easily with most other flowers. They enhance mixed summer arrangements and will also look good on their own using different varieties with their foliage. The variegated foliage is particularly bright. They do best in shallow containers.

The foliage of the oak-leaved pelargonium, *P. quercifolium*, is both decorative and aromatic. The greenhouse-grown Regal pelargoniums produce fine flowers from May to July, making a lot of growth at the same time.

Handling the flowers as little as possible is the best way of making them last in water. See also Geranium (House Plants).

Penstemon/beard tongue
Flower/Su

Rosy-purple, pink, scarlet and blue are typical colours of the long-tubed or bell-shaped flowers of this fairly hardy plant which likes a warm part of the garden. The flowers go well in a vase with delphiniums or other spiky flowers. Dip the stem ends in boiling hot water and give them a good long drink.

Perilla
Leaf

The bronze-purple leaves of *P. frutescens* 'Nankiniensis' are useful for summer flower arrangements. Perillas are half-hardy plants from China. The leaves are fringed and there is a variety with finely cut foliage and another with variegated leaves. Soak the foliage for over an hour in a weak sugar solution.

Pernettya
Berry/Leaf

The bright clusters of pink, purple, red and white autumnal berries of the hardy evergreen shrub *P. mucronata* (commonly grown) are most decorative, different-coloured berries sometimes appearing on the same bush. Hammer the stem ends and immerse the branches in deep water.

Petasites/butterbur
Flower/Leaf

The thick, short, pinky-white flower spikes of *P. fragrans* (winter heliotrope) are sweetly fragrant during the winter months and useful at this time of year with some evergreen foliage. *P. japonicus* 'Giganteus' (giant buttercup) has greenish-white flowers and gigantic leaves which are generally too large for arrangement. Give the flowers a good long drink before arranging.

Petunia
Flower/Leaf/Su

This half-hardy garden flower produces some astonishingly rich colour these days—deep reds and violets with white streaks are among the most striking. The stems are not too long and rather lax and trailing, which makes them suitable for the sides of bowls. There are an enormous number of modern varieties, including such double hybrids as 'Great Victorian Mixed', which has flowers up to 4 inches across. Use them with their own foliage and do not forget to dip the stem ends in boiling hot water and then immerse the stems and leaves in water, overnight if possible.

Peucedanum graveolans/dill
Seed/Leaf/Flower/Su

The aromatic leaves form delicate fern-like sprays and the seeds, rather like fennel, make attractive umbelliferous heads. Dry in an upright position when the seedheads are green.

Pharbitis see House Plants (Trailing Plants)

Philadelphus/mock orange
Flower/Su

Very beautiful intoxicatingly sweet-scented white flowers are typical of this popular, hardy, deciduous shrub. The name syringa, sometimes misapplied to them, is properly attributed to the lilac genus. There are a number of modern hybrids of philadelphus producing arching sprays of double flowers, such as 'Bouquet Blanc' (which is not so tall as the original common mock orange, *P. coronarius*). Remove the leaves, hammer the stem ends, and let the flowers get all the water they can.

Philodendron see House Plants (Trailing Plants)

Phlomis/Jerusalem sage

Flower/Leaf/Seed/Su

There are several different kinds of this evergreen shrub or plant with flowers ranging from purple to yellow. The way the flowers appear between the leaves of some varieties is rather like the common sage. The shrub *P. fruticosa*, Jerusalem sage, has bright yellow flowers at the heads of the stems in single or twin whorls in June and slightly silvery foliage. *P. samia* is a perennial border flower with yellow and orange blooms and seed-pods well worth drying by hanging upside down. *P. herba-venti* looks more like common sage with rather attractive purple and violet flowers. Dip the stem ends in boiling hot water and give the stems a good long drink.

Phlox

Flower/Su

Bright heads of mauves, pinks, purples, reds and whites on long stems of the perennial *P. paniculata* seem ideally suited to vases and groups of other tall flowers, such as lupins, hydrangeas, philadelphus and delphiniums. There are also half-hardy annuals such as those of *P. drummondii*, which includes both medium-tall and dwarf varieties in a wide range of bright colours which mix well in smaller arrangements, or look gay in pots on sills and window boxes. They last well, but hammer the stem ends and give them a long drink, overnight if possible, and once arranged remove the petals which have deteriorated to encourage the younger buds to open.

Phoenix see House Plants (Palms)

Phormium/New Zealand flax

Leaf/Flower/Su

The sword-shaped evergreen leaves of *P. tenax*, which last well in water, may reach over 8 feet long. They are variegated or purplish with cream, red or orange margins and even one or two leaves will look striking, particularly in a green arrangement. They are grown outdoors

Phytolacca clavigera is a singularly useful plant for flower arranging, being decorative in leaf, flower and fruit.

only in milder parts, but they may be potted and brought into the house for short periods. You can cut the leaves from the base upwards to get the size you want.

Phygelius/Cape fuchsia

Flower/Su/Au

Tube-shaped orange-scarlet flowers hang down like fuchsias in a most decorative way. They are rather tender evergreen shrubs which come from South Africa. Dip the stem ends in boiling hot water and give them a good long drink.

Physalis/Chinese lantern plant

Seed

The calyces of *P. alkekengi* look rather like little heart-shaped Chinese lanterns, at first green then drying to a bright orange, when they are used for winter decoration in dried arrangements with dried marigolds, everlasting flowers, ornamental grasses, pressed leaves and seedheads. They go well with the bright moon-shaped seed cases of honesty. They are easily preserved: simply remove the leaves and hang upside down to dry.

Phytolacca

Berry/Flower/Su

The berries of the hardy perennial *P. americana* (Virginian poke weed) form thickly round the

Pinks are not among the easiest flowers to arrange.
Here the bi-colour effect of the pinks has been
picked up by the use of variegated hosta leaves.

spikes and are preceded by white flowers. These dark purple shiny berries are most attractive to look at, but the plant has a nasty smell and the seeds are poisonous so it would not be wise to use the berries for displays which can be reached by young children.

Pieris

Leaf/Flower/Sp

Interesting hardy evergreen shrubs with dark-green long, pointed foliage radiating in a fan rather like rhododendron leaves. Astonishingly the new leaves of some species, notably *P. formosa ferrestii*, are bright scarlet when they form in spring. They resemble the bright red bracts which form at the top of poinsettia plants. They are accompanied by delightful drooping or erect clusters of small white or cream flowers. Hammer the stem ends and immerse the stems in deep water for as long as possible. Spray the leaves with water through an atomiser from time to time.

Pilea see House Plants (Palms)

Pinks

Flower/Su

These include the original cottage pinks which have been crossed to obtain the modern garden pinks flowering from June onwards. Not all of them are pink in colour; for instance, the old favourite 'Mrs. Sinkins' is a double white flower, which has given rise to a pink form. Most of the garden pinks come from *Dianthus plumarius*, which crossed with the perpetual-flowering carnation has produced *D. × allwoodii*, with many outstanding varieties in a wide range of colours. These hybrids are also extremely free flowering and tall enough to go with most summer arrangements. There are several other styles of pinks, including Show pinks, London pinks (largely derived from Allwoodii, garden and Herbert's pinks), 'laced' pinks (with a central 'eye' and zonal edge), Imperial pinks (from Allwoodii and Herbert's pinks).

Pinks go well with most other flowers including roses. They seem to combine something of both a highly cultivated flower with a feeling of

naturalness, so that besides matching the modern hybrid roses they will go with pink thyme flowers and sedums. Cut the stems slantwise, and they do need to be stood up to the heads in water for as long as possible. See also Carnations, Dianthus.

Pittosporum

Flower/Leaf/Wi/Sp

The tiny, scented chocolate purple flowers and foliage of this evergreen shrub or tree look good in early spring arrangements. Unfortunately, it is frost-tender—hailing from New Zealand. Hammer the stem ends and give them a long drink, or spray with a water atomiser. The plants need coppicing (see EUCALYPTUS) to produce long, straight leafy shoots.

Platycerium see House Plants (Palms)

Platycodon/balloon flower

Flower/Su

The campanula-like, bell-shaped, mauve-blue flowers on stems up to 1 foot in height are useful for small arrangements in late summer. There is a taller-stemmed variety which blooms earlier, and there are white and pink flowered forms. Dip the stem ends in boiling hot water after stripping some or all of the leaves and give them a long drink.

Platycodon grandiflorum is the most spectacular of all the bell flowers. The individual blooms measure up to 4 in. across, and can be pink, white or blue.

Platystemon/Californian poppy

Flower/Su

These small creamy-yellow flowers, sometimes aptly named cream cups, belong to the poppy family and mix well with poppies. They are hardy annuals reaching about a foot in height. Dip the stem ends in boiling hot water for a minute and then give them a long drink.

Polianthes/tuberose

Flower

The white flowers of *P. tuberosa* have a powerful, sweet scent (the double-flowered type is even stronger-scented). The tubers are not hardy and

Foliage can be used on its own to create effects as interesting as anything that can be achieved with flowers.

the flowers are generally imported in early spring, or grown in the greenhouse for flowering from autumn onwards.

Polyanthus

Flower/Sp/Su

The garden form of the primula, hardy perennials with primrose-like leaves and flowers. The flowers are in many different shades, sometimes 'golden-laced' (edged in gold or yellow). There are many varieties reaching up to a foot in height. Dip the stem ends in boiling hot water and give them a good drink.

Polygonatum/Solomon's seal, David's harp

Flower/Leaf/Sp

P. multiflorum has tall arching leafy stems from which hang greenish-white tubular flowers like rows of little bells in June. It may be grown as a pot plant and looks particularly good in green arrangements with guelder roses. Give them plenty of cool water before arranging and occasionally spray the leaves with a water atomiser. The leaves may be preserved by leaving them in glycerine solution for a couple of days and then hanging upside down.

Polygonum/Russian vine

Flower/Leaf/Su/Au

A varied group of plants including the Russian vine (*P. baldschuanicum*), a vigorous clambering cover plant which bears white or rose-tinted flowers from summer to autumn. For flower arrangers the neat red to rose-pink or white flower-spikes of the garden border species are more interesting. They last well in water. *P. bistorta* 'Superbum' has creamy spikes of flowers, and *P. amplexicaule* has tall rose-pink spikes of autumn flowers. The pink flowers of *P. affine* and *P. vaccinifolium* appear on somewhat shorter spikes and *P. affine* has bronzy leaves in autumn. The flowers may be preserved by hanging upside down. See also Reynoutria.

Pot Plants see House Plants (Pot Plants)

Potentilla/cinquefoil

Flower/Sp/Su

There are shrubby or herbaceous plants with flowers of bright yellow, rose-pink, red, white, etc. The herbaceous kinds have rather short stems, but the shrubby kinds, such as *P. arbuscula*, 'Logan's Form' and *P. fruticosa* are much taller. Dip the stem ends in boiling hot water and immerse the stems themselves in cool water for a long period.

Preservation and dried arrangements

FLOWERS AND SEEDHEADS Most flowers and seedheads are dried with their heads hanging downwards to encourage straight stems; but such things as achillea and honesty can quite easily be dried standing up. When drying flowers upside down tie them into small bunches and hang them out on a line in a dry, warm room just like washing (space can be gained by hanging some bunches on coat hangers).

Another method of drying is in borax or sand, or both together. Borax on its own can be very quick and must be watched carefully: too long in borax will lead to poor colour developing. Sand alone (it must be silver and very dry to start with) works slowly, taking 10 to 21 days. The weight of sand can be damaging to fragile flowers, so it is mainly used for the larger ones, such as zinnias, marigolds and roses.

A mixture of both is more often used in the proportion of two parts borax to one of sand by dry measurement. Carry out the treatment in strong cardboard boxes or polythene bags, placing the mixture carefully all round the stems to be treated. The stems must not be touching each other; and keep to one kind of flower per box or bag. The flowers should rest in the boxes on pillows of cardboard so that the mixture can be evenly placed around the petals and the weight does not squash the flowers. Make a note of the date of packing and watch development carefully.

Some people prefer to stand the flowers upright and sprinkle the mixture round them, resting each flower in a collar of cardboard.

Alternatively the silica gel method may be used. This involves mixing silica gel crystals with cobalt in the proportions of one pound of silica gel to one ounce of cobalt. Make enough of the mixture to fill the shallow box in which you will be drying the plant material. Line the bottom of the box with the mixture and lay the plants on it, flowers facing upwards. Work the mixture in round the flowers, and leave for a week. Conditions must be dry, and if the mixture turns blue that means that its power to absorb moisture from the plant material is exhausted, and the flowers must be transferred to some freshly mixed silica gel.

Many flowers and seedheads may be dried out standing upright in a vase with little or no water. Look up the best way of treating individual plants under the relevant plant articles. See also Everlasting flowers.

FOLIAGE Glycerine is the ideal material for preserving many types of foliage and it is simple to use. Try to obtain a commercial product or crude glycerine which will be less refined and therefore cheaper to use. It should be made up in a solution of 50 per cent glycerine. Mix in boiling water and allow to cool before using. There are various opinions on what is the correct proportion of glycerine to water. Some say one part of glycerine to three parts water is enough. Others say the ratio should be one part of glycerine to two parts of water. Some experts think that they should be in equal proportions. Some people use the solution hot, especially if the foliage is slightly soft and wilted when treatment is starting.

The sprays of deciduous foliage to be treated should be cut when fully mature or 'ripe'. But sprays of beech can be treated when just turning colour. All foliage should receive treatment straight away after cutting. If left too late in the year, or there is a time lag between cutting and treating, an abscission layer forms and the leaves will drop. Select your pieces for good shape and size. You do not want to treat anything that will not be useful later on, because it is a waste of glycerine. The stems should stand in 6 inches to 10 inches of solution, so choose cylinder type containers. Pack the stems in carefully and leave for a few days. The solution will be drawn up through the stems into the leaves and you should keep adding to the solution as it is taken up. The time taken to absorb this solution will vary with the temperature of the room and the condition of the foliage. The foliage will change colour and take on a shiny appearance which is an indication that it is ready. The leaves often turn beautiful shades of bronze, purple and rust. Remove from the solution and allow the stems to dry. The foliage must lose its stickiness before it is used, otherwise it will pick up all the dust and soon be useless. Oak, magnolia, stripped lime, hornbeam all take well and are most attractive. Young eucalyptus can be very beautiful when treated in this way.

PRESSING LEAVES It is important to get materials for pressing at the right stage of development. If too young they are soft and shrivel badly, and if too old and changed in colour, they become brittle. Each individual frond of fern or leaf should be laid flat between layers of newspaper. For special botanical specimens blotting paper is used but newspaper will do perfectly well for everyday use. Allow several layers to build up and then place them under the carpet where they can remain for a few weeks to dry.

Many types of foliage can be treated in this way and, to my mind, there is only one disadvantage: everything comes out so flat that it must be used with other materials to get interest into the group of dried materials.

Dried materials treated in this way will last for many months, in fact, from year to year provided they are kept clean and stored properly when not in use.

Leaves can be preserved, either under the carpet, as described above, placed between sheets of newspaper (this is ideal for ferns also), or another method is by pressing with an iron set as for synthetic fabrics. Place each leaf between pieces of waxed paper, then coat the whole with sheets of newspaper. When you iron it the wax will melt leaving a protective coat on the leaf. Among the leaves suited to this treatment are caladium, hosta and maple.

Autumn-tinted foliage may be preserved by placing the sprays between sheets of newspaper under a carpet for several weeks until quite dry, but do not allow the foliage to remain on the trees for too long. Remove when the leaves are just colouring, and those of the purple-leaved plants before they begin to wither for they will then remain attached to the stems for some time.

SKELETONISING It is possible to skeletonise leaves, but it is not always worth while. There is such a large number that do not come through the processing and they are easy to obtain from your florist.

The procedure to follow is to boil them slowly in a detergent to soften the green tissue yet leave the veining intact. It is important to end the boiling at the right moment. Once soft, remove the pulpy tissue with a knife blade, but do not tear the venation. After the green tissue has been removed, place them in a bleach solution for a short while (about two hours) to get rid of the colour. This will again need care, because too long in the bleach will disintegrate the leaves, yet too short a time will not clear the colour. Place between paper towels to dry, and when dry press between blotting paper to make them flat.

BERRIES Berried subjects can be treated by brushing over with clear shellac and alcohol in equal proportions. This will be invisible when dry and will keep the berries intact for a long time. Hang upside down to dry. (It is better to do this job out of doors, where drips cannot do any damage, and safely away from fires or naked flame.)

FUNGI Various types of fungi can be dried at a

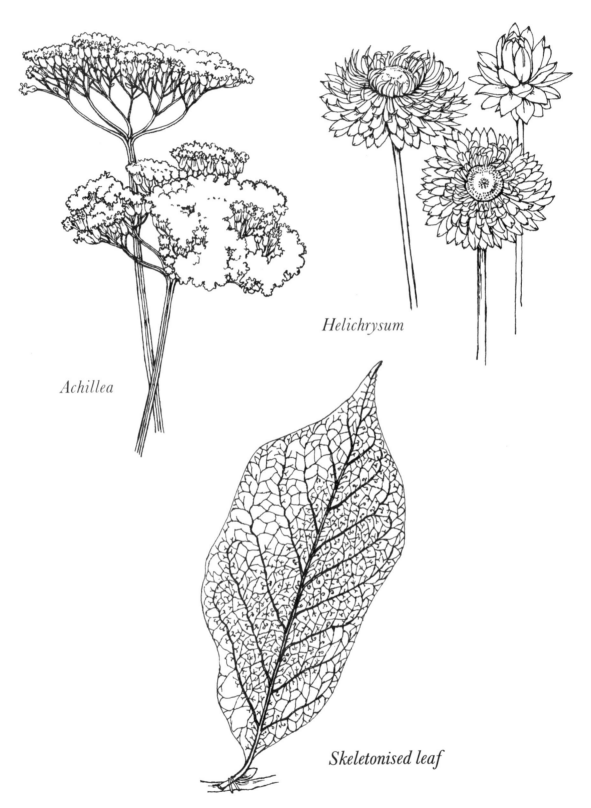

Achillea

Helichrysum

Skeletonised leaf

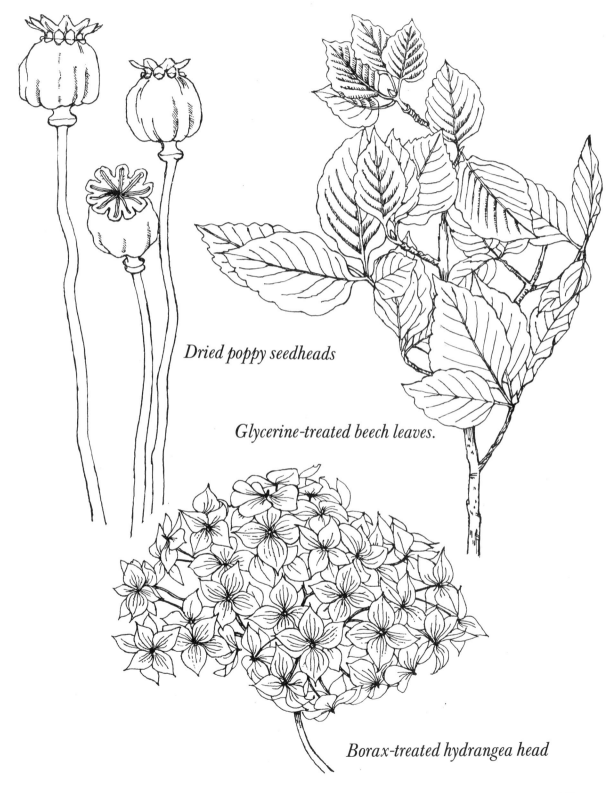

Dried poppy seedheads

Glycerine-treated beech leaves.

Borax-treated hydrangea head

a

Autumn fruits and seed heads can be as effective in their way as flowers. (a) The scarlet berries of *Crataegus corallina.* (b) The feathery seed heads of many clematis species are highly decorative. (c) The translucent pinky-white berries of *Berberis acuminita.* (d) Firethorns (Pyracantha species) produce enormous quantities of yellow, orange or scarlet berries.

b

c

d

Dried seed heads with rose fruits and berberis berries, together with herbaceous peony leaves blend well with late flowering rusty coloured chrysanthemums. The container is a brass oil-lamp stand.

very low temperature in the oven. They may be placed on sheets of brown paper and left three or four hours to dry.

OTHER MATERIAL Acorns, cones and nuts should be allowed to dry out before treating or decorating and moss is dried on sheets of newspaper.

Bulrushes can be sprayed with hair lacquer to stop them splitting. Shellac can also be painted on cones and branches both to preserve them and to give them a lustre.

ARRANGING Dried materials are usually easy to arrange, because one has not to worry about the stems reaching water; in fact, they can be placed into any container that is in keeping with them. As a rule, it is better to keep simple and fairly heavy-looking containers; wood and basket work are excellent, so are copper, brass and heavy stone types. Silver, glass and very ornate china are not in keeping with many of the dried arrangements. Try to sort out your materials into the right colour group for each container. Arranging can simply be done by placing the

stems into the container holding wire netting, or dry Oasis. Sand can also be used for any container that is not well balanced and likely to tip over easily. The same principles apply with fresh flowers. Grade your materials for shape, colour and size; make use of any curved stems and branches to go over the edge of the container. Keep the large flowers towards the centre and get plenty of depth to the vase. No two flowers should be the same length. All stems should flow from the centre of the vase and come out well over the front to break the hard rim of the vase.

DRIED GROUPS The dried flowers used in each arrangement will be chosen according to the shape and type of container and the colouring of the room in which the arrangement is to be displayed. For a colourful display in a stone jug for an oak-panelled dining room, choose from glycerined beech, dried hornbeam, stems of red *Atriplex hortensis*, heads of achillea, poppy and eryngium, a few wood roses (*Ipomoea*) or hydrangea for the centre.

For a narrow-necked cylindrical vase to stand in a niche on a stairway, choose upright stems of oats, wheat, barley and a few stems of other grasses, an arrangment that is all very simple.

A copper trough for a study could be filled

150

with bare branches of beech onto which a few skeletonised leaves have been carefully attached.

For a long-pointed flower group use items of small bulrushes with moluccella and seedheads of poppy or lily. Good round-faced flowers are dried zinnias and achilleas. Another interesting shape is that of the teasel and all these would go together to make an interesting arrangement.

For a table centre, a cone of flowers would be quite pleasing, and this could be made from dried statice, helichrysum, honesty, poppy seedheads, open physalis, small pieces of dried ferns, small imported wood roses, gnaphalium, nigella seed pods, catananche and other fairy flowers (small everlastings such as gnaphalium).

All the arrangements so far suggested have been yellows, reds, browns and straw colours. For an arrangement in a sitting-room requiring pinky colourings, select a chalice vase in a celadon green and into this insert stems of honesty, grasses and statice in mauve and pinks; use wheat and oats for height. The pinky shades of helichrysum help to give weight to the centre; slender stems of rhodanthe also give the right colourings. A few heads of grey poppy, a little dried heather and clematis (if carefully dried) would be quite excellent in a group of this nature. See also Everlasting flowers.

CONTAINERS Wooden containers are particularly suited to simple arrangements of mixed dried foliage, seedheads, wood roses and the yellow-brown flowers of helichrysum. They can take many forms: hollowed out logs, carved bowls, an old tea caddy, etc. At the Constance Spry Flower School there is a beautifully carved top from an old wooden column which has been hollowed out: this is quite excellent for a room with a lot of wood panelling. Baskets of a good simple shape are always popular, and even the ordinary garden trug can look most attractive filled for the winter with preserved flowers, grasses, seedheads and foliage. All manner of baskets are on sale in flower shops and garden centres today: another good source is any shop run by blind or handicapped people's associations.

All the metals are useful; but especially good are copper and brass with their warm colouring that develops over the years from constant cleaning. They will take all the soft browns, greens, yellows and straw colours extremely well. Pewter is excellent for the pinky-mauve colourings found in dried flowers of hydrangea, helipterum, statice, etc.

Preserving Berries see Preservation and Dried Arrangement (Berries)

Primula

Flower/Leaf/Sp/Su/Wi

There are over 500 species of the plant, ranging from the humble primrose and cowslip to the exotic oriental species with their beautiful veined and cut leaves, which generally need greenhouse treatment, and are sold by florists as pot plants for a sunny window sill.

Other hardy species include *P. denticulata* (drumstick primula), which has rather primrose-like leaves and which flowers from March to May with round heads of white or pink on shortish stems. One of the candelabra types, *P. helodoxa* (glory of the marsh) has fine whorls of yellow bell-shaped flowers in June and July and is tall enough to mix in with larger groups. Other beautiful candelabra types include *P. japonica* and *P. pulverulenta*, both 2 to 3 feet high.

The hardy species generally bloom in spring or summer, the greenhouse species in winter or spring. The latter include *P. malacoides*, which has beautiful lavender blue flowers on tallish stems, and *P. obconica*, both of which are available in variety. Dip the stem ends of primulas in boiling hot water and then immerse them in cool water for as long as possible.

Protea

Flower/Seed

Exotic-looking South African shrubs which need greenhouse treatment in areas subject to frost. They are sold by florists. The flowerheads have bright, pointed bracts which look like petals and fibrous-looking centres. Dip the stem ends in boiling hot water and then immerse the stems for as long as possible in warm water.

Pulmonaria/soldiers and sailors, lungwort

Flower/Leaf/Sp

Sometimes the flowers bloom in the late winter when they can be arranged with grape hyacinths or anemones and wild arum leaves or other foliage. The spotted leaves and the flowers, which tend to change their colour from pink to blue (hence the common name), are typical of the genus. Dip the stem ends in boiling hot water and give them a long soak in warm water.

Pulsatilla
Flower/Leaf/Seed/Sp

The flowers and foliage are rather like anemones, except that the foliage of pulsatillas is rather feathery. The flowers have generally similar colours to those of anemones and the hairy seed-heads can be dried by hanging upside down.

Punica/pomegranate
Flower/Leaf/Su

A frost-tender, deciduous shrub which produces rather tubular bright red flowers from June to September. It rarely ripens its fruit in Britain or the north-eastern states of the U.S.A. The rather narrow foliage is attractive as well as the flowers. Hammer the stem ends before arranging.

Pyracantha/firethorn
Berry/Leaf/Flower/Su

The bright orange, yellow or red berries of this evergreen shrub are useful in autumn when they seem to match the sombre colours of autumnal foliage. The white blossom in early summer is also very attractive. Hammer the stem ends and spray or paint the berries and leaves with a transparent cellulose varnish. It will help to preserve the berries, and the leaves will lose less water through transpiration.

Pyrethrum
Flower/Su

This is a member of the Chrysanthemum genus, known as *C. coccineum*. It produces daisy-like flowers in pink, dark purple, etc., which are excellent for cutting and including in mixed arrangements. Dip the crushed stem ends in boiling hot water for over a minute and give the stems a good soak.

Ranunculus
Flower/Leaf/Sp/Su

This genus embraces such humble plants as the buttercup and lesser celandine and the rich double hybrids of the tuberous exotic species, *R. asiaticus*. This species provides the neat rather rose-like flowers of bright red, yellow, pink, orange, or white, which are often sold in florists' shops around Christmas and in spring. They are very attractive and have long been popular with arrangers. The double forms have a compact and shapely look and the single 'button' varieties are also very decorative and rich in colour. Dip the stem ends in boiling hot water and then give them a good soak in cold water. The flowers can be dried in a borax box provided this is done before they are fully blown. See also Preservation (Dried Arrangements).

Reseda/mignonette
Flower/Seed/Su/Au

The hardy annual mignonette, *R. odorata*, has yellowish orange or white spikes reaching up to about a foot in height, and there are a number of varieties with red flowers. If you leave the flowers to go to seed, in October they can be dried by standing in a little water and they will retain their scent for months, or they can be hung upside down to dry.

Reynoutria/knotweed
Flower/Su/Au

These hardy perennials used to be included under *Polygonum. R. japonica* grows quite tall, has woody stems and is often found growing wild. It produces rather feathery-looking sprays of white flowers, usually in autumn. There are a number of cultivated varieties of a more dwarf habit, of which 'Pink Cloud' has flowers with a strong pink colour, and there is another with variegated leaves with patches of creamy yellow, and at first tinged pink. Hammer the stem ends.

Rhododendron
Flower/Leaf/Sp

The brilliant heads of rhododendrons and azaleas (which both belong to the genus *Rhododendron*) are one of the glories of spring, though a few species bloom earlier, such as *R. praecox*, which bears lilac-pink flowers often as early as February.

For large full-shaped flowers of a decorative yellow, *R. campylocarpum* is one of the finest species. Of the hybrids available 'Mrs. W. C. Slocock', and 'Goldsworth Yellow' (apricot to primrose), 'Henry Swaythling' and 'Damaris Logan' (both pale yellow) are good varieties, while 'Hawk var. Crest' is probably the finest yellow hybrid ever raised.

a)

Rhododendrons produce huge colourful flowers which can be difficult to arrange satisfactorily owing to their sheer size and weight. (b) Many species such as *Rhododendron wardii* have much more dainty and manageable flowers than the old hardy hybrids (a).

b)

Of the reds 'Cynthia', a carmine hybrid, has well-formed trusses and 'Doncaster' is scarlet. The lilac 'Grandiflorum' and lilac-with-pink 'Boursault' are both selections of the hardy *R. catawbiense* from North America and have dark green leaves.

The pinks include 'Pink Pearl', a popular hardy hybrid with large flush pink trusses, and 'Mrs. G. W. Leak', which is pink with purplish brown marks. The more humble *R. ponticum* has lilac flowers and may be seen growing in its naturalised state in milder districts.

The Knap Hill and Exbury strains of azaleas are highly cultivated and tall-growing with flowers of many kinds of delicate and exotic colours and shapes. The autumn colours of deciduous azalea foliage are often beautiful.

The Ghent and Mollis hybrids include many fine varieties, such as the double-flowered 'Aida' (rose with a shade of violet). They also include the 'honeysuckle' types, so-called because of the look of the flowers.

The above is only a tiny selection of the different types and varieties from among over 500 species. For the Christmas-flowering azaleas see House Plants (Pot Plants).

Hammer the stem ends and give them a good long soak, occasionally spraying the flowers and leaves, when arranged, with a water atomiser to freshen them.

Rhoicissus see House Plants (Trailing Plants)

Rhus/stag horn sumach

Flower/Seed/Su

The erect flower spikes of the female *R. typhina*, a tree or shrub from North America, stand proudly like dark red Christmas tree candles in autumn. Both the flowers and the seedheads may be used, the seedheads being hung upside down to dry. The autumnal foliage is rich-coloured, but unfortunately does not last well. See also TREES (Rhus).

Ribes/flowering currant

Flower/Leaf/Berry/Sp

The best-known species of the genus is *R. sanguineum* (flowering currant). Like other early-flowering blossoms, such as forsythia, the red flowers can be had earlier by bringing the branches into the house in January and putting them in cold water. Some people do not like their scent but this practice both reduces their aroma and makes their colour more delicate. They can then be used with the early-flowering bulbs. There are several individual varieties of different kinds including a white-flowered variety. There are also a number of other species: *R. alpinum* has bright yellow flowers, others are cream, golden yellow and reddish-purple. The gooseberry, black currant and red currant also belong to this genus, giving decorative foliage, fruits and flowers. Hammer the stem ends and give them a good soak.

Rodgersia

Flower/Leaf/Su

These hardy perennials are really water-loving plants and so want a great deal of attention, which is well worth while for the sake of the unusual foliage and flowers. The pink flowers of *R. pinnata* form their heads at the tops of branching red stems. They can be dried easily by hanging upside down. For fresh arrangements it is best to dip the stem ends in boiling hot water for about a minute and then soak for as long as possible in cool water.

Romneya/Californian tree poppy

Flower/Su

The white satiny flowers of *R. coulteri* are rather like those of poppies with a yellow button of prominent stamens in the centre. The flowers may reach 5 inches across. The slightly untidy perennial plants may be over 7 feet high. Dip the stem ends in boiling hot water before giving the stems a good soak.

Rosa/rose

Flower/Leaf/Berry/Sp/Su/Au

Man's interest in the rose goes back at least 5,000 years and probably a good deal further. As a result, the rose has become one of the most highly bred plants. The magnificent modern hybrid varieties are sometimes rather lacking in scent, but the shape and colour have been refined over the centuries. 'Fold upon fold' was how the poet Shelley described the rose over 150 years ago, and now the colours range with most subtle variations from near blue to all kinds of reds, pinks, whites, yellow and orange. Not everyone

likes the so-called blue roses, such as 'Blue Moon', but there is no doubt that the delicate, often bi-coloured shades of modern roses are a challenge to the arranger.

Nor should all the old shrub roses which reflect bygone tastes be despised. For instance, the old-fashioned roses derived from *R. centifolia* (the rose of a hundred leaves), which can be seen in many paintings of flower arrangements of the Flemish period, will give a period flavour to large groups of summer flowers. The variety 'Fantin-Latour' is named after the nineteenth-century artist who used to revel in painting just such flat, full-petalled blush-pink flowers.

The Bourbon rose was another old-fashioned type which was tremendously popular in the nineteenth century following the introduction of the Chinese strains. 'Louise Odier' has a tidily compact round form of blush pink petals.

R. gallica gave rise to the striped 'Rosa Mundi' (*R. g. versicolor*) in shades of pink and 'Tuscany Superb' with buds of velvety maroon set off on opening by bright yellow stamens comes from the same source. Both are worth trying.

There are many other old shrub roses which will carry a flavour of the past in mixed groups or look delightful on their own. Further introductions of old shrub roses continue to be made, of which 'Constance Spry' (rose pink, mid-summer) has large blooms, a beautiful scent and well-shaped, pointed leaves, coppery when young.

Of the hybrid tea roses which are easily arranged there is a wide choice, including 'Message' (pure white) and 'Super Star' (bright vermilion). Both retain their form well, have good firm stems with not too many thorns. Other good hybrid teas for arranging include 'Beauté', 'Grand'mère Jenny', 'Lady Belper', 'Mischief', 'Miss Ireland', 'Mojave', 'Silver Lining', 'Spek's Yellow' and 'Virgo'. They are all, incidentally, first-class garden varieties.

The modern floribunda roses also provide an excellent choice for the flower arranger. A few of the recommended varieties are 'Apricot Nectar' (light apricot and pink), 'Daily Sketch' (plum red with silver reverse), 'Dearest' (rosy salmon), 'Elizabeth of Glamis' (salmon), 'Evelyn Fison' (red), 'Garnette' (garnet red), 'Golden Treasure' (deep yellow), 'Iceberg' (white), 'Irish Mist' (red), 'Orange Silk' (orange vermilion), 'Paddy McGredy' (carmine), 'Pink Parfait' (pink and cream), 'Queenie' (pink), 'Rosemary Rose' (carmine), 'Sir Lancelot' (apricot), 'Tip

Carnations in an elaborate arrangement using
larkspur, roses and gladioli. The spiky arrangement
goes well with the rather angular wrought iron stand.

An ormolu wall bracket with crystal brilliants makes a sparkling setting for this white rose. It is decorative even when not filled with flowers.

Top' (pink), 'Violet Carson' (peach pink with yellow reverse).

Climbing roses provide flowers for large arrangements. Their long, arching stems when full grown are particularly graceful. Good examples are 'Casino' (deep yellow), 'Chaplin's Pink Climber' (summer-flowering), 'Danse du Feu' (orange-red), 'Golden Showers' (golden yellow), 'Leverkusen' (golden yellow), 'Mme. Grégoire Staechelin' (deep pink, summer flowering), 'Pink Perpetue', 'Swan Lake' and 'Zéphirine Drouhin' (rosy-pink and thornless). The last is one of the old Bourbon roses.

For large decorative heps the species *R. davidii*, *R. moyesii* and *R. rugosa* provide among the best. The variety 'Scabrosa' produces bright orange-red heps, which may be as much as one-and-a-half inches across. See Preservation (Berries).

Miniature roses are difficult to grow in pots indoors but the cut flowers are excellent for small arrangements.

The treatment of roses is a matter of some importance, because, if they are not looked after, their petals will fall all too soon. Pick them when just opening to get the full life of the flowers. Hammer, strip or split the stem ends and remove any foliage which will not be seen in the arrangement. Of all the various chemical or other stimulants introduced into the water it has been found that copper is best. Either arrange the flowers in a copper container, or slip a couple of Victorian 'bun' pennies into the water. It makes it easier when arranging if you first remove the thorns and this also helps to prolong the life of the flowers.

It also helps to dip the stem ends in boiling hot water for a minute and as usual give them a good long soak in slightly warm water which they absorb better. All these preparations may seem painstaking but roses are well worth the time spent on them. Another point worth remembering is that roses will last better the greater the proportion of the stem is in water. A large rose bowl or wide container combined with wire netting mesh is obviously best for the hybrid teas and floribundas so that the relatively short stems receive as much water as possible.

Alchemillas, camellias, carnations, godetias, pinks and sweet peas may mix well with roses. See also Wild Flowers.

Rosmarinus/rosemary

Leaf/Flower/Sp

An evergreen shrub, the common rosemary, *R. officinalis*, has distinctive narrow leaves, dark green above with grey-silvery undersides which are fragrant if crushed. The plants may reach several feet high. The flowers are rather small and generally blue, appearing up the stems between the leaves. There are also lilac and white varieties. Give the leaves a good soak after dipping the stem ends in boiling hot water.

Rubus/blackberry, bramble, raspberry

Leaf/Flower/Berry/Sp/Su

There are a large number of species of *Rubus*, some climbing, others of shrub or creeping habit with both evergreen and deciduous types—almost all providing interesting foliage, sometimes red in colour. The flowers of *R.* 'Tridel' are rather like large white wild roses and appear in May and June. There are a number of ornamental species with flowers, fruits and leaves considerably more attractive than the common blackberry (*R. fruticosus*). They include *R. phoenicolasius*, which has hairy red fruits shaped like heps on red stems. Hammer and dip the stem ends in boiling hot water.

Rudbeckia/cone flower, black-eyed Susan

Flower/Su

This daisy-like generally yellow-petalled flower has a dark centre, and the free-flowering black-eyed Susan (*R. deamii* 'Speciosa' (syn. *R. fulgida deamii*) has a flower with a distinctive purple-black button centre. They are mostly hardy perennials useful for late summer arrangements.

The flowers of *R. tetra* 'Gloriosa' (gloriosa daisy) are particularly large sometimes reaching over 6 inches across in various colours and double forms on firm stems, all of which make good cut flowers lasting well in water. Dip the stem ends in boiling hot water for a minute or so and give them a long soak in cool water.

Rumex/sorrel

Seed/Flower/Su

Some types of sorrel are generally regarded as weeds, but the tall green flower spikes of other varieties are distinctive in green arrangements. The arrow-shaped light-green leaves of *R. acetosa*, which may be eaten raw or cooked like spinach, look good in small arrangements. Dip the stem ends in boiling hot water for a few seconds without allowing the steam to reach the leaves and, when arranged, spray occasionally with a water atomiser.

Sorrel seedheads can be dried by hanging upside down. Remove the leaves and pick the stems for drying before they reach full maturity. The red types, such as *R. sanguineus*, are particularly good.

Ruscus/box holly, butcher's broom

Leaf/Berry

The evergreen small pointed 'leaves' of *R. aculeatus*, the native shrub, are good for winter and Christmas decoration and the berries on the female plant are a bright cherry red. The foliage can easily be painted silver for Christmas decorations.

Ruta/rue, herb of grace

Leaf/Flower/Su

The tiny, delicate leaves of this dwarf-sized medicinal herb are often a deep glaucous blue and are excellent for winter arranging. The bright yellow four-petalled flowers last well in water.

Salpiglossis/painted tongue

Flower/Su

The flowers, which are mostly delicately veined, are orange-yellow, violet-yellow, crimson, yellow, etc., and last well in water. The 'Splash' F_1

hybrid is a vigorous free-flowering variety which makes an excellent pot plant under glass. Dip the cut flower stem ends in very hot water (not actually boiling) for a few seconds and then give the stems a long soak in cool water.

Salvia/clary, sage

Flower/Leaf/Su

The most commonly seen salvias are the ones grown for summer bedding with bright red flower spikes and dark-green, deeply veined leaves. These belong to scarlet sage (*S. splendens*) and there are several varieties. There are over 700 species of *Salvia* including the common sage (*S. officinalis*) with its narrow aromatic leaves and blue, purple or white flowers. Like *S. argentea*, it flowers in June or July. *S. argentea* has bluish-white flowers with ornamental silvery foliage, and the perennial *S. haematodes* has light blue flowers from June onwards and interestingly wrinkled heart-shaped leaves. Other salvias with beautiful blue or purplish flowers on fairly tall spikes include *S. virgata*. *S. carduacea*, the thistle salvia, has magnificent purple heads on thick stems. *S. grahamii* gives showy crimson flowers from July onwards. All these flowers are excellent for mixed summer arrangments, and the leaves of many give off a strong scent when rubbed.

The plant known as clary (*S. sclarea*) with lilac flowers and pink or white leaf-like bracts has produced many varieties which can be dried and are also very decorative when cut. The various forms of *S. pratense* with blue or rosy-purple flowers are also very beautiful. Dip the stem ends in boiling hot water and give them a good soak.

Sambucus/elder

Flower/Berry/Leaf/Sp

The bushes or trees of *S. nigra* provide the white flowers and black berries for making elder-flower and elderberry wine, and can be seen growing fairly commonly in hedgerows. The aroma of the flowers which appear in June is rather pungent, but the fruits do not smell and the leaves of some varieties are variegated or distinctively indented. If you want to use the flowers, pick them early in the day to avoid petal fall. To keep the foliage as long as possible dip the crushed stem ends in boiling hot water and soak overnight.

Sanguisorba/burnet

Flower/Leaf/Seed/Su

The flowerheads of the great burnet, *S. officinalis*, look a bit like dark red bottle brushes at the heads of their long stems. The toothed leaves are a bright green but tend to curve inwards showing their paler undersides. *S. obtusa* from Japan has rather mop-like flowerheads and its seedheads can be dried standing in a little water. For cut flowers dip the stems in boiling hot water for a little over a minute.

Santolina/cotton lavender

Leaf/Flower/Su

The finely divided, bushy foliage of these dwarf evergreen shrubs is a useful standby in winter. It is greeny-grey in colour and seems to match that season of the year. The yellow round flowers are like small everlasting flowers and can be dried as such.

Satureja/savory

Flower/Leaf/Su

Summer and winter savory are favourites for flavouring in cooking, and the winter savory has evergreen leaves. There are a large number of other species, including a number of ornamental types sometimes known as *Calamintha*. Dip the stem ends in boiling hot water and give both leaves and stems a good long soak in cold water.

Saxifraga/saxifrage

Flower/Leaf/Sp

The saxifrages comprise over 350 species and are plants with often interesting foliage and delicate flowers. Their dwarf habit restricts their use to some extent, but the mat-forming varieties sometimes provide foliage for lining hanging baskets as it does dry out as easily as moss if supplied with a peat compost. It can also be used to cover the wire netting in arrangements.

S. umbrosa is the well-known London pride; its star-like pink flowers on slender stems may be used from May to July. *S. longifolia* is one of the finest species with tall arching flower stems covered with flowers which sometimes reach up to 2 feet. They look best in the garden planted in big bold clumps, and are very effective as edging plants to borders.

Scabiosa/scabious

Flower/Su

The perennial species of *S. caucasica* are best known. They flower all the summer and into autumn in delicate pincushions of white or shades of blue and mauve. Even finer open-petalled flowers somewhat resemble anemones: a good variety 'Clive Greaves' has large rich mauve flowers and 'Miss Willmott' is a fine white variety. All are good for cutting.

Schizanthus/butterfly flower, poor man's orchid

Flower/Su

The flowers of this Chilean plant are beautiful in tall sprays of various colours. In cool temperate regions they are usually grown in a cold green-house when they will flower in winter or spring, but may be bedded out. They last well as cut flowers after the stem ends have been dipped in boiling hot water and been given a good soak.

Schizostylis/Kaffir lily

Flower/Au

The value of these South African plants lies in their late-flowering quality. The best-known species, *S. coccinea*, has tall spikes of crimson flowers but there is also a fine pink one called 'Mrs. Hegarty' and the late-blooming 'Viscountess Byng' is also useful. They all last well in water.

Schlumbergera see House Plants (Cacti and Succulents)

Scilla/squill

Flower/Sp

The delicate flowers of these bulbous plants are blue, rose, violet, mauve, lilac, etc. Many of them are like bluebells, which used to be included in the same genus but are now classified under *Endymion* (see Wild flowers). The Siberian squill (*S. sibirica*) is not unlike the bluebell but a much deeper blue. They appear on short stems early in the year and can be arranged with other spring bulbs and with wild arum leaves, etc. Plunge the stem ends in boiling hot water for a minute as soon as they are picked. This should help to keep the stems erect.

Scindapsus see House Plants (Trailing Plants)

Scrophularia/figwort

Leaf/Flower/Sp

The figwort is a somewhat nettle-like looking plant, and the variegated variety *S. aquatica* 'Variegata' has opposite leaves marked with creamy white. There is another cultivated species *S. chrysantha* with yellow flowers in March. Some species have a rather strong smell and they are not very long lasting so dip the stem ends in boiling hot water for over a minute and spray the leaves occasionally with a water atomiser to freshen them.

Seasonal arrangements

What more pleasing arrangement could there be at Christmas time than an elegant small table vase arranged with *Helleborus niger*, the Christmas rose, variegated holly, berries of tree ivy with a few leaf trails and finished with a good quality red velvet ribbon. The holly may need to have a few leaves removed to get the full display of berries. If a slightly more exciting effect is required, lightly frost the foliage with the addition of a little glass glitter. Another suitable arrangement could be done in all foliages, using a large up-right urn-shaped vase. Get the background filled in with bare alder branches, branches covered with lichen and some long slender conifer branches. Into the centre of the group add branches of variegated and green holly well berried, also stems of privet berries or hawthorn. At the base have a large stem of *Mahonia bealii* and a group of wired up fir cones to add interest. Over the sides and trailing down the front, a few pieces of tree ivy with berries finish this arrangement. This can remain natural looking or can be lightly 'snowed' with a small white paint spray or brush for a festive effect.

In the early spring one cannot do better than to have a 'garden on a plate'; this is made up of small flowering and foliage plants carefully arranged and planted together with rock and moss to make the garden. This idea can be used all the year round, but springtime is particularly good because of the wealth of bulb plants and small flowering shrubs. One immediately thinks of the Roman and Dutch hyacinths, dwarf tulips and narcissi, crocus, snowdrops, polyanthus, primroses, grape hyacinth, erica, baby Japanese

I

Seasonal arrangements. (i) Spring. Narcissi, catkins, Lenten roses, variegated ivy and *Arum italicum* 'Pictum' combine to make a delicate spring arrangement. (ii) A summer arrangement with all the opulence that might be expected at that season. The gilt goat's head jardiniere is grand enough to carry such an arrangement. (iii) An autumn arrangement using chrysanthemums, autumn berries and the fading foliage of the royal fern. (iv) The simplicity of this arrangement, as well as the actual materials used, reflect the starkness of this season. The plant is *Garrya elliptica*.

II

III

IV

Bouquets. A beautiful Christmas bouquet created by the Constance Spry School, London, with Christmas roses, frosted holly leaves and Irish lace.

azalea, saintpaulia, kalanchoë and primula, to name but a few which last very well under these conditions. There are many types of foliage plants. Ivy in variety, helxine, scindapsus, chlorophytum, various ferns, tradescantia, peperomia and begonia give a wide selection of colours and shapes. To add interest to these plants use lichen on branches, cork bark, stones, rock, sand, pebbles and bun moss, which all help to make a garden full of interest. The secret is not to place the plants too close to one another. Each should show up as an individual. The extras, such as moss and stones, help to fill· the gaps.

The ideal container for this is the old-fashioned meat plate, or a dish on small legs, to lift it off the ground and to stop damage from condensation at the base. A depth of 3 inches is ideal so that the ball of the soil round each plant can be covered and is not disturbed too much when planting. These miniature gardens will last (depending on the care they receive and the plants used) for many weeks. Flowering plants should be replaced as soon as the blooms start to fade. The flowering plants you can use in the summer are all much bigger and not so attractive, but a very pretty and cool effect can be obtained from an all-green 'garden on a plate', using foliage houseplants and small ferns.

In spring one has a wide choice of flowers from which to pick and a real basket of all the

first flowers is most gay and exciting. Make use of such things as hosta foliage and flower clusters of the hellebores: *Helleborus niger, H. orientalis* and *H. foetidus* are all attractive. Blue and gold polyanthus, chalky auricula, striped tulips of the type seen in Dutch flower paintings and the elegant, pointed lily-flowered tulips are excellent. A few clusters of forget-me-nots and sprays of the first tree and shrub blossoms all add interest and widen the colour range.

The first daffodils with their own foliage (if you can bear to pick them) look bright and cheerful arranged as a growing group in a shallow dish. A branch or so of hazel catkins make a fine back group, and at the base of the stems a few clusters of primroses. The rest of the vase area is covered with moss.

In late spring you cannot do better than have large vases of tulips and lilac or azalea with the many colour ranges available today, from yellow through cream to white, pink, apricot, scarlet and all the in-between shades. All these flowers can be used in vases on the table, for large room decorations in the house and also for special

Seasonal arrangements – summer. The pale acid greenish-yellow of lime flowers can make a stunning arrangement against a dark background. Note how shallow the actual container is.

occasions such as wedding groups in churches. It is often difficult to decide when the spring flowers are over and summer flowers are with us, because the seasons vary so much, and today flowers are carried long distances to extend the market supplies.

What could be more pleasing than a large grey china tazza-shaped vase arranged with the following? Pale pink peonies, cool yellow lilies, deeper pink muted tones of oriental poppy, blue-grey spikes of delphinium and foxgloves together with silver grey foliages and a touch of that excellent golden philadelphus, *P. coronarius* 'Aureus': a very pretty combination of interesting-shaped flowers and delicate colours.

During the hot spells in the early English summer, one can get great pleasure from a white and green group arranged on a pedestal, or in a large Bible box. Sprays of single and double philadelphus, partly stripped of foliage to encourage them to last longer; long elegant stems of 'Iceberg' roses with buds; candidum lilies with a few white delphiniums to give extra height and, perhaps, if they have lasted, a few remaining white peonies for weight low down in the vase. Many foliages can be chosen to add to this arrangement. The early leaves of artichoke would be excellent at the centre and perhaps such things as *Phormium tenax* as an outline at the back with some young fennel.

One should not let a summer pass without one arrangement of old-fashioned shrub roses, which are a complete decoration on their own, and there is nothing more beautiful than the rose 'Constance Spry'; a modern variety named after the person who popularised the old-fashioned rose and helped its return to the gardens of so many flower arrangers today. See also Rosa.

The sweet pea is perhaps more pleasingly arranged alone with its own foliage. It is not long lasting; but what a joy it is as a table decoration, delicate, sweet-smelling and in a wealth of colours.

For autumn, there is a vast choice from fruits, flowers, berries, and a great number of foliages, changing through all the autumnal shades. For an exciting group for a buffet table, choose from seedheads, such as foxgloves in seed and a few late flowers like grey secondary stems of delphinium. Try nerines in the new hybrid forms, *Begonia rex* leaves as a focal point, with sprays of blackberry, *Cobaea scandens* and a few long trails of the last purple clematis; add to this a few

fruits of tomatoes, gourds and any other striking material available in this colour range. All this would look well arranged in a bronze or black urn or vase on a foot or raised base, to provide room for the trailing materials.

Michaelmas daisies give a wide range of colour and can be most attractive when well arranged. Not long-lasting unless carefully picked over from day to day, they are perhaps better arranged on their own and massed carefully, getting as many colours as one can and grouping them well.

It is in autumn that you can most enjoy the chrysanthemum which is now grown in so many varieties that it comes in nearly all colours except in the blue range. The spray varieties and single blooms look well together, but one must pick varieties with care to help them to set each other off when arranging. Some of the sprays are so heavily crowded with clusters of flowers at the ends that they need thinning before they can be arranged properly.

Seaweed

Fresh seaweed is sometimes used in glass vases, rather in the manner of crumpled chicken wire, to support or balance flower stems. Used in this way it does not look unattractive. It can also be used for covering the base of an arrangement, when it will keep its freshness if the roots are allowed to dangle in water.

Beachcombers may come across fantastically coiled pieces of sea wrack dried by the wind and sun, which may be used in plaques, along with shells, sedges and other seaside plant material. Seaweed can be dried like most other types of plant material in a warm airy room or placed on newspaper in the sun.

Sedges and rushes

Though closely related, they differ from each other in that the flowers of the true sedges (*Carex*) have neither petals nor sepals; and they differ from grasses in that the stems are triangular and are not hollow. The false bulrush, *Typha latifolia*, is of a different family, *Typhacaea*, the reedmace family. It is an aquatic perennial, frequently seen on the margins of rivers and ponds, which grows to a height of 4–5 feet tall, its female flowers appearing as a terminal chocolate-coloured cylindrical spike of about 1 inch diameter and 6 inches long. It is most attractive when used as indoor decoration especially to provide contrast to green flowers, e.g. *Amaranthus caudatus* 'Viridis' and *Nicotiana* 'Lime Green'. The display may be enhanced by the use of *Briza maxima*, quaking grass, with its graceful spikes of small nodding 'lanterns'.

The wood club rush, *Scirpus sylvaticus*, is equally suitable for indoor decoration. It is widespread in ditches and damp woodlands where it grows 2–3 feet tall. It bears numerous olive-green spikelets spirally arranged in a much-branched head, with which orange or yellow flowers may be allowed to intermingle. The clustered club rush, *S. holoschoenus*, present on sandy shores in south-west Britain and the Mediterranean, is equally attractive. It grows 3–4 feet tall and forms a widely branched head. It bears its pale brown flowers in cone-shaped clusters.

The galingale, *Cyperus longus*, which may be found in Europe and North America, is most effectively used with orange and yellow dahlias which bloom at the same time. It has bright reddish flowers arranged in a widely branched head.

The sedges are more readily obtainable and one of the best for decoration is the drooping sedge, *Carex pendula*. It is common in damp woodlands and bears its flowers early in summer. They are of a combination of green and brown and are borne in elegantly drooping spikes about 6 inches long. When used for indoor display, they more resemble the greenish-yellow male catkins of the hazel which they follow shortly after. The flowers of the pond sedge, *C. acutiformis*, are of rich purple-brown colouring and are borne erect, 4–6 to a stem. These resemble the catkins of the pussy willow and are enhanced by the grey-green stems and leaves. Usually found close to fresh water, where it grows 3–4 feet tall, it is one of the loveliest of all British native plants.

The moorland sedge, *C. binervis*, is similar, but the individual flower spikes are less conspicuous. It is found on heaths and moorlands everywhere and grows 2 feet tall. It forms a striking contrast where used with white flowers, especially with white delphiniums which bloom at the same time, for its flowers are jet black.

Also in bloom at the same time is the hop sedge, *C. pseudocyperus*, usually found near fresh water. It is one of the most handsome sedges, growing 3 feet tall with bright olive-green leaves

and stems and drooping flower spikes, also of bright green. They resemble the flowers of *Sanguisorba obtusa* (syn. *Poterium obtusum*), the bottle brush plant, being similar to the brushes used to clean babies' feeding bottles (see Sanguisorba in main list). The bladder sedge, found in marshy places, is equally attractive. It is *Carex vesicaria*, and grows 2 feet tall, being deep green throughout. The flower spikes which resemble dark green cones are formed almost at right angles to the main stem along which they are liberally and evenly placed.

The tussock sedge, *C. paniculata*, of fenland woodlands is entirely different in habit and appearance. It makes a dense tussock 3–4 feet tall and almost as broad, and bears its flowers in a loose graceful spike like those of the rough meadow grass, but denser. It will add its individual beauty to an arrangement of sedges and grasses.

Sedum/stonecrop

Flower/Leaf/Seed/Su/Au

The popular *S. spectabile* has cold fleshy leaves and produces pink flowerheads in the late summer and autumn. It is a hardy perennial plant and one of a family of 600, which includes *S. éroseum* (roseroot). Roseroot has lovely yellowish-green flowers in summer and blue-green leaves. Other plants in the genus have dark-red or purple leaves and dark-red or pink flowers which blend well in autumn arrangements. Hang the ripe seedheads upside down to dry.

Sempervivem see House Plants (Cacti and Succulents)

Senecio/ragwort

Flower/Leaf/Su/Au

The yellow, daisy-like flowers and greyish soft leaves of the hardy shrub *S. laxifolius* are well known, but the family contains well over 2,000 species, including the popular pot plant, the cineraria. The pot cinerarias range in colour from blue to pinkish red and are produced from *S. cruentus*. They appear in florists in great numbers in early spring. If you want them to survive till the following year the winter temperature must always be over 40°F (4°C) and the plants should not be over-watered at this time. The half-hardy *S. cineraria* (dusty miller), and the tender *S. leucostachys* provide delicate, silvery foliage.

Setcreasea see House Plants (Palms)

Shells

Shells collected from beaches may be used in arrangements with a sea theme, along with dried starfish, seahorses, coral, seaweed, etc. Sea shells are very often useful for covering the base of an arrangement. Newly collected shells should be washed in warm water and left to dry out. Sea urchins and starfish shells must be cleaned by very gingerly opening up their bases and gently scraping out their insides. Shells can be glued together to make fantastic and attractive constructions. They may be polished with a soft cloth and varnished with clear, cellulose varnish. Large tropical shells make excellent containers, and smaller shells and half-opened double shells can be used to make tiny miniature arrangements by filling them with a piece of Oasis or Florapak.

Shows

Flower arranging is a sociable activity and it is no wonder that many people in Britain, and very many more in the United States, belong to clubs and societies for the purpose of flower arranging. What could be better than to discuss ways of flower arranging and exchange ideas with fellow flower arrangers? Undoubtedly the chief of all the activities organised by clubs and societies is the flower arrangement or floral art show.

Such shows generally have two sections, one competitive and the other purely for exhibition purposes. It is true that for many people the best way to improve is by entering the competitive field, working alongside others, having one's arrangements assessed by judges, and finding out mistakes and new techniques through the judges' comments. However, there are many people with a talent for flower arranging who have no inclination to compete. They may do magnificent exhibition work, they enjoy flower arranging for its own sake and for the sense of artistry and pleasure in self expression it brings, but they find taking part in competitions abhorrent.

Floral art and flower arrangement shows require careful planning, hard work and enthusiasm. They are often organised by flower arrangement clubs to raise money either for club funds or for charity. Other show organisers, such as agricultural show committees, arrange floral art sections as a popular attraction, and they usually finance each exhibition section and give prize money with or without trophies for the competitive classes.

Having found a suitable hall, or suite of rooms, maybe even a marquee, it is essential to begin by designing an overall plan, usually related to the show title chosen. If it is not possible for a single designer to prepare the initial plan, then the show areas should be handed over to a number of individuals or groups to design.

Muslin, hessian, hardboard, pegboard or screens may be used for backgrounds, so long as they are immaculately staged. Consider fire regulations in your choice of materials. Furniture and stagings should be carefully chosen to present a pleasing effect and enhance, not dominate or detract from the flower arragements. Colour schemes and special lighting are worth experimenting with to produce outstanding effects and here some professional help may be required. Where dried arrangements are to be staged it is essential to have good lighting or they will look extremely dull.

In the competitive section a separate work table (to be removed before judging) should be provided for each entrant. Competitors' cards in numbered and sealed envelopes should be placed beside the entries and judges' comment cards also provided. Competitors should receive a competitions badge or card admitting them to the staging area and allowing them to uplift entries after the show. In a large show this is absolutely necessary to avoid things going missing. Water should be within easy reach of the staging area. Competition stewards should ensure that competitors finish arranging their entries in time for the area to be cleared and swept ready for judging, since the judges have to complete their work in time to allow the Press to obtain the results before the show opens to the public.

The rules for the competition section are almost always strictly based on those laid down by the National Association of Flower Arrangement Societies of Great Britain. N.A.F.A.S. was founded in 1959 and includes 1,000 British societies with a total membership fast approaching 100,000. In America the rules for the competition section are strictly based on those laid down by The National Council of State Gardening Clubs Inc. of U.S.A. The two associations are mutually affilliated and in America the total membership vastly outstrips that of N.A.F.A.S. There are affiliated organisations in many other countries as well.

The association's magazine *The Flower Arranger* includes illustrated articles on shows and much other news. A coloured photographic record of national festivals, etc., may be hired in sets of slides from the N.A.F.A.S. headquarters. Among the association's publications the schedule definitions are most valuable to show organisers and competitors. Terms in general use are defined and brought up to date and rules, schedules and competition regulations are included in continually revised editions.

When entering for a show read the schedule twice to make quite sure you know the rules and understand what it requires. No judge enjoys disqualifying an otherwise good entry as 'not according to schedule'. Decide which classes you wish to enter, taking into account the time allowed for staging and your own speed of work. Do not enter too many classes so that you end up by not being able to complete the staging of some of your entries. You do not do your best work when trying to beat the clock, and you may have prevented another entrant from getting a place in that particular class. In addition, nothing is more disappointing to organisers than to have gaps in the staging in the middle of a class as a result of entries failing to be staged.

Think carefully about each class: what container will be suitable in style and the right proportions for an arrangement in the space provided, and what accessories, if any, you will require. A common mistake is to use an accessory which answers to the schedule but is not in scale with the overall size of the arrangement. Collect containers and accessories together a week or two before the show. If you have access to garden plant material have a good look round and decide what will be available.

When you have chosen your container, etc., set a table up against a wall at home marking off the measured area you are allowed for staging and then work on the ideas you have for your proposed arrangement. If flowers are not readily available use foliage or dried plant material as substitutes. The important thing is to work to the shape and size in which you will finally create your entry.

Arrange your accessories, changing them where the size and shape are not pleasing, finding a means of raising the placement if that helps to enhance the arrangement. Varying drapes should also be tried for their effects. It is now possible to obtain a small adjustable stand to hold drapes. This avoids any necessity to attach the drapes to the background (and anyway this is not always permitted). Bases too should be carefully considered and covered to tone into the scheme if necessary. It is useful to have one or two extra neutral bases which can be used to adjust the height of the arrangements if things do not work out quite as planned.

Remember that your arrangement must come within the given area, not rise above it or stick out over the front edge of the staging, and the tips of the plant material must not touch the sides of the niche. Care should be taken to cover as much of the mechanics of an arrangement as possible. It is simpler to do this with some moss, stones or foliage, depending on the type of container, before making the design. When completed it will then look an integral part of the whole and not something added.

When you are satisfied with your overall design attend to details, such as polishing a shiny metal container. Wrap each item carefully and pack ready for transporting. If it is necessary to display a title and lettering is not your forte, find someone who can help. Failing that buy some self-adhesive lettering which can easily be used to make a neat title. Pack the title card with care, covering it to keep it clean. Smudged or tatty cards detract from the whole presentation.

Next prepare your container with the pinholder, 2-inch mesh chicken wire (with the side edges cut away), 'Oasis', or whatever other medium you have chosen to work in, ready to be soaked or filled with water at the show. Pack scissors, or flower cutters (two pairs if possible), a small watering can, plastic bucket, atomiser spray if you have one, a few pieces of wire if you are using grapes or anything needing anchoring, plasticine or 'Bostic' to anchor pinholders, clamp for driftwood, a few cocktail sticks if you need to position fruit, and an extra block of 'Oasis' besides what will be needed for your entries in case of emergencies. Some florists' cones may be required if a particularly tall arrangement is planned. Cigar tubes make good substitutes used together with fine canes

Shows: Arrangements can vary from the sublime to the ridiculous. An arrangement for a show class entitled 'Picture': the arrangement looks exactly like a Dutch master's still life.

Shows: Another still-life type arrangement, but this
time without the picture frame.

Shows : A clever arrangement made inside a hanging
birdcage. Show judges like to force exhibitors to
exercise their ingenuity.

Shows: A highly successful arrangement using a birdcage and incorporating a mechanical singing bird. The diagonal axis helps the arrangement cohere.

Shows: An arrangement using candelabra. Such themes are popular at shows throughout the U.K. and the U.S.A.

Shows: Many show classes tend towards the
gimmicky. In the arrangement the drapes have
become visually more important than the flowers.

Shows: An even more gimmicky arrangement
incorporating modern wallpapers and other
strictly non-floral elements.

A show arrangement in the Japanese style. It is worth
comparing this arrangement with a genuine
Japanese one.

and rubber bands or clear tape. Sticking plaster is often needed when fingers are snipped in mistake for stems. Lastly a plastic sheet on which to work makes clearing up easy and simplifies the final emptying into a rubbish bin.

Drapes must be placed on a cardboard roll after ironing or they will show creases. Cover them with polythene for transporting.

Two days before the show start collecting plant material. Select the foliage carefully and condition it according to its type. Some leaves respond better to total immersion, woody stems require scraping before soaking, others require the tips of the stems to be dipped in boiling water for a few seconds then stood in cold water, yet others prefer warm water. Choose the colour and shape of any fruit used which will best suit your design.

The day before the show cut your flowers or collect them from the florist. Always make sure you have one or two blooms to spare. Remove thorns from roses, defoliate where necessary, but certainly remove the lower leaves, saving any which you may use separately, condition and keep in a cool place.

On the day of the show pack your flowers and foliage carefully. Florists' boxes are best for this purpose. If they have to travel far line the boxes with polythene and cover flowers and foliage with it to prevent the plant material from drying out in transit.

In addition to all these preparations it is always advisable to recut the stems before arranging at the show. Finally, think of yourself and take along a vacuum flask of coffee and a few sandwiches.

Arrive at staging time or shortly afterwards—you may not require all the time given but if you have the time in hand and anything goes wrong (you may break your best bloom) you can probably do something about it. Find out from the competitions secretary where your class positions are and where you are to work. Place your belongings as neatly as possible under the table. Try to relax completely before you start to work. Do the simplest things first, then tackle the more complicated arrangements once you have got into your stride. Be pleasant and polite to those around you, but try not to become involved with what they are doing and do not invite comment on your own work. It only causes confusion in your mind to do this, and gamesmanship is no more unknown in flower arranging than in any other form of competition.

When you begin to flag, stop, even in the middle of an arrangement, have your coffee and sandwich and perhaps walk round, and go back to your task refreshed and relaxed. When you have completed your work, and are satisfied you have done the best you can, pack your belongings, clear the work area, put the rubbish where requested or take it away, have a brief word with acquaintances, and leave. It does no good to hang around and have second thoughts—they are usually wrong anyway.

After judging, whether you have won or not, have a good look round the entries and consider the judging. Try to put yourself in the judges' place and go over all the entries in a class, and eliminate from your choice any not in accordance with the schedule and rules. Then consider the quality of the design, the suitability and condition of the plant material (an unusual colour may be an asset, a grub-eaten leaf is not). A pot-et-fleur which has been planted up with anything and everything will not have gained approval. Take account of the suitability of the container, the interpretation of the title, the colour harmony and whether the material is properly set in water or a water-retaining material, and reduce your choice to two or three entries and finally look for points of distinction. The judges will have looked for that indefinable something, a special distinction which so often separates the award of the first and second places.

You may not arrive at the same decision as the judges: inevitably preferences for colours or different tastes in draped fabrics will influence choices, and on these finer points it is hard to say who is right. Nevertheless there is much to be learnt from this exercise and studying the judges' comment cards can be invaluable in future.

If you have a genuine complaint about the judging take it to the secretary and have it dealt with according to the rules, rather than talk to friends about it. If you particularly admire an arrangement seek out its creator. You will find that as well as learning from others, flower arrangers are on the whole the most generous people, and many a root or cutting has been given or exchanged as a result of a show bench meeting.

Shrimp Plant see Beloperone Guttata (House Plants)

Sidalcea

Flower/Seed/Su

Beautiful pink, white, red or rosy-purple petals borne on graceful stems are characteristic of these plants, which are in the same family as the hollyhock and mallow. They are hardy perennial plants from North America which will grow in any sunny border. Dip the stems in boiling water and keep them in deep water. The seedheads may be hung upside down to dry just past bud stage.

Silene/catchfly

Flower/Leaf/Sp/Su/Au

There are 500 species of silenes (some being rather weed-like in habit), including such wild flowers as the perennial sea campion (*S. maritima*), of which there are cultivated varieties with large white or white-pink flowers. Another cultivated perennial, *S. schafta*, has lovely rose-magenta flowers and is useful for small summer arrangements. Various silenes bloom at different times from May to October, *S. schafta* flowering from June onwards. A taller flower and one that provides a cloud of white flowers on delicately branching stems, *S. inaperta*, is less well known. The annual *S. armeria* is an old favourite garden flower. It has bluish-green lance-like leaves and heads of rose-pink or white flowers reaching over a foot high. Dip the stem ends in boiling hot water for a minute.

Silybum/milk thistle, holy thistle

Leaf

S. marianum produces dark-green prickly variegated leaves covered with a beautiful network of white. This is excellent foliage for summer arrangements. Dip the ends of the stems in boiling water.

Sinningia see House Plants (Pot Plants)

Smilacina/false spikenard

Flower/Sp

These small, whitish flowers which appear on 6-inch sprays are useful for lightening arrangements. Although they flower in May, they may occasionally be obtained later from florists. The leaves are sometimes very long, slender pointed and downy underneath. Dip the stem ends in boiling hot water.

Solanum/Christmas cherry, winter cherry

Berry/Flower/Su

S. capsicastrum is best known as a greenhouse pot plant bearing orange-scarlet berries around Christmas. See HOUSE PLANTS (Pot Plants). A similar shrub *S. pseudocapsicastrum* (Jerusalem cherry) is also grown as a pot plant. The wealth of plants in this family includes the potato and the aubergine, the fruits of the latter having ornamental value. The flowers of *S. jasminoides*, the potato vine, appear in summer and have bluish-white flowers with yellow centres. If you use them, dip the stems ends in boiling water or even pure alcohol first.

Solidago/golden rod

Flower/Seed/Su/Au

This is the tall showy plant producing arching sprays of yellow flowers like oriental fans, which are often seen growing wild on old garden sites. There are a number of varieties—not all as common as the familiar golden rod, but of greater interest to the flower arranger—such as 'Golden Wings', which has a warmer colour and even longer stems than usual.

Sparganium/bur-reed

Berry/Leaf/Flower/Su

An unusual pond-side plant, the bur-reed has dark rounded fruits and long fleshy leaves which look startling in any kind of arrangement. *S. erectum*, the common bur-reed, has leaves which may grow to over 3 feet long.

Spartiannia see House Plants (Palms)

Spiraea

Flower/Leaf/Seed/Su

This is a deciduous shrub which produces sprays of rather foamy pink, purplish-red or white flowers. The leaves of some species take on beautiful autumn colour, such as *S. macrophylla*. The plants will grow in sunny positions in almost any soil. The flowerheads of the early varieties look good in spring displays. 'Anthony Waterer', which flowers about July, is a popular wine-red variety. The seedheads of spiraea can be dried in a flower display in a warm room. Hammer the stem ends for cut displays.

Spry, Constance

Constance Spry made very clear her conviction that flowers, if they were to be used for arrangement at all, should be allowed to show their beauty naturally. Her style, essentially direct and simple, puts out of countenance any patently bogus ingenuity that from time to time is applied to flower arrangement. The object of 'doing the flowers' at all, to her mind, was to enjoy them. She grew them herself for pleasure, made several gardens in her lifetime and wrote about them lovingly. Many of the things that she cultivated as a gardener and used in her early decorations had not customarily been considered particularly beautiful or even decorative or quite suitable to the fashion of the day, but her ideas suddenly caught the imagination and stirred a conventional atmosphere into life with a touch of magic. Her influence first began to make itself felt in the 1930s. Over 40 by then, she had previously won distinction in another occupation, as principal of a London County Council school in the East End of London, and her enlightened contribution to what was a challenging educational experiment of the local authority of the time is still remembered. Her subsequent fame however spread about the world, and the artistry, which happily she could impart to others, has had its impact further abroad than America and Australia, where she toured as a lecturer; pupils come to her schools in Britain from Japan, India and Africa as well as from European countries.

The business Constance Spry built up started as a very small shop behind Victoria Station, London. It was called 'Flower Decorations' and its name made the title of the first of a dozen books,

Here Constance Spry shows what can be done with a little imagination. The snowdrops have their stems embedded in wet spaghnum moss instead of in water.

Constance Spry has an eye for the unusual. Here the
relationship between the vase and the flowers
is as interesting as the flowers themselves.

This container was designed by Constance Spry herself. The stand is of wrought iron with a bevelled, smoky mirror base.

including a famous cookery book, in which a fluent expression of ideas provides entertainment for the uninitiated and for experts. As a decorator of great places for great occasions she was held in the highest esteem and made an O.B.E.; her sparkling enthusiasm enlivened a trade and still inspires countless amateurs. She designed vases, carpets and made lifelike artificial flowers and taught other people how to do such things for themselves.

Constance Spry founded not only the shops and the floristry school that bear her name but, with Miss Rosemary Hume of the Cordon Bleu, founded Winkfield Place, Berkshire, a residential training school where she lived and taught, and these perpetuate the achievements through which her name not surprisingly became a household word.

Stachys lanata/lamb's ear, woundwort, hedge nettle

Flower/Leaf/Su

This is a useful plant for its leaves which are covered with a thick mat of soft hairs, which look silver when they catch the light. The flowers are bright purple and appear as erect spikes. Do not wet the leaves but give them plenty to drink. If you allow the seedheads to hang upside down they will be useful for dried arrangements—their grey stems being particularly effective. The plants will grow in almost any soil, make a good border, and reach up to 18 inches tall.

Stephanotis

Flower/Leaf

A favourite flower at weddings, its fragrant waxy-white, star-like flowers indicating purity and innocence. The dark evergreen leaves set off the flowers, and the whole effect is one of elegance and beauty. Hot greenhouse conditions are needed for growing stephanotis, which is a climber from Madagascar. The only species cultivated is *S. floribunda*. When cut give the stems plenty of water, but keep the flowers dry or they will turn brown.

Stones

Stones are often useful in covering the base, or weighting down a top-heavy arrangement. Gravel or sand may also be used, and natural or coloured stones or sand can be very decorative.

Larger stones or rocks of an unusual shape or colour will often match a piece of driftwood, and both will be objects of interest for the flower arranger who is fond of collecting. Stones and pebbles of different kinds will suit different sorts of arrangements. Flintstone has a cool effect and sandstone is 'warm'. Large slabs of stone or slate make excellent bases, and hollow-shaped stones may be used as containers.

Succulents see House Plants (Cacti and Succulents)

Sweet corn

Berry/Leaf

This heading includes several kinds of maize grown either for food or decorative purposes, known under such names as squaw corn, strawberry corn, or corn-on-the-cob. Squaw corn has variegated coloured cobs, but the shiny, yellow cobs of corn-on-the-cob are often included in ornamental fruit arrangements. Strawberry corn cobs are smaller and dark brown.

Sweet peas

Flower/Sp/Su

The fashion for growing and displaying sweet peas did not begin until towards the end of the last century. They remain some of the most fragrant and colourful flowers, in beautiful pastel shades and darker crimsons and blues, some with delightful 'picotee' edges. When cutting from the garden, plunge the stems straight into a container of water and handle them as little as possible. You can dip the stem ends in boiling water for a second or so. The effect of cutting seems only to stimulate the plant to produce further blooms, and they do not need to be mixed with other flowers or foliage to make a beautiful display. The fragility of the flowers makes them a prerogative of those with gardens—and all the more reason for growing them. New varieties seem to be available every year, but 'Air Warden', 'Frolic' (picotee), 'White Ensign', 'Elizabeth Taylor' and 'Leamington' are all powerfully fragrant and good exhibition varieties.

Symphoricarpus/snowberry

Berry

The white berries of this hardy deciduous shrub are loved by children, who delight in the popping sound made when they are pressed between the fingers. The berries appear in autumn and last well into the winter. Remove the dead or unsightly leaves before arranging the berries in white cascades with other foliage.

Syringa/lilac

Flower/Sp

Not to be confused with the mock orange, which is the very sweet-scented, white-flowered *Philadelphus*. There are many varieties of lilac, a tree

Sweet peas are everybody's favourite and need some contrasting foliage, such as the lambs' ears to add interest.

or shrub flowering in shades of purple, violet, primrose-yellow, carmine, pink, mauve and blue, as well as white and cream. 'Preston' hybrids are favourites with flower arrangers. Try the flowers in masses or mixed with other spring flowers, remembering that the shorter the stems and fewer the leaves the longer the flowers themselves will last. After hammering them, dip the stems in boiling water or steep in hot water for some time before arranging.

Tagetes/African marigold, French marigold

Flower/Su

These must be distinguished from the English or pot marigolds (see Calendula). They make fine, long-lasting cut flowers and mix well. There are many different varieties, including both single and double flowers, 'pompons' and shades from creamy-white, pale primrose and lemon to golden-orange, brownish-yellow, scarlet, deep red and maroon. A popular garden variety of *T. patula*, the French marigold, is 'Dainty Marietta', which has golden-yellow flowers blotched maroon, but the stems are only six inches long. More popular with arrangers are varieties of the African mari-

gold, *T. erecta*, such as 'Crackerjack', in mixed colours from gold to yellow, which are over two feet high.

Thalictrum/meadow rue

Leaf/Flower/Su

These plants have rather fluffy heads of flowers, generally pink, lavender or yellow, and dainty foliage. Some species, such as *T. minus*, which has fern-like leaves on thin but strong stems but uninteresting yellow flowers, are grown primarily for decorative foliage. Others have unusually attractive blooms, such as *T. dipterocarpum*, which has lavender-blue flowers with long yellow stamens.

Tradescantia see House Plants (Trailing Plants)

Trees

From trees of woodland and hedgerow and from those of the garden, the flower arranger can obtain much basic material throughout the year, green leaves in summer and winter, and foliage which takes on rich colourings of red and yellow in autumn. In winter, evergreens provide valuable material.

In autumn and winter the hips and haws of the

Lime flowers and lilies make a stunning combination in this arrangement against a background of pinewood panelling.

wild roses of the hedgerows are available; as well as the berries of the mountain ash which are borne in generous trusses of crimson or yellow; the fruits of the holly, pryacantha and cotoneaster are also useful.

Bearing its berries of sealing-wax-red while still carrying its crimson-tinted leaves, the rowan or mountain ash *(Sorbus)* is popular for indoor decoration, but the equally handsome variety, *Sorbus aucuparia* 'Xanthocarpa', is not so well known. It has striking yellow berries. *Sorbus cashmiriana* retains its white and pink berries until long after the leaves have fallen. The handsome trusses of scarlet berries of the tree-like *Cotoneaster frigida* appear in autumn, but are long lasting if not eaten by birds. The orange berries of the female flowers of the sea buckthorn are equally long lasting on the trees. They will retain their form and colour when indoors almost through the winter if the berries are coated with varnish after removal from the trees. See PRESERVA-TION (Berries).

The fruits of the horse chestnut (conkers) enclosed in their thick green protective cases and those of the quince, *Cydonia oblonga* (the latter are deepest green mottled with white and of similar size), may be used in flower arrangements with surprising results. They should be removed from the trees early in September before they fall and while still attached to their long stems. As with berries, varnishing will prevent them from shrivelling during winter.

Sprigs of oak with the acorns still attached will also provide interesting material in autumn, but the acorns should be gathered before they part from the cups. In autumn the hop-like trusses of the hop hornbeam *(Ostrya)* are particularly attractive.

In spring, numerous trees yield catkins which retain their beauty when in the home for many weeks and the sticky buds of the horse chestnut and balsam poplar are also useful.

Among the most useful of the catkin-bearing trees are the willows, *Salix medemii* being the first to bear its large golden tassels in February before the leaves. *S. caprea*, the 'palm' or pussy-willow, bears its catkins covered in silvery 'fur' soon after. In addition, the willows provide colourful twigs in winter, none being more striking than *S. vitellina* (syn. *S. alba* 'Vitellina') which has twigs of brilliant gold, and those of *S. daphnoides* are plum-coloured, and covered in silvery 'bloom'. The bright yellow handsome male catkins of the hazel appear in February and measure almost three inches long. In early April, the silver birch bears its slender tubular catkins as the leaves unfold, and is excellent for spring displays. The alder provides yellow catkins tinted with red.

Similar to the wind-pollinated catkin bearers are the conifers, which with their glaucous foliage are invaluable for display, none more so than the Scots pine. The young golden-yellow cones forming early in summer are as colourful as when they have matured to a deep chocolate brown. The cluster or maritime pine with its almost globular cones, and the Austrian pine, with long elegant cones shaped like cats' tails, are also attractive.

The leaves of many deciduous trees, such as the sweet chestnut and beech, may be retained by removing them towards the end of summer while still fresh and the sap is active. This is important for they will then be able to absorb the glycerine and water solution which will enable them to retain their freshness throughout the winter. If removed later than the end of August, they will have lost the power of absorption. See also PRESERVATION: Foliage. The shoots of the evergreen *Buxus* (box) may be cut in August and treated with glycerine. The box is one of the most useful trees for decorative leaves.

Those trees and shrubs which retain their foliage through winter will be indispensable to the flower arranger, and one of the most useful is *Pittosporum tenuifolium*, which reaches small tree-like proportions only in warm gardens and usually in sight of the sea. It has jet black stems and small glossy grey-green leaves with attractively waved margins. It is grown commercially in warmer districts, made into bunches and sold in large quantities to leading florists. The firs *(Abies)* are useful for their cones and leaves.

The Portugal laurel, *Prunus lusitanica*, with its glossy dark green leaves, will also reach tree-like proportions where grown in a rich loamy soil and in a warm garden and is a valuable winter evergreen for the arranger. Likewise the rhododendron with its elegant long glossy leaves which turn almost black when given the glycerine treatment.

The holly *(Ilex)* with its dark green leaves, crinkled and spiky at the edges will bear berries only if male and female trees are growing near each other, but the foliage alone of several varieties makes it worthy of cultivation. *Ilex aquifolium* 'Silver Queen' has leaves variegated with gold and the variety 'Golden King' has a contrasting margin of deep golden-yellow. The upper leaves of long-established trees will have almost lost their spiny edges, for at a height of more than 10 feet grazing animals cannot reach them and here the leaves are more easily removed and used for decorative purposes. If the spiny leaves prove troublesome to use, the small dark-green leaves of the evergreen oak, *Quercus ilex*, often silvery on the underside, should be obtained instead. Used as a hedge, it withstands clipping and sprigs may be removed as required throughout the winter. *Quercus suber*, the cork oak, has leathery oval leaves and its rough cork-like bark makes an attractive winter decoration if removed with care. *Quercus cerris*, the Turkey oak, also has interest for the arranger for it has deeply lobed leaves 4–5 inches long, tapering to a point

In an arrangement of this type the table is as much a part of the overall picture as the flowers. The ingredients are simple: rayonnante chrysanthemums, gum leaves and leaves of *Magnolia delavyi*.

and acorns of similar length which ripen to a polished mahogany colour and are held in large cups. The variety 'Variegata' has its leaves edged with silver.

For winter green, the *Cupressus* and *Chamaecyparis* species are invaluable and are obtainable in all shades of green and gold. The sprays may be removed at almost any time and if placed in the open between sheets of wet paper or beneath bracken or leaves, they will retain their freshness for several months. The evergreen *Arbutus* has handsome, leathery leaves of deepest green.

Most trees retain the colour of their twigs all the year round and even when the leaves have fallen, they make their contribution to flower arrangement. Most striking are the shoots of *Cornus alba* which are of bright red, turning crimson at the approach of winter, and those of *Szlix purpurea* (purple osier) are deep purple. *S. vitellina* has twigs and bark of brilliant orange. For contrast, use *Betula papyrifera* (birch) or *B. populifolia* which are white, or *Abutilon vitifolium*, its young wood being covered in white down. The twigs of *Salix babylonica* and *Alnus incana* 'Aurea' (alder) are glowing yellow and the young shoots of *Populus canescens* (poplar) are deep pink. The variety 'Aurora' is a remarkable sight in spring when the new leaves unfold for they are deep green speckled with silver and enhanced by the rose-pink wood. At this time, it makes a striking display used with delphiniums and with other blue flowers of the border. And with them use the clear golden-yellow leaves of *P.* × *serotina* 'Aurea' or those of *Catalpa bignonioides* 'Aurea' (Indian bean tree) which are large and striking and always create interest.

Also golden in leaf is the hazel, *Corylus avellana* 'Aurea'. The variety 'Contorta' has curled and twisted wood and bears buff-coloured catkins. giving it considerable value for floral art. Very similar is *Salix matsudana* 'Tortuosa', which has bright yellow-orange twigs in winter.

Of the invaluable purple-leaf trees, *Prunus cerasifera* 'Atropurpurea', the ruby-red leaves of spring turning deep purple-bronze in autumn and 'Trailblazer' with its glowing mahogany-purple foliage and edible red cherries borne in autumn are worthy of inclusion in every small garden. Their neat foliage makes them ideal for floral art. Others with purple foliage include the copper beech; *Malus* × *purpurea* (flowering crab) and *M.* 'Red Glow', its broad leaves having purple veins: *Acer platanoides* 'Goldsworth Purple', the purple

maple; *Fagus sylvatica* 'Purpurea' (beech), and *Cotinus coggygria* 'Royal Purple'. The latter is enhanced by the feathery inflorescences of smoky-purple which may be made to last several weeks if sprayed with hair lacquer when cut and taken indoors.

Quite different in style are the leaves of *Fremontia californica* (now *Fremontodendron californica*) which makes a small tree in a warm garden, the heart-shaped leaves and shoots being covered in rusty down. Interesting too is *Gleditschia triacanthos*, closely related to acacia with handsome pinnate foliage and flowers which are followed by long twisted seed pods. These are retained through the winter when they are much in demand for decorative purposes. The young foliage of amelanchier is covered in silvery grey down.

The flowers of trees have only limited value in floral art for mostly they are insignificant and quickly die when placed indoors. Those flowering in winter and spring have greatest value, for flowers are then scarce, and in a cool room they will retain their freshness for a greater length of time. The winter-flowering trees bear their blossoms on leafless wood and are all the more striking for this reason. Magnolias are delightful in early spring but flowers do not generally last long indoors.

Prunus communis, the common almond, bears its sprays of pale pink flowers early in March when *P. conradinae* 'Semi-plena' is in bloom, its deep pink buds opening to double flowers of pale pink. *P. subhirtella* 'Autumnalis' is earlier into bloom, opening its flowers late in autumn and intermittently throughout winter, likewise the hybrid Japanese cherry 'Fudan Zakura', its pale pink buds opening to pure white flowers.

Cornus mas, the Cornelian cherry, begins to show its tiny yellow flowers towards the end of winter and these are followed by large crimson fruits. Also winter flowering is *Parrotia persica* which makes a small tree 15 feet tall. It bears small neat clusters of red flowers on bare branches. For the wonderful autumn tints of its foliage this plant is supreme. Like the wych hazels of the same family, this tree requires a lime-free soil. The flowering twigs, like those of *Hamamelis mollis* (wych hazel), may be removed when the buds show colour and if the ends are placed in damp sand in a warm room, they will quickly reveal their delicate beauty. See also Acacia, Eucalyptus, in main list.

A typical spring arrangement using daffodils and narcissi. The basket which holds the container is straw coloured and harmonises well with the colours of the flowers.

Triteleia/Ithuriel's spear, brodiaea

Flower/Su

A flower which used to be known under the title *Brodiaea laxa* but which is now more correctly known as *Triteleia laxa*. It has deep purple-blue rather tubular shaped flowers which are delightful for small early summer arrangements. Except in severe climates the corms are hardy enough to grow in well-drained sandy loam.

Brodiaeas all come originally from Western North America. The genus has been split into sub-genera, of which *Triteleia* is one, *Ipheion* is another. See also Ipheion.

Trollius/globe flower

Flower/Leaf/Au

These are water-loving plants with attractively lobed leaves and globe-shaped flowers, in colour and shape rather like huge double buttercups. Some varieties, such as 'Golden Queen' from China, have orange flowers and are nearly three feet tall. Dip the stem ends in boiling water and arrange them in deep water if possible. They will grow in moist soil in most gardens.

Tropaeolum/nasturtium

Flower/Su

These bright dwarf annuals and perennials are one of the delights of country walks in warmer country districts in summer, when their trumpet-mouthed, red, orange and gold flowers can be seen trailing over garden walls and banks. They can be exciting indoors too, if allowed to cascade from bowls in long trails of foliage and flowers. Or the flowers make neat but cheerful table decorations placed compactly in a low bowl. There are some wonderful double varieties and the flowers last well in water.

Tulipa/tulip

Flower/Su

There are thousands of different varieties of tulips which bloom in April and May in colours ranging through almost the whole spectrum. Perhaps the most beloved of all are the delicately shaped lily-flowered varieties, such as the satin-textured 'China Pink', which reaches a good height in even the poorest soil, the red 'Queen of Sheba' and the pale yellow 'Ellen Willmot'. One or two blooms of these varieties can be used in conjunction with a few curving leaves and smaller flowers to make an interesting display. Generally, however, tulips are exciting in masses.

Other useful types for flower arranging are Bijbloeman, Bizarre and Rembrandt tulips. Rembrandts have large cups which are striped and streaked. Bizarre tulips have yellow flowers with brown and purple markings; and Bijbloemen are white with purple, rose or violet markings. The large blooms of Parrot tulips, in maroon, purple, yellow, red and orange are also excellent for cut flowers. So are the Viridifloras with unusual green-coloured flowers tinged with pink ('Greenland'), red ('Hollywood'), or yellow ('Viridiflora Praecox').

The stems of tulips have a way of bending—not unattractively. However, if you wish to keep them straight wrap each stem in a wet newspaper for about four hours before arranging. The flowers last well in water. See also House Plants (Pot Plants).

Ulex/gorse, whin

Leaf/Flower/Sp/Su/Au

This is the common gorse of the heathland with vivid pea-like flowers and sharp spines. The double variety is often found in gardens. The evergreen foliage provides dark backgrounds for arrangements. Using industrial gloves strip off the lower spines, hammer the stem ends and strip off some bark. Different varieties bloom at different times from spring to autumn, but the flowers need careful handling as they can easily drop off.

Vallota see House Plants (Pot Plants)

Verbascum/mullein

Flower/Leaf/Seed/Su

Bright flowers including yellows, purples and reddish-browns are in contrast to the beard-like white or silvery hairs which grow on the stems and leaves of many species, and which will carry droplets if you do not remove the fleshy substance at the bases of the leaves when placing them in water. The flowers are generally on tall spikes rather like hollyhocks. *V. bombyciferum* (syn. *V.*

'Broussa') has lovely soft yellow flowers and silvery down and reaches up to six feet. *V. chaixii* has free-flowering yellow flowers on tall spikes. *V. thapsus*, Aaron's rod, is a densely woolly species. Mostly biennial verbascums will grow in almost any sunny spot in the garden.

Verbena

Flower/Su/Au

Showy half-hardy annuals or perennials, the flowers are mostly purple, lavender or violet in dense heads usually not very tall. One or two species are particularly brilliant, such as *V. peruviana*, which is bright scarlet, and *V. × hybrida* (florists' verbena) which has many varieties in pink, red, blue, often with buds open in water, and if the stem ends are dipped in boiling water the flowers should last.

Viburnum/guelder rose, laurustinus, snowball tree, wayfaring tree

Flower/Leaf/Berry/Sp/Su/Au

Generally deciduous shrubs with white sweet-scented flowers, of which some species, such as the evergreen *V. tinus* (laurustinus) and *V. fragrans*, are handy for providing flowers for winter arrangements. However, *V. opulus* (guelder rose) and *V. opulus* 'Sterile' (snowball tree) bloom in May and June. The guelder roses are a beautiful white with a tinge of green and the leaves of *V. opulus* are rich red in autumn. The flowers of the snowball tree appear as green globes that turn white. The native British *V. lantana* (wayfaring tree) also produces its flowers in spring and its small red berries slowly turning black are quite decorative too. *V. carlesii* and *V. fragrans* (another winter flowerer) have slightly pink flowers. One or other variety of viburnum is providing scent and flowers, leaf or fruit all the year round.

Vinca/periwinkle

Leaf/Sp

The variegated creamy-white evergreen leaves of *V. major* 'Variegata' and *V. minor* 'Variegata' are useful as trailers to set off flowers or other plant material in a vase or bowl. Dip the stem ends in boiling water and spray the leaves with water from an atomising sprayer.

A stunning late summer arrangement incorporating red hot pokers, sun flowers and hydrangeas, arranged on an ornate pedestal. Note the floral inlay on the top of the round table.

Viola/violet

Flower/Sp/Su/Au

The bunches of 'sweet violets' that used to be cried in the streets of London for a penny may be a little more expensive, but are still fragrant and exquisite flowers for bouquets and arrangements. There are many named varieties of *V. odorata*, all scented and in different colours. A good one for cutting is 'Czar' which has blue flowers with long stems.

The plants can be flowered in winter under a cold frame, so it is possible to have blooms for the greater part of the year. The flowers should be fully open when arranged and it is a good idea to spray the flowerheads with an atomiser and dip the stem ends in boiling water.

Viscum/mistletoe

Berry/Leaf

Traditionally mistletoe stands for peace and friendship which is perhaps why couples kiss under sprigs of it at Christmas. The symbolic origins of the plant go back to the time of Druidism, a Celtic religious cult. Considering its berries and leaves are so long-lasting and gay, it is surprising it is not used more often for arrangements.

Vitis/vine

Leaf/Berry

Grown mainly for flower arrangers for the interesting-shaped leaves, which tend to be especially rich in colour in autumn. The flowers are inconspicuous, but the fruits may be very decorative. *V. coignetiae* is perhaps the most ornamental species—the leaves turning to crimson or orange in autumn. Varieties of *V. vinifera* have also got very decorative foliage, such as 'Brandt' which has crimson, orange or pink autumnal leaves. *V. v.* 'Purpurea' has red-purple autumn leaves and decorative fruits. Dip the leaves in boiling water. Leaves of interesting colour can be preserved by pressing.

Contrasting foliage forms and colours make the use of flowers unnecessary in this arrangement. Foliage includes leaves of bergenia, iris, peony, vine and *Begonia rex*.

Vriesia see House Plants (Palms)

Washingtonia see House Plants (Palms)

Water

Water is essential to plant life. Growing plants with roots attached and cut stems and branches are dependent on moisture for keeping the cells in the stems and leaves fully turgid. Plant tissue will wilt from time to time when conditions are such that the dry atmosphere takes more moisture from the plant than the roots can take up from the soil. This is a partial wilt, which is rectified as the temperature changes during the late evening, or more water is received by the plant. The same thing will happen with pot plants when the soil becomes dry. The flowers or foliage farthest away from the roots will wilt first, and if seen in time, can be treated and brought back into good condition. If the plant becomes dry for a long period, no amount of treatment will restore it. The foliage may respond, but the softer flower tissue will remain dead. It is the early recognition of this partial wilt which is so important. Immediately it is noticed, plunge the plant into a bucket of warm water until all the bubbles cease to rise from the soil. Then lift it out of the bucket to allow surplus water to drain away, and at the same time, saturate the foliage and flowers with a fine mist of water and then cover with damp tissue paper. Stand the plant in a cool place to recover. After a few hours, the flowers and foliage should be back in a good turgid state. This can be done a few times, but the good plantsman never allows it to happen.

Over-watering can also have serious consequences, and many plants are killed in this way. The foliage usually shows yellowing at the leaf tips and many leaves falling prematurely. No plant should stand in water for long periods. After being thoroughly soaked it should then be allowed to drain. A good idea is to stand plants on a little gravel or ash. This allows for a moist atmosphere around the foliage, a cool root run, but with no chance of the plant roots becoming drowned.

Plants and cut flowers benefit from a fine spray overhead. It helps to keep the foliage clean and stops the pores on the surface being clogged with dust, and it certainly freshens up cut flowers. Spraying should be done well away from any polished or delicate surface, and make sure that no drips fall from the saturated leaf surface. Spraying bulbs and young growing shoots will encourage growth (it helps soften the bud caps) and if the temperature is correct, it gives the atmosphere of an April day.

Cut flowers, as soon as picked or unpacked, should be placed in clean water. Tap water is better than rainwater, because there is little or no bacteria present. All foliage which will be below water level should be removed straight away. If cutting from the garden, take a bucket round with you so that the flowers have no chance of drying out. Once back in the house, they should be treated according to their type.

Wedding decorations

Flowers always enhance this occasion, but much will depend on the style and type of church as to what flowers will be necessary. The interior of some churches are very ornate and others are quite plain. Some will require the florist to bring all the necessary equipment such as vases and plinths while others will have these available and like to have their own used.

The flowers should add to the beauty of the church and look a part of the overall inside decoration. As a general guide it would be fair to say that six groups normally will suffice and the size of these will depend entirely on the size of the church. Some need to be very large to show up well and have to be arranged with the aid of tubes or flower cones. Again, certain colours will be better than others and blue and mauves may well be lost at a distance in a church with grey-stone wall interiors.

It is usual to have a pair of vases on the altar one at each side (some ministers will not allow flowers on the Holy Table) but a lovely group in the centre of the altar is most effective. It is certainly usual to use the altar vase belonging to the church and then the flowers can be left if the rest of the flowers have to be cleared after the ceremony.

Two large groups usually stand either side of the choir stalls or at the chancel rail. A smaller pair may well stand at the back of the pews either side of the aisle.

If it is a large wedding, it is nice to have a group in the church porch or just inside the door. Another good site is at the back of the church, so often an area of oddments—vases left from festivals, broom cupboards etc.

(b)

(a)

(c)

Wild flowers. What are weeds in one country are often cultivated plants in another. So far as flower arranging goes wild flowers provide just as much floral material as cultivated plants. a) Lords and Ladies. b) Bindweed. c) Lilium *paradalinum*. d) Tansy. e) Primroses. f) Snake's head fritillaries. g) Trilliums.

(e)

(d)

(g)

189

(f)

Wedding reception arrangement. A single white peony is the visual centre of gravity in this arrangement. The container is an inverted meat dish cover on a wrought iron stand.

Another good place to display flowers to good advantage is on the window sills. They are up out of harm's way and can be seen by all. Pew ends are sometimes used; these are posies of flowers which can be hung carefully at the end of certain pews. Don't over decorate—it is not a flower festival, and never from choice garland pillars, it is always very difficult to fix garlands without defacing the stonework.

The colour scheme within the church will usually follow that of the bridal party. White and greens show up best especially on the altar. Extra colour can be added to the large groups; remember that big flowers look best in clean-cut groups and it is necessary to get good backing foliage to make the flowers show up well.

Wild flowers

What are weeds in Katmandu are exotic plants at Kew, and the wild flowers of Florida are house plants in New York. Basically there is no difference between wild flowers and cultivated flowers, except that in general cultivated flowers came originally from some other part of the world. Therefore, as far as flower arranging goes, wild flowers are just as beautiful and just as useful as many cultivated flowers.

However, a word of warning: over the last fifty years there has been a serious decline in some genera of wild flowers and some have come close to extinction. In a few cases some of these wild flowers are now protected by law and may neither be picked nor dug up. Local natural history or conservation societies will tell you which flowers these are.

Bold arrangements must incorporate more delicate material. Here the airy tracery of rose bay willow herb contrasts with the lushness of eucomis flowers and foliage.

Wild flowers can be picked and used in flower decoration in just the same way as cultivated flowers. When gathering them it is always better to cut the stems rather than to break them. The flowers should never be pulled as this may leave a hole in the centre of the plant where the water can collect and rot the crown of the plant. This applies particularly to bulbs and succulents. Flowers picked in the wild should be taken home in plastic bags containing a little damp moss. The bag should be blown up with air and knotted at the top.

Many wild flowers will thrive in gardens. The important thing to remember is that they must be given conditions in the garden as similar as possible to those in which they were growing in the wild. Never dig up a single plant growing on its own: only take plants from places where there are many of them growing together and always make sure that there are plenty of undamaged plants left behind. Alternatively many wild flowers can be grown very easily from seed.

The best way to find what wild flowers there are in your neighbourhood suitable for floral decoration is to ask at your local library for a book on the flora of your neighbourhood.

Wisteria

Flower/Sp

Beautifully scented, deciduous climbing shrubs which produce brilliant purplish-blue flowers nearly one foot long. They will not keep in water but are irresistible to the eye.

Yucca/Spanish bayonet, Adam's needle, sword lily

Flower/Leaf/Su

The sword-like leaves are evergreen and useful for winter arrangements. Several varieties are hardy and the creamy-white flowers are magnificent.

Zantedeschia/arum lily, calla lily

Flower/Wi/Sp

Beautiful pure-white trumpet-shaped flowers with large arrow-shaped leaves make this a marvellous plant for large displays. *Z. aethiopica* (lily of the Nile) is tender in most cooler districts, but can be planted out in summer. It is excellent for cut flowers.

Zebra Plant see Aphelandra

Zebrina see House Plants (Trailing Plants)

Zinnia

Flower/Su/Au

Half-hardy annuals and perennials which generally produce large tall daisy-like flowers in rich colours of orange, bronze, red, green and pink as well as white. Dip the stem ends in boiling water for over a minute before arranging. The flowers can be dried by a borax treatment just before they reach full bloom.